*Observing and Recording
the Behavior of Young Children*

OBSERVING AND RECORDING
the Behavior of Young Children

Dorothy H. Cohen
Formerly Senior Faculty, Graduate Programs
Bank Street College of Education

Virginia Stern
Formerly Research Associate
Bank Street College of Education

with Nancy Balaban
Director, Program in Infant and Parent Development
Graduate School of Education
Bank Street College of Education

THIRD EDITION

Teachers College, Columbia University
New York and London

Published by Teachers College Press, 1234 Amsterdam Avenue, New York, N.Y. 10027

Library of Congress Cataloging in Publication Data

Cohen, Dorothy H.
   Observing and recording the behavior of young children.

   Bibliography: p.
   Includes index.
   1. Child psychology—Methodology.   I.   Stern, Virginia.
II.   Balaban, Nancy.   III.   Title.
BF722.C63 1983   155.4   82-19560

ISBN 0-8077-2713-X

Manufactured in the United States of America

88 87 86   3   4   5   6

CONTENTS

PREFACE TO THE THIRD EDITION

At the time the first edition of this book was written, the practice of observing and recording the behavior of children as it was happening was pretty much confined to a small handful of early childhood teachers who were fortunate enough to have been trained in the tradition of child study. The tradition began in the nineteenth century, when some psychologists studied children, often their own, through recording their activities. The technique was applied to the study of children in educational settings just after World War I, when it was pioneered by early proponents of a developmental approach to curriculum. Although early childhood teachers accepted the principle of record keeping based on observation, the practice failed to become widespread because the skills were not taught at most institutions preparing teachers. The original edition of *Observing and Recording the Behavior of Young Children* was a first effort at translating these skills into teacher terms.

In the years between the first and second editions, interest in young children escalated, and research brought to our attention fresh information about how children learn and how their language develops. At the same time, there was a resurgence of interest in natural observation, probably because young children so stubbornly and persistently resist being captured by the more commonly used standardized tests. Since then, innovations in the field of preschool education have come about through the passage of legislation and the accumulation of new knowledge about children resulting from research on changes in social attitudes and roles that influence family life and, therefore, young children. This new edition is a response to those innovations. Without in any way altering the basic approaches or premises concerning the study of children, we have added new materials that reflect recent information. In addition, we have included records that capture some of the different styles of responses from today's child.

Additions to Chapter 5, "Recording Children's Behavior in Dramatic Play," and the additional material relating to the capacity for symbolic representation in Chapter 9, "Observing Children Develop the Power to Think," are the result of research that provided increased detailed knowledge about young children's dramatic play.

Chapter 11, "Observing and Recording the Behavior of Infants and Toddlers," stems from a striking change in preschool education, that is, the increasing number of settings that have opened their doors to toddlers and infants.

Chapter 12, "Recording the Behavior of Children with Special Problems," has been added because of the passage of the Education for All Handicapped Children Act of 1975, which requires that the education of handicapped children take place in the "least restrictive environment," that is, as much as possible within a regular class. This law encompasses both private and public schools attended by school-age children. Federally funded preschool centers, such as Head Start, are also required to accept some handicapped children.

Although, fortunately, men are now entering the field of early childhood education, the teacher is referred to mostly as "she," because the overwhelming majority of teachers of young children are still women.

We hope that this third edition will increase the usefulness of the book to teachers and that through it they will become more aware of children as the whole and integrated people they are. Special thanks are due to the many students at the Bank Street College of Education whose efforts at learning to observe and record appear in this volume and give it its contemporary validity.

We have revised this edition without the very special insights of Dorothy Cohen, who died before this effort came to fruition. Dorothy's commitment to children was complete; her knowledge of development, both profound and encyclopedic. Her philosophy, which is reflected throughout this book, has provided thousands of teachers with a fundamental tool of the trade. Dorothy's death is a great loss not only to the field of education, her colleagues, and future students at Bank Street, but also to this edition of our book.

1

GETTING STARTED

WHY RECORDS?

EACH OF US has known at some time the gl w of satisfaction that comes with reaching through successfully to a child. Having applied just the right touch at the right moment, we have warmed to the smile of pleasure and trust a child bestows on us when we have understood what he or she feels and thinks. And each of us has known, too, the frustration of using to no avail tested wiles and approaches, of being baffled and irritated because we have felt completely ineffective with some children. All teachers want to understand their children better. Many have tried to keep records of children's behavior in an effort to gain insight into why they do what they do. But all too often even records conscientiously kept seem to reveal very little, and we fall back on our hunches and our intuition as bases for judgment.

This manual on record-taking describes recording techniques that will help teachers of young children toward their goal of understanding children's behavior. The manual does not tell how to interpret behavior, but it does suggest the details to look for that will be meaningful in explaining behavior. The manual tells how to gather data and how to make the best use of data. It discusses principles of observation rather than principles of diagnosis. If we could say that understanding a child is like unraveling a mystery, then taking records is the gathering of clues. Like experienced detectives we must recognize the significant clues; we must develop special skills.

Teachers of young children do not get very far when they ask

1

children to explain themselves. Nor can they use the personality tests and questionnaires that might help in understanding older children. For the present, our best technique seems to be the careful gathering of evidence via the on-the-spot record. To the writers, this means recording details that not only describe the action but reveal how a child feels about what he is doing: details on *how* he does something as well as what; the *quality* as well as the quantity of her interrelating with people and materials; and, of course, what she says.

The most complete recording of this kind, but not necessarily the best for our purposes, would be done by someone who knows short-hand and is not responsible for the life of the group. Obviously it is impossible for teachers to achieve near-perfect written records of all the details they actually see. Nevertheless, there is benefit to be gained from an awareness of what to look for in those odd moments when a teacher can whip out a small pad and let her pencil fly. Every teacher can get some records, and over the months even occasional jottings add up to something impressive! More important is the fact that knowing what is significant makes one generally more aware of the nuances of children's behavior, even if it is not always possible to write things down.

A Teacher Needs to Be One Part Scientist

In suggesting that teachers study children by careful observation and recording of behavior, we are borrowing from research a tool that has aimed at achieving the utmost objectivity and dispassion. For teachers observing the children with whom they work and live, absolute objectivity is impossible, and objectivity itself becomes a relative thing. As a matter of fact, it is to be hoped that no teacher would ever try for so much objectivity that she would cease to be a responsible and responsive adult to her group. It is far better for a child to have a warmly interested teacher who has kept no records than a meticulous observer with no warmth! But if we do not strive for the kind of absolute objectivity that eliminates all feeling, we do seek awareness on the part of the teacher of the kinds of personal, subjective feelings that tend to color records. The picture of a child that is influenced by such teacher involvement might not be a true picture of the child at all.

Suppose we look at a child with this in mind.

Here is Johnny. He is five. He lives on Third Street. He comes to school every day. To Teacher A he is a lovable roughneck, sturdy, and full of fun. To Teacher B he is a sloppy child, wild, and un-disciplined. For Teacher C he hardly exists. To Teacher D he is one big appeal for mothering. Which Johnny is the real Johnny? Does anyone know what Johnny thinks about himself?

Apparently people do not see children with unbiased eyes, or everybody would see the same Johnny. We need to examine these biases, or personal involvements, if we are to have some degree of accuracy in our record-taking.

Our Conception of What Children Should Be Like Was Shaped in Childhood

When we ourselves were the butt of adult directions, we were told in definite terms what behavior would be tolerated and what would be punished. Within our families, within our communities, there were traditions and opinions, standards and values, set up as guides for our youthful consciences. To be clean was virtuous, to be dirty was naughty. To be polite was to merit love, to be rude brought on a spanking. But family goals were not always the same. Sobriety and thrift formed a code for some people, conviviality and relaxation as serious a code for others. To become a scholar was the goal for some, financial success for others.

When we are little, the teachings of the important adults are impressive. So impressive do they remain, in fact, that when we become adults and teach children in turn, we fall back with greater security and sense of rightness on what our parents taught us about how children *should* behave than on what research tells us about how they *do* behave. That is why Johnny's sloppiness stands out for Teacher B and his good humor for Teacher A. Teacher C can hard-ly admit that such creatures as Johnny exist because to her way of thinking little boys are just not as nice as little girls! But Teacher D forgives all precisely because he is such a little boy.

If we were to measure fluid milk in pounds and potatoes in quarts, we would be more accurate than if we measured children's behavior in terms of adult virtues and aspirations. While children will, when adult, take on adult ways of behavior, as children they are governed by somewhat different laws that are peculiar to this stage in the life of a human being. We know that a caterpillar is a stage in the life of a moth and it cannot fly. We know that a calf cannot give milk, although some day it will. But all too many people expect the human child to behave as adult as possible, and the sooner the better! In point of fact, we can be much more successful in guiding a child toward mature adulthood if we are clear about the nature of childhood.

Perhaps the thing that fools us about young children is the fact that they can speak. Because this special human ability is achieved so early in life, it is easy to assume that the thinking that lies behind the speech is surely the same as ours. By this reliance on children's speech as the key to understanding them, we close off too many meaningful avenues of communication between children and ourselves.

How many times do we say to a child, in anger or in sorrow, with insistence or with sweetness, "Why did you do it!" And in anger or in sorrow, belligerently or helplessly, the child answers, "I don't know." The truth of the matter is that children do not know, and cannot tell us why they do as they do. When we don't know either, that leaves us both confused!

Children Reveal Themselves in Special Children's Ways

There are reasons for a child's behavior, of course, plenty of them. Sometimes it is hard to decide which is the most likely of several possible reasons for the same kind of behavior! But while every bit of behavior is caused by something, we must sadly admit that what that something is for the particular child who is the enigma is often a mystery. That is why as teachers we must gather good clues that will lead to understanding. Only by learning to see children as they are, and especially as *they see themselves,* will we get our clues. It is not as simple as it sounds.

Young children are still operating out of strong physical and emotional bases. Their bodies not only move into pretzel shapes with fluidity; body movement, body processes, and feelings loom large on the horizon of their existence. Young children *think* with their *hands* (they *touch* to find out) and *socialize* with their *feet* (stamping and kicking noisily are fine acts of comradeship!). Or, they might think with their *feet* (what happens to a worm?) and socialize with their *hands* (what will happen if I touch him in the eye?). If we would record their growing and learning, we must record what they do with their bodies, even as we listen to what they say with their mouths. And we must listen without our grandmother's prejudices peering over our shoulder!

Thus, even though the speech of a young child is a wonderful thing indeed when it occurs, it is far from complete for a long time for all the help it is to adults trying to understand childhood meanings. It is not too good a tool for expressing feelings and thoughts, for example, although it fast becomes highly skilled at expressing *wants*. (Even this is not true of all children.) Does a young child say, "I feel sad," or does she hang her head, cry, or stare into space (all *physical* expressions)? If we wait for her to grow to the stage where she is mature enough to pinpoint her emotions and tell us about them, we shall wait a long time indeed! We must learn, therefore, to recognize other behavior as clues to thought and feeling.

Children communicate with us through their eyes, the quality of their voices, their body postures, their gestures, their mannerisms, their smiles, their jumping up and down, their listlessness. They show us, by the way they do things as well as by what they do, what is going on inside them. When we have come to see children's behavior through the eyes of its meaning to them, *from the inside out,* we shall be well on our way to understanding them. Recording their ways of communicating helps us to see them as they are.

THERE ARE MANY KINDS OF RECORDS

There are many ways of keeping records of children's behavior to suit different purposes and situations. Some records are frankly *impressionistic* and this is perfectly acceptable at times. When a new boy or girl enters school, a teacher cannot help but react, and size up the child in her own terms. If she writes down her impressions, she will have a record to turn to later when she has developed another perspective on the child. How correct are her early impressions? To what extent are they borne out by more knowledge?

Some teachers keep a *log* or *diary* about their group. At the end of the day, or perhaps during rest hour, they put down what stood out that day in as much detail as they have time and energy for. This is an excellent way of recording the activity of the group, its shifts in leadership, its ideas and interests, its accomplishments. It is an invaluable aid to planning. Some teachers do the same thing but with less regularity and only from time to time, spot-checking in a sense. There are charts and checklists that help a teacher remember which children have not used paints for a while, which should get a turn at the workbench, and which are taking a large share of social responsibility. And of course there are snapshots and drawings, movies and tape-recordings (too expensive for most of us!). One can also keep track of the number of times a certain kind of behavior took place, like how many times Amy hit someone, and how many times she threatened to hit but didn't; or with whom and with what Orrin was playing at 10:30 every day during a three-week period. All these techniques are good and can be used profitably. The use of any recording technique, however, must be determined by our purposes.

What Are We After? Why Are We Taking Records?

We are here suggesting a recording technique that will show a fairly full and realistic picture of one living, breathing child, as he (or she) responds to life in his own unique way, as he interacts with people and materials and functions at his own stage of maturity and growth. It is hard to focus on a child as an individual in this manner when one has grown accustomed to planning for an entire group. But while a group has its own laws of interaction that are surely worth studying, the study of individuals in the group leads to greater awareness of what is significant in human growth and development. The technique of studying one child in detail leads to deeper understanding of the one child and broader knowledge of all children.

Records, however, are not a panacea. They are no more than a means by which a busy teacher can take hold of a squirming, slippery, smiling, screeching, intriguing, and bewildering child and hold her still long enough to examine her carefully. This procedure, taking on-the-spot records of behavior as it is occurring, we call, for want of a better name, the *on-the-spot running record.*

Recording Behavior As It Happens

It is comforting to know that there are practically no fixed rules in this job of record-taking. The whole technique is relatively new to education; it has its creative aspects and its weaknesses. There will undoubtedly be modifications and changes as the technique becomes more widely used. We are going to be suggestive for the most part, and the rest is up to you!

Since your primary responsibility is to be the teacher of the group, your times for recording will literally have to be snatched. Children's needs come first, and you may have to drop your pencil to race to someone's rescue. It helps to have pads, cards, or a small notebook in your pockets, on shelves around the room, and up your sleeve, too. Never miss out on a choice bit because no pencil is handy! Be casual and unobtrusive about it all. Get close enough to hear things, but not so close that you interfere with the play. Notes can be rough and full of abbreviations, to be filled in and cleaned up later. Get the date down and the child's name as well as where the action is set. Should the children ask you what you are doing, don't let them in on the secret because they may become self-conscious. Be nonchalant and say something noncommittal, like "It's teacher's work," or "It's writing I have to do."

Take records of a child at as many different periods of the day as possible, although not necessarily all in one day. You will want to record behavior at arrival and dismissal, at toileting and at rhythms, at wash-up and at story time, at free play and with creative materials. You will want to see what a child does indoors and out, alone and with others. Recording in a variety of situations will show up all-pervasive behavior, such as relationships with children and adults, adjustment to school, feelings about routines, position in the group, etc.

Often it will seem that these everyday records are not getting anywhere, and it is easy to become discouraged. But when, after a period of time, details of similar character are grouped together, patterns of behavior emerge, and we begin to see what it is a child is really doing. Be patient and let the thing grow. Recording behavior is, after all, recording growth, and since children are in transition between stages much of the time, you will need many stills before you see the common movement running throughout.

A Word of Caution

Never, never allow records to lie around in public view. Treat them the way a doctor treats data about patients. Even the most inconsequential information about a patient is kept confidential, and we must do the same. Unless there is a professional reason for doing so, tell your funny and delightful stories about children *without identifying the particular child or family*.

LANGUAGE AS A TOOL IN RECORDING

The language of recording presents its own difficulties, especially for people unaccustomed to writing. It is easy to feel the challenge too great and to give the whole thing up as a bad job. Since the important nuances of behavior cannot be recorded adequately without some use of descriptive terminology, it is worth exploring this aspect of the recording technique. It is not at all impossible to grow in skill if you consider that almost everyone has a larger passive vocabulary than an active one. As a beginning, suppose we joggle our memories for verbs, adverbs, adjectives, and phrases that can be used descriptively.

Verbs

Some of us could think of a dozen synonyms for the word *walk* in a matter of seconds—

amble, stroll, saunter, clomp, stomp, march, strut, ramble, etc.

Others of us get paralyzed at the challenge. Yet the distinction between one child's actions, or gross movements, and another's may depend on the correct synonym for the word *walk*.

Look at it this way: A turkey walks. A cat walks. Are they the same? A one-year-old walks and an octogenarian walks. Their movements are obviously dissimilar. Johnny walks and Susie walks, and we must record the quality of each. To find the exactly characterizing word, we might say the turkey *struts,* the cat *slinks,* the baby *waddles,* the old man *totters,* Johnny *lopes,* and Susie *minces.* The word walk tells us *what a person does* but not *how he does it.* No two children walk across a playroom or over to a child or toward the teacher in exactly the same way. As teachers, we respond to the *quality* of the behavior as we watch the child. We respond to the child who walks frantically because we sense trouble, and we feel in our own muscles the swinging walk of a child who is full of joy.

Here are some synonyms as a starter for verbs commonly used in records. There are many more with which to become familiar.

Run—stampede, whirl, dash, dart, gallop, speed, shoot across, bolt, fly, hippety-hop, dash
Say—whisper, bellow, shout, scream, roar, lisp, whine, demand, tell, murmer
Cry—wail, howl, whimper, fuss, bawl, sob, mourn, lament, weep

Adverbs

Adverbs are one means by which pedestrian verbs can be given character when the exact verb is elusive. They are somewhat interpretative in that we define the mood and feeling of the behavior when we use them. But they are not used to pass judgment on the child. They describe an action, a part of the body, a look, a smile. For example, we can say, "She smiled bitterly," "He tugged determinedly," "She looked at the teacher vacantly," and not in any way describe the child as bitter, stubborn, or stupid. The descriptive word is a one-shot assessment of a single aspect of the child at a particular moment. Thus, going back to the verb *walk,* we can say walked merrily, jauntily, heavily, etc. Or the ordinary verb *talk* can be narrowed down meaningfully when excitedly, pleasantly, sourly, resentfully, cheerfully, cheerily, laughingly, etc. are tacked on.

At the same time, the consistency within the child becomes a safeguard against erroneous generalizations from a single gesture, smile, posture, or movement. For example, if a recorder writes at the same time that a child "whined" in describing the voice and "grinned" in describing the mouth; or walked "merrily" with "tearful eyes," it is clear that that recorder is not really observing.

As we indicated earlier, teachers cannot be absolutely objective, since they themselves are part of the total situation in which the recording occurs. Yet in trying to capture the quality of *how* a child builds, sings, jumps, cries, fights, paints, speaks, or whatever, we may use the descriptive language of *how* a child does *what* without courting an unnecessary or biased interpretation of the child as a person.

Adjectives

We need a good supply of adjectives too. For example, is every smile a cheerful smile? Could a smile be joyous, tearful, wholehearted, toothless, toothsome, forced, heart-warming, wavering, fixed, reluctant, etc.? Could a child with a reluctant smile possibly be feeling the same way as a child with a tearful smile, or a timid one? Here are special shades of *happy:*

> jubilant, joyous, gay, bubbling, bouncy, sparkling, effervescent, delighted, cheerful, contented, etc.

Here is *sadness* qualified:

> mournful, wistful, depressed, downhearted, gloomy, heavy-hearted, melancholy, downcast, sullen, dejected, discouraged, etc.

Phrases of All Kinds

Still another descriptive tool is the little phrase that has the telling action in it. Although these have their place, one must be careful to avoid becoming too dependent on such phrases; sentences can be cumbersome when too many phrases weigh them down. Here are some phrases to give character to the verb *walk:*

he walks

dragging his legs	with head turned to the sky
scuffing his toes	looking neither here nor there
swinging his arms	with boredom on his face
hunched and bent	intently observing
hands in pockets	with an awful clatter

In mentioning the language of the record, it seems as though we are adding more hurdles to the ones teachers already face while taking records. Certainly there are not enough good opportunities for recording, the speed at which one must work is frustrating, and sheer muscular endurance plays its part in the difficulties too. Even though the challenge of using descriptively precise language may be still another hurdle, the problem of good use of language in recording is one we must overcome. We are not accustomed in our culture to being colorful and descriptive in our everyday speech, although we may enjoy such language when reading. Nevertheless, records that are truly pictorial are so in large part as a result of imaginative language. If you feel too discouraged, try looking in Roget's *Thesaurus* or the dictionary for synonyms for some of the most commonly used action words and feeling tones. You will be surprised at the number of descriptive words you actually know and can put into your active command with a little joggling. Just make sure that the descriptive word you use really characterizes the quality of the action.

2

RECORDING A CHILD'S BEHAVIOR DURING ROUTINES

ORGANIZING THE INFORMATION

SINCE WE NEED a starting point, let us start with observing a child at tasks and behavior that make up so much a part of a young child's life—the routines. At school we generally think of these as cleanup, toileting, snack-time, lunch, rest, etc. These are the "uncreative" but necessary aspects of the program that are repeated day after day, the activities around which many a program revolves. Let us look at a child about to become involved in a routine—for example, getting dressed for outdoors. Although this seems to be a simple and obvious activity, let us look at a child with the following questions in mind.

What Is the Stimulus for the Activity?
* How does it happen that the child is dressing now?
    Did the teacher ask her to, individually?
    Did the teacher make an announcement to the class?
    Did the child notice others and follow suit?
    Did he just get an impulse and begin to dress himself?

In a word, we want to know what set the child off on the dressing process. We could call this spur to action the *stimulus*. It might come from within or outside the child. It might be obvious (the teacher told the child to get dressed) or not obvious at all (apparently an unexplained impulse).

What Is the Setting?
* What's going on around the child while he is dressing?
    What is the physical setup affecting the activity?

(cubbies or lockers are near or far away, there are chairs to sit on, children crowd into small space, etc.)

Who are the significant people nearby and what are they doing? (adults who are important to the child, her friends and "enemies," a visitor about whom she is concerned, etc.)

This enveloping activity would be the *setting* in which the behavior takes place, since obviously nothing happens in a vacuum.

What Seem to Be the Child's Reactions?

- If the activity was teacher-initiated, how does the child react?
  Does he accept the idea?
  (willingly? cheerfully? with annoyance? with complaints? silently?)
  Does she resist the idea?
  (openly and directly? indirectly?)
- If the action seems child-directed, how is it carried out?
  (eagerly? stealthily? hastily? calmly? dreamily?)
- Does the child show any special attachment to his clothing?
  (clutches jacket anxiously, fondles gloves lovingly, glares suspiciously at children who examine her hat, etc.)
- How seriously does he take the process? How much interest does he show?
- How does the child handle herself?
  (skillfully, clumsily, awkwardly, easily, etc.)
- Is his ability equal to the task?
- Does she have specific abilities?
  (can put on hat but not buckle it, fasten buttons, zipper jacket, etc.)

It sounds as though each of these questions requires an answer, as in a questionnaire. On the contrary, the questions are only reminders of things to be aware of as you are observing. One item may be far more important than another for a particular child. Some items may call for lengthy description and others for none. It all depends on how a child happens to approach her task.

With your two hands alone you are undoubtedly "short-handed" as you attempt to help a group get dressed for outdoors, and it may be hard to get anything written down. On the chance that some occasions do arise when this is possible, a brief description of behavior that includes some of the above points might read as follows.

As dressing time was announced, Ian shouted, "Goody!" and beelined to his locker. He plopped his hat on his head, scooped up his coat and ski-pants, and shuffled over to where the teacher was sitting ready to help the children. "Yippee," he gloated. "Here's my pants. Put 'em down for me!" The teacher laid them out straight and Ian pretzeled into a sitting position, dropping his coat on the floor. With lightning speed he forced first one foot and then another into the legs of the ski-pants, then wiggled himself into a standing position. Still wiggling his torso, he hauled the straps over his shoulders and reached down for his coat. He looked at it speculatively a moment and then handed it to the teacher. Turning his back to her, he waited for her to hold it in position. As he pulled it up, unmindful of the tucked-in collar, he fumbled with the zipper in an obvious effort to make haste.

There are still other reactions to be aware of in routine situations because they extend the implications of the action.

• Does the child seem to want to function independently?
    How do you know?
• How does she or he behave in relation to the group situation?
    Can he proceed in the midst of group activity?
    Does she withdraw? Does he get silly or otherwise disruptive?
• What are the external factors that may be influencing the child's
    reactions?
    (This is the dynamic aspect of the *setting* mentioned above.)
    Does the teacher sit in one spot and expect the children to come
    to her?
    Are the children expected to sit in their chairs and wait for the
    teacher's help?
    Are the children expected to do the job alone?
• How much individual attention is offered?
    As much as the child wants?
    As much as the teacher thinks the child needs?

We include these many details because everything children do is a response to *something*, whether it be to feelings within themselves or to situations and people *outside* themselves. To describe only the action, such as "child runs around the room," and not comment on the entire situation leaves us in the dark as to what the action means. Running around the room at rhythms is one thing, at lunch another, at dressing or cleanup still another! A child responds to a total situation, and this includes people, things, the physical environment, the demands to be met, etc. A boy or girl responds as a total person, with thought, feeling, and physical activity.

See how different is the response of two children to getting their clothes off when they arrive at school (and how differently their mothers treat them).

> Four-year-old Lisa came into class, hands in pockets, walking next to her mother. Her mother unbuttoned her coat—Lisa did not attempt to help; her body was very limp as her mother did this. Her eyes were roving around the classroom. When her coat was off, she walked into the room, still looking all around—she completely ignored or forgot about her mother's presence. Her mother quickly left without saying goodbye.

> Three-year-old Ted arrived with his mother and Jamie (another child in the class with whom Ted regularly goes to and from school). Ted stood facing his cubby, his back to the classroom, his mother behind him. He pulled his hat off his head with his right hand and placed it on the top shelf. He pulled down the zipper of his coat and took it off, struggling with it but eventually removing it by himself. His mother did not offer assistance, nor did he request it. He was talking to Jamie as he undressed, but I could not hear what he said, nor could I see his face. Once his coat was off, he tried to hang it on his hook. He grabbed a handful of cloth in the back of the coat, placed it on the hook, and let go. The coat fell. He picked it up in the same way, holding the material of the back of the coat. He tried to hook it, but it again fell. He tried the same thing a third time, with the same result. Now he began laughing. Jamie laughed, too. As he and Jamie were laughing, his mother picked up his coat and hung it on the hook without saying a word. The boys stopped laughing and walked in together. Ted's mother followed silently.

What Does the Child Do Immediately After?

When the dressing is over, we note what the child does then and thus complete the sequence of events from the first stimulus to the last concluding act. Sometimes what a child does immediately after the episode we are observing tells us quite a bit. For example:

> When Lisa's mother left, the teacher offered her chalk (a new classroom addition) to draw with, but Lisa said in a decided voice, "I want play dough." She walked over to the play dough shelf, took the play dough, and put it on the table. She then took a seat that allowed her to see the entrance to the room. She began rolling balls very dis-

tractedly—she did not look at the dough at all but kept her eyes fixed on the door.

As we observe a routine, we ask:

- Does the child accept the group procedure that follows, such as sitting on a chair, on the floor, waiting at the door, etc.?
- Does she run out without waiting for the group or the teacher?
- Does he rush to get the first place at the door?
- Does she show the children what she has done?
- Does he cry? Does he sing? Does he chortle to himself?

This may seem a lot of questioning about so simple a procedure as getting dressed and undressed. But there are important clues here for us to pick up, as we shall see when we examine the feelings with which a young child invests these selfsame routines.

THE MEANING OF ROUTINES TO YOUNG CHILDREN

Do you ever wonder why some children stand patiently to be buttoned and belted but others scream with rage if you make a move to help them? Why some children are utterly confused by the dressing process and others use the occasion for mad dashing around the room? Why some children burst into tears if they cannot find a mitten and others reveal a fine carelessness about everything connected with their clothing?

Of course we know that individual children are different from one another. But *all* children are different from adults generally, especially in this matter of routines.

For adults, routines are a means to an end. We wash for breakfast, we clean to get a place ready for work again, we dress quickly to get to work. But children understand time and schedule only hazily. Nor are these the criteria by which they guide their activities. For young children, routines are either an end in themselves or a deterrent to the important business of living. For example, washing hands does not necessarily have any connection with lunch at all—it might very well be an opportunity to explore and savor the properties of water, and perhaps of soap and paper towels too! It is an occupation in its own right, with its own enticements. Or it is a silly obstacle in the path of food when you're just too hungry! In the same way, cleanup may have nuisance value because it keeps one from having a last chance at the slide; conversely, it may be a cozy way of feeling groupness with peers under the warmth of your teacher's approval. In any case, the sense of responsibility that motivates adults is at its barest beginnings in early childhood and hardly a reliable ally for the teacher.

The pleasure principle is very, very strong in young children, so that "I want to" is as good a reason as any the teacher might think up, and "I don't feel like it" is a really compelling force. To children, routines have a meaning all their own, and it is not an "adult" meaning. In addition, individual children may add to the meaning a special flavor out of their own experience. Yet with all this, they want to, and will in time, learn to behave as we do.

The Mechanics Come with Attitudes

Children learn how to behave at the table, the sink, or in any other routine from the adults in their lives. For some adults, efficiency *per se* is so important that adult standards are held up as a model with a certain amount of fretfulness and impatience. For others of us it becomes simpler and easier to do the job ourselves than wait for a child to bungle through it. Still others of us love to do things for children because we enjoy being good to them in that way. In some homes there isn't much time for children, and they must shift for themselves. Quite unconsciously, therefore, as children learn the mechanics of the routines, they absorb attitudes, too, not only toward the carrying out of the routine, but toward *themselves* as functioning people. Willy-nilly, from the attitudes of the adults during their learning years, children build up conceptions concerning their level of achievement and their potential abilities, without the chance to compare themselves with other children of their own age and experience.

All this children have under their belts by the time they get to school, and careful observation of their behavior at routines will reveal a good deal of it. In addition to their handling the mechanics of living, we may well see something of their feelings about being dependent on adults, or whether being independent of them means anything to them. Perhaps, too, their feeling of trust or suspicion of adults will appear. These general attitudes come through in relation to the specific tasks we call routines. However, the different routines lend themselves to unique mannerisms and behavior reactions intrinsic to their function, and need to be looked at separately for this reason.

RECORDING EATING BEHAVIOR

In observing an eating situation let us bear in mind the intimacy of mother and child in the child's learning to handle foods. In the back of our minds we might tuck away the observation of pediatricians that most eating difficulties stem from anxiety, pressure, or ineptness on the part of the parent. Something of the child's attitudes toward herself or himself is bound to come through as well as the degree of smoothness of functioning. It is certainly an indication of self-confidence and social strength, for example, if children take care of their own body needs when they are well enough coordinated to do so.

Details to Observe

- Setting (table setup, other children, teacher, service, etc.)
- What is the child's reaction to the eating situation?
    Is she accepting, eager, resistant, choosy?
    How seriously or casually does he take eating?
- How much food does he eat?
    (rather little, two helpings, lots of meat, no vegetables, never gets enough, big portions in comparison to others, etc.)
- What is the manner of eating?
    How does he hold utensils? Does she eat with her hands?
    Does he play with food, throw food, hold food in his mouth?
    Is she systematic and well organized in her attack on food?
    Is he messy, fastidious, etc.?
- Does he socialize, and how much?
    To whom does he speak? How else does he make contact with children?
    Is the socializing more meaningful to her than the eating?
    Does she manage both socializing and eating?
    Does he talk only to the teacher, to a special friend, to no one, etc.?
- Does the child show interest in food?
    Has he special likes and dislikes?
    Does she comment about the food?
    What is her pace (speed or slowness) of eating?
- What is the adult's role?
    What group procedures are laid down?
    How much and what kind of individual attention are offered?

- What is the sequence of events?
    What does the child do and say?
    What does the adult do and say?
- How does the child leave the table?
    (talking eagerly, smacking lips, stonily, in tears, etc.;
    pushes chair back easily, knocks chair down, etc.)
- What does the child do then?
    (runs around the room, stands around talking, stands and
    waits for the teacher, gets a book or toy, goes to the toilet,
    goes to food wagon to help clean plates, looks into bowls
    for more food, etc.)

How Selective Shall We Be?

Since young children are as likely as not to be unconcerned about
table manners, we may find ourselves recording activity that is not
socially acceptable, with the uneasy thought that putting it down
on paper somehow carries our approval. Neither approval nor disapproval plays any part in recording technique, although they may
influence what we do or say as we respond to children. To guide
children on the long road to maturity we must start with them
where they are, which means, first of all, noting accurately what
they do without moral bias or judgment. To deny the reality of
their behavior because it is displeasing to us or because we are
showing them better techniques is to limit ourselves unduly as
teachers. It is only human to be subjectively selective about what
we observe and record; therefore we must take pains to incorporate
a little of the scientific approach into our professional selves. Whatever a child does is part of that child and should be recorded. How
we deal with the behavior is another matter.

Eating Records

The following records, one of a three-year-old and the other of a
five-year-old, reveal how much more than simple ingestion of food
is involved in an eating situation.

> Erin is sitting at the table with a napkin in front of her, waiting for
> juice and crackers. She is holding the cup over her chin. She gets the
> juice pitcher, holds the handle in one hand and the bottom of the
> pitcher with the other hand. She pours very carefully, her tongue
> licking her top lip. She puts the pitcher down gently and takes the
> basket with crackers, which has just been passed to her. She knocks

the basket into the cup and spills her juice. She looks at the teacher with concern.

The teacher suggests that she get a sponge. She goes to the sink where the sponges are, reaches for the paper-towel dispenser and struggles to get a towel out. The aide asks her if she wants any help but she finally gets the towel out. She is holding a cracker in her mouth the entire time. She starts wiping up the juice, spreading it all over the table. Her napkin has gotten wet and she states matter-of-factly, "I need a new napkin." The teacher gives her one and she starts shredding the old one. She crumples it into a ball and puts it on a shelf. The teacher asks her to throw it in the garbage and she does this without any question.

She returns to her chair and another child says, "More pear juice!" Erin asks, "Is it pear?" The teacher answers that it is banana and apple juice and she quietly says, "Oh." She sits chewing on her cracker, with crumbs all over her mouth. She stands up and sits down again for no apparent reason, then states, with disgust, "There's crumbs in there." She is holding her cup over her head and looking through the clear bottom. She says, with the same tone of disgust, "I don't like it!"

She gets up, walks quickly over to the sink, and pours out her juice. She returns to the table to finish her cracker. She picks up her empty cup and napkin and throws them away. She is still chewing her cracker as she bounces off to her cubby to get her mat for rest time.

It is lunchtime, and Sara bounds over to the table she customarily sits at, a smile of rapture overspreading her face as she spies the repast spread out before her. Not having partaken of the mid-morning snack, she is inordinately hungry and eager to begin the meal. However, she patiently awaits the arrival of the other children, seven in all. With arms outstretched and body straining to reach the platter, she carols out, "Pass the tuna fish!" There is no response and her request goes unheeded. Sara then more forcefully and insistently repeats her plaint, but is astounded when Samuel, ignoring her, removes the platter to his side and unhesitatingly proceeds to serve himself. Sara waits her turn without protest, nevertheless.

At the first opportunity, she dishes out a moderate portion (approximately three tablespoonsful) of tuna fish salad for herself and passes the rest to Gabriel at his request. Eating slowly but with good appetite, she pauses to gaze with fascination at a slowly spreading puddle of milk that Kenneth has accidentally spilled onto his plate, then reaches over to help him blot it up. "Where should I put this?" she inquires, pointing with distate at the soggy napkin and dropping it with a splat on the plate.

Both children resume their eating until interrupted by Leonard's resounding cry of "Whoever eats peanut butter is a rotten egg," which Sara repeats lustily with obvious delight and agreement. Leonard, apparently piqued because the attention has shifted to Sara, grimaces ferociously and punches her swiftly and squarely on the arm. Neither flinching nor crying out, Sara appears unmoved by the sudden attack. Instead, having little by little consumed her tuna fish, she is ready for the next course, calling out, "Please pass the bread, please." No one complies. Then, as if thinking aloud, she declares, "I'm going to open this milk" and pours a small amount into her glass, sipping it slowly. Becoming slightly impatient, she repeats more loudly and insistently, "Pass the bread," and is finally handed a slice of rye bread. It is petulantly refused as unsuitable for sandwich purposes, as it does not match the slice of white already on her plate. Confiding to the observer, she pronounces, "Mommy says I'm not allowed to have more bread." T: "Why not?" Sara replies matter of factly, "I don't know. Give me that other piece of bread," then carefully spreads peanut butter in small dabs.

She then peers inquisitively into the container of milk and says in a puzzled tone of voice, "Nothing's in here." She shakes the container vigorously, looks up with a happy smile on her face and concludes, "Oh, there *is* something in here." With that, she pours out the rest of the milk and gulps it down. Replete and content, Sara surveys the table and observes brightly, "This is the quietest table."

RECORDING TOILETING BEHAVIOR

As in eating, the toileting routine has its specifically important aspects, such as a child's attitude toward his or her own body and the important question of whether the child sees body functioning and control as a source of pride in achievement or a bond to babyhood.

Details to Observe

- What set the child off? (What is the stimulus?)
  (child's own need imitation of a friend, response to group practice, request by the teacher, wet pants, etc.)
- What is the child's reaction—acceptance or resistance?
  (he might obviously need to go to the toilet but refuse to use the school toilet; she might not go when the group goes; he might go cheerfully, absentmindedly, hurriedly, casually, etc.)
- Are there signs of tensions? fears?
  (stiffness of body, clutching at genitals, whimperings, etc.)

●How interested does the child seem to be?
●How seriously or casually does the child take the toileting procedure?
●How does he handle himself? Are her coordination and skill up to the task?
(Is she competent? awkward? smooth? clumsy? slow? fast?)
●What is the child's manner like?
Casual? Excessively modest? Exhibitionistic? Does he show awareness of sex differences? Does she show interest in sex differences or similarities? What kinds of contacts with children, if any?

Of course, the behavior has to be seen against the background of the group procedures and teacher role to which the child is reacting at the moment. As in other episodes, we record the sequence of events from beginning to end and, if possible, we include the language of the child exactly as we hear it (or note its absence in everything we record). These illustrations may make this clearer.

Toileting Records

First, Lorna, age four-and-one-half:

Riding on a seesaw with Priscilla. Hops off. "I almost wet my pants." She runs inside, Priscilla following. Both pull down their clothing and sit on toilets, singing. "Skit, scoot, skit, scoot." Lorna flushes toilet, pulls up underwear and pants. "I think I'll wash my hands." Removes jacket. "See I have two shirts, isn't that funny? Are you going to wash your hands too, Priscilla?" Washes quickly. "Now I'll go into the dressing room and see how I look."

Four-year-old Robert is not so casual:

Robert is in the play yard, standing on top of the packing case, holding his pants and jiggling up and down. Sees teacher and says, "I want to go into the building."
T: "All right. Do you want to go to the toilet?"
"Yes." Climbs down hastily, saying, "I don't want you to watch."
T: "I'll close the door. Do you want the seat up?"
Robert frowns for a moment. "No, I don't know yet what I'm going to do. I want the door all the way closed."
Teacher closes the door and waits. Robert calls out twice, "I'm not through yet." After several minutes, he shouts, "I'm finished now." Flings open the door and struts out.
T: "Do you want to wash your hands?"

Robert's brows go up in surprise. "No, 'cause then I'd be ready for juice and crackers and it isn't time." Skips out to play yard. Plays in water tub, splashing hands madly. Holds up hands, fingers spread wide. Grins. "Look at my hands—clean!"

Another view, this time of some three-year-olds:

At the end of the story, the teacher reminded the children to go to the toilet if they had to, before washing up for snack. Martin got up slowly, dreamily, curiously watching the others as they clamored, "I did. I didn't." He says nothing and suddenly walks over to bathroom, by which time three girls were already in it. Lois and Paula are on the seats and Wendy is standing waiting. Martin edges past Wendy into a tight little corner between the sink and the wall. He is completely absorbed in watching Lois, who is now wiping herself. She wiggles off the toilet. "Wendy, I'm finished," she says and begins to pull up her underwear. Martin comes out of the corner just then and kneels down in front of her. Without saying a word, he holds down her slacks and panties with one hand, and pulls up her skirt with the other. She watches him. He has a look of innocent wonder as he carefully, with one finger, pokes her navel. She is as absorbed as he. They say nothing. The other children are by now watching him. The teacher says to Lois, "You had better move out of there, Lois, because these children are waiting." Martin and Lois both look up at her and Lois pulls up her pants as Martin walks out to wash. He did not go to the toilet.

RECORDING BEHAVIOR AT RESTING TIME

Rest as a routine has its own particular kind of responses, too. Along with such reactions as showing trust in adults and acceptance of group patterns, is the matter of body tensions and ability to relax. This is especially significant for the child who is new to the school situation. Even after adjusting to school, however, some children continue to need comfort and support during rest hour, while others have their most successful social experiences then, and still others just drop right off to sound slumber. It may help to see the meaning of resting time to a child in the following terms.

Details to Observe

- How does the child happen to be resting? (What is the stimulus?)
  Did he sprawl out by himself, or is there a prescribed time?
  Did the teacher decide the child was tired?
  Does rest automatically follow lunch hour?
  Does the child seem to understand what is expected of him?

- What is the child's reaction?

  Accepts (in matter-of-fact fashion, with pleasure, etc.)?

  Resists (dawdles, talks, does not respond, frequently asks to go to the toilet, frequently requests water, etc.)?

  Refuses (cries, runs around the room, runs out of the room, etc.)?

- Does the child require special attention from adult?

  (patting, sitting nearby, given lollipop, taken to separate room, etc.)

- Are there any signs of tension while resting?

  Body tensions (amount of movement, restlessness)?

  Comforting devices (thumb-sucking, masturbation, ear-pulling, etc.)?

  Special attachments (dolls, animals, handkerchiefs, blankets, pillow, diaper, etc.)?

  Leaving cot frequently on one pretext or another?

- What seem to be the child's bodily requirements for rest?

  Are there evidences of fatigue?

  (yawning, red eyes, peevishness, frequent falling, etc.)

  Does he sleep? For how long?

  Does she need something to play with (book, doll, etc.)?

  If he does not sleep, does he seem relaxed?

- What is the child's reaction to group during rest?

  Is it disturbing and disrupting?

  (shouts, sings loudly, runs about, crawls under children's cots, pulls up blinds, annoys children, etc.)

  Is there social activity?

  (talks to neighbor, signals, etc.)

  Is she conscious of other children's needs?

  (whispers, walks quietly, etc.)

  How does he wake?

  (smiling, talking, whimpering, crying, tired, refreshed, etc.)

  What does he do when he wakes?

  (lies quietly, calls the teachers, rushes to the bathroom, starts to play, etc.)

Rest might look like this:

Teacher is seated near a group of five four-year-olds who are lying quietly on their cots. Jeff is having a little difficulty getting comfortable. He tosses restlessly about, occasionally playing with his hands and feet. Near his head is a Teddy Bear which he tosses up into the air from time to time and tries to catch, unsuccessfully, with one hand. With a jerk and a grumble he is under his blanket and out again. He stretches onto his side, with finger in his mouth and looking tired. All of a sudden he is hidden again under the blanket, whispering barely audibly to himself. At times one of the other teachers walks through the room to the coat closet. Jeff raises his head long enough to watch her get her purse and leave. Then he drops back onto the cot, repeating his starting performance—playing with his hands and feet, as well as the fringe on the edge of his blanket. He stares dreamily at the chairs and beds around the room, all the while playing with his hands, feet, or blanket fringe. Suddenly he starts to clap loudly. Teacher cautions him about this, explaining that this is rest hour and children are sleeping. He stares at the teacher for a moment and then lies back without as much as a sound until the end of rest hour.

PATTERNS OF BEHAVIOR

Observations of children's behavior during the daily routines at school reveal behavior at any given moment in a child's life. Many such on-the-spot observations, added up over a period of time, reveal that which is consistent and repetitive in a child's responses to similar situations. We can then see the particular patterns of response, which may be similar to or different from other children's but, in any case, are true of that child. A pattern of behavior may be fixed and steady, even to rigidity, or it may be shifting and changing, even to the point of utter unpredictability. Over a really long period of time (six months to a year) the records may reveal sharply changing patterns as the child learns to handle routines differently, with maturing and experience. The importance of the on-the-spot record taken over time is the evidence that is accumulated to support or dispute the generalizations we usually feel able to make after we have known a child for a while. This is a basic reason for attempting frequent recording, even though admittedly it does not come easily in the life of a teacher.

This is one child's *pattern of behavior* at rest hour:

Tony's face always puckered up when he saw the shades drawn, although the look of distress never developed as far as tears. Not until the teacher came to sit with him did he relax, and then noticeably. He never asked for anything to comfort him, like a toy or a cracker, and never said anything. But as the teacher sat quietly near his cot, he would fall asleep in five minutes.

A *changing pattern* is revealed in this end-of-the-year generalization about a child's behavior at dressing time:

> At the beginning of the year Nancy would rush to get to the door the minute her outdoor clothes were on. She would lean against it stiffly with arms and legs outstretched and look like a formidable opponent for anyone who might challenge her. Many times she fought verbally with Ralph and John, the only ones in the group who dared question her right to be "first" all the time. As her friendship with Susan and Kate grew, she began to urge them to hurry and be first with her. Since Susan and Kate enjoy conversation too much to be hurried, she got nowhere with this. She would look anxiously at the door as she prodded them and eventually run off to her coveted spot. But one day Nancy stayed and waited for Susan and Kate. Triumphantly she confided to them, "We don't care if we're not first, do we, huh?" This was a great day for Nancy!

The patterns do not always rise to meet us. We may have to hunt for them deliberately. It helps to go back, say after two or three months, and tease out the items pertaining to that aspect of behavior we are trying to check. We might do something like this:

Episodes of resting —9/13, 9/21, 11/9, 1/8, 3/14
Episodes of toileting—9/14, 9/27, 10/17, 12/7, 3/14
Episodes of dressing—9/17, 10/3, 1/22
Episodes of eating —9/24, 10/12, 1/8, 4/13
    (etc.)

Listing the highlights of the individual episodes helps make the pattern become clear.

Highlights of Tommy's resting behavior:

9/23   Tommy cried when he woke from rest.
9/30   Tommy clung to teacher as he woke.
10/6   Tommy would not fall asleep without teacher sitting next to him.

The consistency of behavior is rather obvious. Tommy's rest time at school is fraught with feelings of uncertainty at this point.

GENERALIZING FROM THE RECORDS

A child is all of one piece, but different situations may cause any child to react in different ways. In finding the pattern of reaction to different routines, we might find similarity in all—or positive or negative reactions to different ones. For example, a child might be cheerfully cooperative in all school routines, or silently withdrawn; or she might be a fine group member until toileting, or eating, or rest. A child's reactions in any case are uniquely his or hers, and the record tells us about these unique responses to the life situations at school. In gathering evidence bit by bit and then seeing the patterns emerge, we really begin to see the child as he or she actually is. These persistent or changing patterns of behavior can be grouped under broad generalizations. The following are useful in understanding a child's behavior during the routines.

Persistent or Changing Patterns of Behavior in Relation to Routines: A Summary

- Usual attitudes at beginning, throughout, and at end of routine
  - Accepts easily, complies, resists directly or indirectly, shows signs of tensions, fears
  - Degree of interest
- Dependence or independence as evidenced in routines
  - Has to be reminded or told
  - Acts on own responsibility and initiative
  - Accepts or rejects assistance
- Consistent emotional reactions to routines
  - (excitement, silliness, relaxation, self-confidence, etc.)
- Coordination and abilities, tempo and time length
- Effect of child's behavior on group functioning
- Routines as social experience
- Adult participation and child response
  - To group procedures established by adults
  - To individual attention
- Expression of physical functioning
  - Amount of food eaten, length of sleep, frequency of urination, ability to relax, need for rest
- Awareness of and interest in own sex and sex differences revealed through routines
- Special problems (excesses)
  - Excessive modesty or exhibitionism at toileting, dressing, and undressing
  - Attachment to clothes
  - Extreme choosiness at eating time, retaining food, not eating, inability to eat solid foods, etc.
  - Dreaminess

Excessive physical tension and inability to relax

Fetishes

Excessive need for attention from teacher

Special ways in which teacher handles this child, and why

Wetting, soiling (in relation to age and frequency)

Records Showing Teachers' Generalizations

The following are illustrations of records in which the teacher has generalized about the child's behavior at routines on the basis of many on-the-spot records and the patterns that emerged.

Upon entering school, Lee resisted vigorously any and all routines, gradually accepting them one by one. He has never had a toilet accident at school, but called for the utmost privacy in toileting and usually postponed the process until he reached home. It was not until December that he went willingly without signs of stress. I was delighted last week to have him come to me and say, "You know, I went to the bathroom twice already." He knows when we wash hands and washes his in methodical fashion. He eats his snack matter-of-factly, placing cup and napkin in wastebasket when finished. He rests quietly after settling down on his rug. He dresses and undresses himself, asking for help only when necessary. He knows where to hang his clothes, and is careful to hang them up correctly.

Kim is fully independent now in dressing and undressing and no longer asks for help. Toileting is handled entirely by herself and even our presence is not required. Resting is still a time for socializing but for the most part without too much giggling. If she has been playing hard, she usually stops periodically to sit and look at a book or just watch what is going on around her as she sits. The rest period sometimes lasts for ten minutes, then off she goes again.

In routines as in other activities Nora at first did everything for herself and did it well. Could dress and undress herself with a minimum of help, even to buttoning. When given stool to stand on, she could turn on faucets after she had been shown how. In few records available on toileting, I have noticed no great curiosity as to differences of sex, with the exception of mentioning that she sits down to make and Craig stands up. She does not even look too much, but shows great interest in how fast the water or urine runs down the toilet and "how down it goes." Toileting time for Nora is noted to be a time for socializing. In the beginning she didn't want anyone to wash with her, but at present will wash in bowl with two others. Teacher on duty says Nora at this time very often talks about happenings of the morning past and most often has a remark about the fol-

lowing juice and rest routines. These remarks themselves have a repetitive quality. "Juice is good." "I sleep on my rug." "Show you my
rug." As to juice routine, Nora in the beginning watched the children
to see how they acted, what they had, what they did with their cups,
etc. If someone singled her out for attention, she acted coy or
grimaced or performed for the child, but hesitated when she noticed
adults looking. Now for the most part she eats quickly and wants to
hurry up to rest. Nora passes the basket with cookies in it to each
child in order around the table, then on to the next table, until all
three tables have been served. In comparison with many of the four-
year-olds' procedure, this is much more systematic. She has never
rested quietly on her mat, but at first she flopped up and down on her
tummy, pulling on others' rugs when they did this to hers. Now she
has a very hard time to lie on the mat at all, but wants to stand and
grimace and dance before the floor-length mirror. When reminded to
get on her mat, she drops down quickly, rests rigidly for a few seconds, and very often never does more than just sit. In all routines
Nora appears to enjoy socializing. She seems to feel comfortable in
following routines, even most of the rest periods. During rest, if
Nora's rug is where she is less likely to disturb the group, we do not
enforce rest on her as long as she is just moving and not talking. She
does not seem to be tired or need rest.

The generalizations based on what we see happening tell us
something about matters that are of vital importance to young children. Adults who developed social acceptability in these areas long
ago, and perform correctly with ease and without thought, are likely to overlook their significance in children's growing concepts of
themselves as people in a social environment.

3

RECORDING A CHILD'S USE OF MATERIALS

THE MEANING OF MATERIALS TO CHILDREN

WE TURN NOW to another area of functioning in the life of a child, experiences with materials. Play materials are as integral a part of school life as routines, but their function in the development of personality is somewhat different. If we tend to see play materials as a means of keeping idle hands busy, or if we evaluate their use in terms of work, we are likely to miss the special role they do play. Surprisingly, a good part of that role is its function in supporting children's cognitive growth, specifically in symbolization. The following brief record shows the beginning of this role:

> Three-year-old Suzanne and Jamila are sitting next to each other working with the play dough. Both have small rolling pins stuck straight up out of the dough. Jamila starts singing, "Happy birthday to you. . .," and they both stand up and fall back into their chairs giggling and laughing in high-pitched voices. Suzanne puts a blob of play dough on the end of an ice cream stick, and Jamila watches her with her index finger inside her mouth. Suzanne offers the stick to Jamila, and Jamila pretends to lick the play dough off the stick. They again break into laughter kicking their feet under the table.

Most people tend to interpret symbolic activities quite narrowly as the ability to write and to read the writing of others. While reading and writing are symbolic processes, they reflect only half of our symbolizing capacities. They are part of the more common, *verbal* half. The *nonverbal* half gives us our art—painting, sculpture, dance, mime, music, and drama (which combines both verbal and nonverbal). Nonverbal symbolization is an important way of com-

29

municating, even if it is not the most common, because many experiences, feelings, and thoughts either cannot be or are too difficult to be put into words.

Few people become artists, yet the nonverbal symbolizing activities are a necessary aspect of the learning process in childhood. Experience in nonverbalizing activities, such as dramatic play and the use of materials, is the basis for children's ultimate use of the more abstract forms of symbolization, such as letters and numbers. The reason for this is that young children use language primarily for social purposes and considerably less for intellectual conceptualization than we would like to believe. Until about the age of seven (give or take a year for individual differences), children's understanding is markedly limited by what their senses feed back to them, and their language is a reflection of that. They can and do make simple comparisons as they approach four and five, but on a concrete level and in a personal way. "My painting is better than yours," they say. "Yours is yukky." "That truck is bigger than the old one we had." It is too hard for them to be objective or analytical because they are still so egocentric. They find it almost impossible to deal with concepts that are not somehow related to their experience. As a result, what they can express or uncover through language is limited, too. This does not mean that children do not talk about real, important, and valid experiences. It is rather that their thinking, and therefore their talking, is tied to concreteness, to physical reality.

Nevertheless, children do begin to have an awareness of abstractions, even if they cannot fully grasp or explain their half-formed, shadowy understanding in words. They gain an intuitive sense about abstract concepts from the relationships and transformations they themselves cause in the materials they use in their play. In the following record it is apparent that two five-year-olds are absorbing the concept of relative height, an abstraction, in their typically personal, physically involved way. They are building with blocks.

DAN: Boy! This is getting high!

CHRISTINA: Mine too.

DAN (glancing at Christina): Mine is higher because I started mine first. (He continues to make his taller as he talks.)

CHRISTINA: That doesn't matter.

DAN: Measure. Mine is higher. (He holds his arm out and levels it with the top of his building. With slow, steady steps, he goes to

Christina's building.) See. (He extends his arms out on either side of himself for emphasis.)

CHRISTINA: So—I can reach higher. (She stretches up on tiptoes.)

DAN: See how high I can reach? (He stands right next to her and looks upward, trying to see whose hand is higher. He is unsteady and lurches backward, but catches his balance and prances to the shelf for more blocks. He begins to put another level on his structure As he works, he boasts.) Mine is still higher. Mine has floors.

CHRISTINA: Mine will have floors soon, just after I . . .

DAN (interrupting): Mine already does. (He speaks proudly, smiling as he hops back to the block shelf.)

Thus, as children use materials to replicate experience, they are spurred on to increasingly subtle levels of symbolization without being handicapped by their as yet inadequate verbal power. This in no way downgrades the role of language. It merely recognizes the reality of how children learn, which is through their senses, with language a secondary reinforcer that helps to define and extend their learning rather than to initiate it. Not until they are well past their early childhood and near the end of middle childhood can they learn about concepts primarily through words. For this reason, nonverbal forms of symbolizing activity can and should be well advanced before a child is asked to deal with the more abstract forms of symbols such as letters, words, and numbers.

Here are two children learning a variety of concepts through their use of materials:

Larissa is a two-and-one-half-year-old at an infant–toddler center who is finishing what she calls "stick-down," collage work with two-inch, precut pieces of paper. Her concluding efforts involve getting more glue out of the squeeze bottle. She does this by turning the bottle upside down, grasping it with both hands, and pressing very hard with her thumbs. The top of the bottle appears to be clogged because she applies a great deal of pressure for a long moment, accompanying the force with a quiet but determined grunt and a strained facial expression—jaw set, teeth clenched, head averted slightly as if anticipating that she might be squirted. A drop finally plops out onto the paper, Larissa looks satisfied and puts the glue bottle down, relaxing her face and her previously tensed shoulders. She then picks up a piece of wallpaper carefully with thumb and index finger of her left hand and places it down with the fingertips of both hands. She turns to the teacher and says, "I finish now."

Could she have understood through a verbal explanation about the flow of glue what she learned intuitively by using it? See what five-year-old Nan is learning in the sandbox without a word on her part or her teacher's. She is working by herself, not joining the ongoing conversation of the other children.

Nan pours sand through a large funnel and observes the running sand from the top, putting her head almost into the mouth of the funnel, and then lifts the funnel to see the sand run out of the bottom. Then she fills a large bucket and shakes it, watching the action of the dry sand. She pushes down hard with her hands on the sand in the bucket. She pours the sand through a sand mill the other children are using, steps back from the box, smiles broadly, and says, "All right, I've got the baby food."

The other children continue pouring sand through the mill and announce that it is a volcano machine. Nan pours sand into the machine with a small shovel and remarks to no one in particular, "We're going to build the biggest volcano in the world." She pours sand into the machine from the bucket and then the funnel. Edward takes the funnel from her and removes the machine off the pile of sand. Nan does not object but takes a bottle and fills it with a scoop, then pours the sand from the bottle onto the pile. She fills the bottle from a jug, pouring from different heights. She empties the bottle by shaking it backwards and forwards in an arc, watching the patterns of the falling sand.

The teacher announces cleanup. Nan starts to level the sand with a cardboard comb. The other children leave and Nan levels the sand again with wide movements of her whole arms reaching for more space. She flips the sand to and fro with flicking motions of the wrist of one arm and sweeps through it with both arms describing a semicircle before she leaves to join the group.

At the same time that children use materials for learning, they use them to express and cope with feelings of all kinds. Their bodies can exert more or less pressure, gentleness, or anger; their nails can scratch, their muscles can pound; their fingers can manipulate with care and composure or with awkwardness and distress.

Materials, ordinary play materials, are a bridge between children's inner selves and the outside world. They are the means by which children capture impressions of the world outside themselves and translate them into forms they can understand; they are the means of pulling out of themselves what they feel and giving it concrete expression. Materials (toys, blocks, sand, paint, clay, wood, paper, crayons, pencils, etc.) help children to

- Transform feelings into action:
    Anger or high spirits get pounded into clay.
    The desire to be big and strong goes into building "the tallest building in the world."
    The mood of spring sunshine is gently painted in pinks, yellows, and pale greens.
- Translate ideas into forms, concepts into shapes:
    A house of blocks, like a real house, has to be closed in and around; a road of blocks rambles on and on; a bridge is high up and across.
- Turn impressions into products:
    A cookie of clay must be round and flat; a crayoned grownup has long legs and a big smile.

Even if their impressions of a tree, a cow, or daddy all come out looking like a blob of red paint, children feel they have made a good try! Through their use of materials, children externalize impressions and feelings, develop muscles and skills, grow in powers of reasoning and logic. They gain in inner strength as they clarify hazy, incomplete understanding of the real world of objects, phenomena, and people.

Children approach materials as they approach life itself, with directness or shyness, with attack or withdrawal, with fear and hesitancy or with courage and self-confidence. Do all children plunge into soapsuds with the same zest? Do all children build daring block towers? Do all children sprawl paints across every inch of paper? Don't we all know the tidy child who handles clay and paint almost daintily? Or the cheerful little person who is never willing to stop playing and put toys away, who makes the most mess at the clay table, carries the mess over into an orgy of soap and water in the bathroom, then disappears just when it's time to clean up! And what of the many others who confine themselves to a limited few of the materials we offer them, as though starving themselves in the midst of plenty? Or the sad child who does not play with anything? There is a consistency of style and approach to materials that reveals much about children's responses.

Children will take any material, shape, or form and breathe a bit of themselves into it. The more shapable, or "unstructured," the material is, the better it serves for them to project feelings and ideas. At first contact, a material is something outside oneself, and a curiosity for that reason. It has to be explored as an item of the world outside of self. Then there is experimentation with it for its own sake: What are its properties and possibilities? Does it stick, stretch, break, fall, crush, smear? Eventually the material becomes a medium for expression and projection, and it is *used* for the child's own purposes.

When a child is fairly well able to break down the details that pertain to objects and people, and has the physical coordination for detailed work, materials are used representationally to crystallize that clarity. If a child is confused about some details, the confusion is set down too. Interestingly enough, if feelings are stronger than intellectual curiosity or creativity, a child may seem to misuse the material, as when a boy or girl makes mud out of clay or uses a doll for poking and throwing, or deliberately breaks block buildings. At such a point, children may need materials that are especially suited to their individual needs.

Materials that have a specific use and function, like dolls and bikes, are "structured" materials. Children use these for the implied purpose, but they will also project feelings onto them. (The doll is naughty and rebellious or is crying and upset.) Or children use them as a means for carrying out ideas, desires, or fantasies. (The bike is a plane, the doll is a traffic officer, the lotto cards are tickets, etc.)

Semi-structured materials, like blocks (not as fluid as paint or clay, nor as finally formed as a toy car), give the satisfaction of construction and three-dimensional solidity.

But beyond this analysis, there remains the wonder of children's imagination: If they need a plane, a car or a stick can become one. If they want to make a person, they will struggle with the material until the essence of *person* is there.

In short, materials are used by children in the way children themselves need and want to use them. The manner and style, however, is unique to each child.

DETAILS TO OBSERVE IN RECORDING A CHILD'S USE OF MATERIALS

THE SETTING
- Include the nearby significant people and activities, as in routines, and also such things as the abundance or scarcity of

materials, availability of supplies, amount and kind of adult supervision, etc.

THE STIMULUS

- How does the child come to use the material?
  (teacher-suggested; group procedure; imitation of another child; self-initiated; suggested by another child, etc.)

RESPONSE TO PAINT

- What colors does the child use? Does she mix colors (in jars, in coasters, or on the paper)? Are the colors separated on paper?
- Does she paint one color over another?
- Is he able to control the drips?
- Does he try to control the drips? Does he deliberately drip?
- Does he confine himself to one small spot or bit of space, or does he spread out? Does she paint off the paper?
- What forms, if any?
  (vertical lines, curves, circles, fill-ins, letters, dots, numbers, blotches of color, representation, etc.)?
- Does the child paint over the forms?
- What kind of brush strokes?
  (scrubbing, dotting, gliding, etc.)
- How many paintings? Does she paint quickly? Does she work for a long time on one?
- Does he name the painting? In detail? In general?

RESPONSE TO CLAY

- How does the child handle the clay physically?
  (pounding, rolling, pulling apart; squeezing, poking, making mush; making balls or snakes; slapping it, stamping on it; patting, stroking, scraping, etc.)

- Does she use supplementary tools, such as tongue depressors, sticks, toothpicks, scissors, beads, etc.?
- Is there representation?
  (naming; size of products; accuracy of detail)
- How does he use material in the space available?
  Does he work in his own area or does he spread out (off the board, over the table, etc.)?

RESPONSE TO BLOCKS

- What blocks does the child select?

(size and type of blocks; supplementary materials—dolls, small blocks, cars, wedgies, etc.)
- What forms does she construct?
  (up in the air, crisscross, along the floor, piling, enclosures, recognizable structures, etc.)
- How does he use space?
  (confined or spread out; close to shelves; aware of obstacles; etc.)
- How flexible is the child in solving problems? Does he/she try different approaches? Repeat the same ineffectual ones? Repeat a successful approach again and again?
- Does the child verbalize while working?
- Is the structure named? Is it used in dramatic play? Is the child interested primarily in the process of building?
- Is there a repeated theme? Are themes changeable and varied?
- Does any kind of imaginative play develop while the building is going on? After it is finished?

LENGTH OF TIME SPENT WITH MATERIAL

The length of time spent can reflect concentration span, interest, distractability, disinterest, feelings of inadequacy, tolerance for struggle, tolerance for challenge, response to something new, age, etc.

RECORDS OF USE OF MATERIALS

The following two children are getting something very different out of their play with materials. First, two-year-old Penny at the sandbox:

> Penny runs to sandbox carrying tablespoon, empty orange juice can, and toy plastic teacup. She climbs down into sandbox, sits down in corner, and silently and intently begins to fill can with sand, using spoon. She is oblivious to several other children around her. She stands up, dumps sand from can onto asphalt outside sandbox. She bangs can down on sand several times, then gently pats sand with open palm, saying "Cake." René, age four, comes up. She starts to take can from Penny, saying, "Can I have that?" Penny pulls the can away and stands still, staring at René.
>
> Teacher gives René a small spoon and plastic cup. She stands beside Penny and they both begin to spoon sand, occasionally smiling at each other. Penny climbs out of the sand and goes to bench where teacher is sitting. She dumps the sand onto the bench and then spoons it back into can. She dumps it onto the bench again, and pats

it gently. "I'm making cake." She takes a spoonful of sand and puts it on teacher's hand. She looks up and sees Patty on the swing. She runs over to her, carrying spoon with her.

Manuel, five-and-one-half, is in an after-school group who are waiting for their working parents.

Manuel thrust his hand into the clay bucket. As he pulled out a large piece of clay, his face took on an expression of mock nausea. He uttered one loud and spirited word, "Yuck." He walked over to where Stephanie, Johanna, and Lora had already started their work, and threw his clay upon the board vigorously. Immediately, he started to pound and slap with his hands. Then, using a flat piece of wood, he quickly slapped the clay into a flat, circular shape. His gestures were made even more forceful by the lunging movements of his body, which was stretched across the floor.

Manuel picked up a roller and began rolling out his pancake, stopping every now and then to use the wooden stick to shape the edge into a smooth, circular form. He then dropped both tools and began slapping the clay with his hands. Once again he used his whole body while chopping with his hands at the clay in the manner of a karate expert. "Kawabunga!" he shouted. Stephanie and Lora joined in the action, and a chorus of voices chanted, "Kawabunga!" Manuel's fingers began scraping the clay off the board. His hands began shaping the formless mass into a cake-like form. His body stretched out, and he assumed a more contemplative posture as his fingers smoothed the sides of the shape.

He then picked up one edge of the clay and began to roll it up slowly. This done, he squeezed the roll with his hands and shaped the clay into a ball. He slapped the ball down and flattened it out. His fingers spread out and pushed the clay in a long, sliding movement back and forth over the board. He picked up a clay hammer and, with full strength, delivered a blow on the flat piece of wood. "Kawabunga chop!" he yelled over the noise of the loud hammering.

"My ears are hurting," the teacher said. "Don't hammer on the wood, Manuel. It makes too much noise." He continued hammering directly on the wooden piece. The teacher moved closer. "What did I say to you?" she asked.

Manuel looked up at the teacher, hesitated, and then repeated, "Don't bang on the wood." He dropped the hammer and discarded the wooden piece. Then he rolled the clay into a ball with a slow, twisting motion. He pressed his fingers into the clay, picked it up, now pie-shaped, and flipped it into the air. Then he picked up a hammer, pushed the clay, then pounded it. He rubbed his palm into the board as his mother made a quiet entrance into the room. Alerted by the other children, he greeted his mother gleefully and went off to wash his hands in the bucket.

THE UNIQUE QUALITY OF THE CHILD, OR
HOW THE CHILD DOES *WHAT*

Thus far we have recorded children's use of materials in such a way as to get a fairly inclusive picture of *what* they are doing. But we must also note what the special meaning of the experience is to an individual child. We must get down *how* a child does what he or she is doing. We must consciously and deliberately include, along with the actual action itself, the signs that show feeling.

When we record *gross* movement, such as "she reached for a block," "he lifts the brush," "she grabbed the sponge," we are recording actions completely objectively, but without their life-pulse, or even our own response to their meaning. A child might be reaching for that block stealthily, hesitantly, or victoriously; perhaps she grabbed the sponge angrily, defiantly, efficiently, or just quickly; and he could lift the brush suspiciously, hastily, or absentmindedly. It is not enough to record what he or she *does* (i.e., reached for a block), we must tell *how* a child does the *what*. In the above descriptions, the meaning of each activity is different with each qualifying word. The descriptive adjective or adverb indicates the unique character of the gross action.

As we live and work with people, we react spontaneously to their range of feelings without ever thinking about how we know they feel as they do. We just sense it. With children, we certainly sense when they are delighted with themselves, when they are unhappy, when they are tense, when they are completely at ease. Actually, we take into our mind's eye a wide variety of cues that the other person sends out and get a composite picture that we then interpret according to our own experience and associations. Often we jump to conclusions before we get all the clues. It helps, therefore, to break down the nuances of behavior so that we are able to include them in the record. Even though something of our own interpretation will be there, the evidence to support us will be there, too.

As indicated in the discussion of the language of recording, there is a difference between the subjective interpretation that *labels the child:* "He is hostile," "She is stubborn," "He is anxious," "She is greedy," and the interpretation of one small piece of the total behavior: "He gave the teacher a *hostile look*," "She *replied stubbornly*," "He showed an *anxious smile*," "She *reached greedily* for the cookies." The difference is more than semantic. Labeling children defines them and confines them within a total appraisal. Interpreting a piece of the whole, such as a gesture, a smile, a posture, a voice quality, etc., leaves room for the gathering of many such expressions of feeling within a variety of situations. One can have hostile feelings under certain conditions and not be a hostile person. One can be stubborn about certain convictions and not be a generally stubborn person. One can feel anxiety about particular occurrences and not be an anxious person. One can even be greedy about one or two things and yet not be totally greedy at all.

Describing *how* a child does *what* adds up in time to clues we seek in order to understand children's motivations and feelings. These clues to feeling are the involuntary, noncontrolled, nondirected movements and gestures that accompany any gross action and give it its character. They are unique for every child and every action, for no child works at materials, or is involved in any form of play, ·without a variety of accompanying behavior. Thus, as we pick up the child's action and at what or whom it is directed, we note other things as well.

- We include the sounds a child makes and the language a child speaks.

  If the voice is being used, what is it like?
  —Loud, soft, ringing, well-modulated, high-pitched are descriptions of the *physical quality* of the voice.
  —Jubilant, wavering, whining, reassuring, hesitant, gleeful, nonchalant, casual, fretful, smug describe the *feeling tone* of the child's voice.
  What does the child say? (Pick up direct quotes if possible.)
  Does the child chant, sing, use nonsense syllables, phrases, tell stories, etc., while working?
- We note the movements of the body as a child uses materials.
  What is the posture like?
  (erect, rigid, hunched, floppy, straight, curled, squat, etc.)
  What is the rhythm of the body movements?
  (jerky, smooth, easy, jumpy, staccato-like, flowing, etc.)
  What is the tempo of the body movement?
  (rapid, sluggish, measured, slow, swift, leisurely, deliberate,

speedy, hasty, moderate, unhurried, etc.)
How much and what kind of effort does the child expend?
(a great deal, excessive, very little, moderate; strained, laborious, easy, vigorous, forceful, feeble, etc.)
What kind of freedom does the child show in his/her body movement?
(sweeping movements; cramped, tiny movements; free-flowing; restrained, tight, restricted, etc.)
• We identify the details of facial expression.
—Eyes (glint, dullness, brightness, shine, teariness, blinking, etc.)
—Mouth (grin, quiver, pucker, tongue between lips, biting lips, smiling, wide open, drawn tight, etc.)

From these details we can surmise the child's emotional response to the materials, e.g., excitement, contentment, frustration, self-criticalness, confidence, squeamishness, stimulation, overstimulation, taking in stride, intense interest, preoccupation, etc. Feelings come through clearly in this next episode.

> Angelita, four-and-one-half, was sitting next to the teacher, playing with Tinkertoys. One of the other children held the box. In a very annoyed voice, Angelita blurted out, "I want to use that." She had a look of strong concentration on her face as she took each piece and pushed it forcefully into place. She took time choosing which piece to use next. The teacher got up and walked away, but Angelita did not seem to notice. She kept on working in the same way, thoughtfully and forcefully, without talking to any of the other children at the table. Her construction was large and intricate. When the teacher told her it was cleanup time, Angelita said, "No!" in a determined way and continued working. Later, when the teacher told her that she could keep her finished work on a shelf, Angelita very carefully carried it there. When she noticed a child going toward the piece, she screamed, "Don't touch that!"

Reactions to People While Working

The feelings that children reveal may be reactions to things other than the materials they are using. We include in the record, therefore, what we see of their reactions to the people around them.

• Is there any socializing with children as the child uses materials?
How does the child show awareness of children nearby?
(talking, showing materials and products, touching others,

etc.; using products in dramatic play; helping others, criticizing; calling for attention to what he/she is doing, etc.)
Does the child work alone or with others?
• What are the child's relations to adults while using materials?
Does he call for help, approval, supplies, etc.?
Is he suggestible, defiant, indifferent, heedless, mindful, etc., regarding adult offers of help, adult participation, reminders of rules and limitations, offers of suggestions, etc.?
• How does the experience end?
What events and feelings follow immediately after?
(puts things away, puts work on the storage shelf, destroys own work, shows things to the children or teachers, leaves everything and goes to another activity, dances around the room, etc.)

RECORDS ILLUSTRATING DETAIL

The following records all show attention to detail and nuance. The first is primarily a recording of gross movements and sequence of events.

Yvonne, age five:
Yvonne came directly to the outdoor table on which teachers had prepared a basket of scissors, crayons, paste in a six-ounce jar with a spoon in it, and small paper cups. The children were encouraged to help themselves to the paste and to put it in a cup. There was also a stack of paper and two aluminum plates filled with paper collage, string and wool, and cloth collage in various shapes. "I wanna paste, I wanna paste, I wanna paste."

Teacher, busy with another child, "Yes, Yvonne. It's Bill's turn now . . . It will be yours next. Help yourself, Yvonne." (She can be very self-sufficient, but now and again becomes completely helpless, usually with a smile on her face as though she knows she is acting.)

Standing in the same place, and not looking at teacher, Yvonne says, in a babyish, whiny tone, "I wanna paste, I wanna paste." She looks along the table at the others who are cutting, crayoning, pasting. She moves around a child, and helps herself to the entire basket of crayons, placing it in front of her seat. She helps herself to paper, sits down, and makes a few crayon marks. As though realizing that this was not what she had planned to do, she calls, "Mrs. M.?"

"Yes?"

"I wanna paste."

"The jar is down at the end of the table, Yvonne."

Yvonne goes for the paste and gives herself some. Back at her seat she pastes a piece of collage on her paper, helps herself to another piece, and pastes that. She works intently, lips parted. Spends more time than needed pushing her finger around and around in the paste on the paper, as though enjoying the feel of it. She pastes wool, lace, paper, and cloth. A piece of string frustrates her. Teacher approaches.

"May I help you?"

"Yes," whiny and a little pouty. Teacher puts a short line of paste on the paper and lays the string on it.

"Now you show me how you want your string to go and we will put some paste there." Yvonne accepts this idea.

"Now you put the paste where you want the string to be." She does.

"I'm finished!"

"O.K."

She smears the paste around on her hands. "I wanna wash."

"There's water and towels on the tree stump," says the teacher.

Yvonne washes and runs off to the trikes. She had not spoken to any child while she worked.

The second record has more of the "qualifying" details, and reveals the mood of the child more successfully.

Winky, age four-and-one-half, at the paints:

Winky points to the window and with radiant face calls in delight, "It's snowing cherry blossoms! First they are white, then green, then red, red, red! I want to paint!" He goes to the easel and quickly snatches up a smock. Sliding in beside Wayne, he whispers to him caressingly and persuasively, "Wayne, you want blue? I give it to you, okay? You give me red because I'm going to make cherries, lots of red cherries!"

After the boys exchanged paint jars, Winky sits erect, and with a sigh of contentment starts quickly but with clean strokes to ease his brush against the edge of the jar. He makes dots all around the outer part of the paper. His tongue licks his upper lip, his eyes shine, his body is quiet but intense. The red dots are big, well-rounded, full of color, and clearly separated. While working, Winky sings to himself, "Red cherries, big, round, red cherries!" The first picture completed, he calls the teacher to hang it up to dry. The next picture starts as the first did, dots at the outside edge, but soon filling the whole paper. He uses green too, but the colors do not overlap.

Still singing his little phrase, Winky paints a third and fourth picture, concentrating intently on his work.

The other children pick up his song and Wayne starts to paint blue dots on his paper. Waving his brush, Winky asks, "Wayne, want to try my cherries?" Swiftly and jubilantly he swishes his brush across Wayne's chin. Laughing, he paints dots on his own hands. "My hands are full of cherries," he shouts. He runs into the adjoining room, calling excitedly to the children, "My hands are full of cherries!" He strides into the bathroom emphatically to wash his hands. Nellie follows him in, calling, "Let's see, Winky." "Ha, I ate them all," he gloats as he shows his washed hands with a sweeping movement. He grabs a toy bottle from the shelf, fills it with water and asks the teacher to put the nipple on. He lies down then on a mattress and contentedly sucks the bottle, his face softly smiling, his eyes big and gazing into space, his whole body limp with satisfaction.

This record shows us something of a child's need to relate to others while working.

Freddy, age five, at clay:

After hanging up his snowsuit Freddy entered the playroom in a manner which for him was thoughtful and quiet, a great contrast to his voluble propulsion, as if shot out of a cannon. He edged into a chair at the end of a table where no one else sat, his eyes dreamily watching in an unfocused manner the actions of others at two other tables as they rolled, punched, and pounded the clay they were using. Like a sleepwalker he accepted a hunk of clay and in an absent manner rolled it under the palm of his right hand, his head turned to the side, eyes directed toward the ten or twelve in the room.

A few minutes passed thus. Then he picked up the hunk of clay and let it fall "kerplunk" on the table. Instantly his mood changed, like pressing a button and changing a still picture into an animated one. "Boom!" he shouted, "I got a ball! Look at my ball, teacher! Bounce! Bounce!" He banged it down a few times. Then he started rolling it into a long thin piece. "Here's a snake. I'm making a rattlesnake. Are you making a rattlesnake, Donna?" he asked the child nearest him at the other table.

To David, who had a moment before entered the room and started to work at Freddy's table, "That's a snowman, David. Now I'm making a snowman. ... Now I'm making a snake big as Edward's." Freddy held it up and chortled with glee. "Hee-hee-hee."

"Look what I made. I twist it here." He dropped it on the table and began pounding it.

"Now I'm making a pancake. Look at my pancake. Taste my pancake, teacher."

Flop! he dropped it on the table again, rolling it over and over,

faster, faster, his motions in keeping with his words. Head and shoulders were hunched over the table, his lips and tongue stumbled over
each other in an effort to increase the speed of his words. "Chee—ee
—ee—eeeeeeeee..."

Everything slowed down. He was quiet, absorbedly working for a
moment. Then in sharp staccato and prideful tone: "Look what I
made, teacher.... Look what I made, Donna.... Look at my wrist-
watch."

At this point it was necessary for the teacher to help another child,
and she was in a stooping position, with her back to Freddy. He
poked her insistently in the back to add emphasis to his exhortation.
"Look at me, teacher!"

She turned to find the clay covering Freddy's upper lip. His head
was tilted back to prevent its slipping off. "It's a mustache. Ha-ha-ha
(he laughed uproariously). Now it's a hat." He quickly transferred
the clay to his head. "Teacher, look at my hat."

It seems that Freddy's satisfaction in all he does comes not only
from his creative use of materials but from the response of individuals, especially adults, present.

INTERPRETATION—THE LAST DIMENSION

Even though we spot the separate, small parts of an action, we
actually respond to the whole, integrated behavior of a child, such
as his anger, joy, surprise. Our response follows a spontaneous,
unspoken assessment of the child's feeling which is drawn from our
personal experience and understanding. To some extent we must
rely on this subjectivity to define or interpret a child's behavior. We
are dependent, however, on correct descriptive words about significant details to place that feeling on record. The value of a record
that includes details such as those suggested in the preceding sections is that our interpretation (he is happy, he is sad) is rather
better bolstered by objective evidence. We are therefore less likely
to be assuming that a feeling is present in a child because we happen to be identifying with him as the underdog or victim, or because we are reacting with subjective antagonism to an aggressor or
uncouth person, or because for any other reason we are putting
ourselves into the situation irrationally. Interpretation represents
the sum total of our background of understanding. Professionally
valuable interpretation relies heavily on objective data.

A Note of Caution

It is impossible to get everything into every record. No child ever does everything possible in human behavior at any one time, nor could a teacher get it all down if a child did. Don't try to use the suggestions for details to record as a checklist! While the teacher is busily checking off what seems important to look for, the child may be doing something we never thought of at all, and that would be missed. Keep your eyes on the youngster, not on the printed page! It is not *how much* you record, but *what* and *how,* that makes a record valuable.

On-the-Spot Records Lead to Supported Generalizations

The review of children's use of materials over a period of time will be a mirror of their growth in this area. We will get to know many things about them that we might have missed without these concentrated observations of their activity. We will see a profile of their tastes and ideas and learn how much confidence they have in their own imagination and capacity. We will note their dependency on adults and children, their concern for standards or indifference to them, their pleasure in doing or their anxiety about doing things wrong. These responses are evaluated best when seen against the backdrop of a child's general coordination, maturity, experience, and age, as well as against the usual behavior of children of the same age group.

PERSISTENT OR CHANGING PATTERNS OF BEHAVIOR IN RELATION TO MATERIALS: A SUMMARY

As with the summary on routines, we look for patterns of behavior —overall patterns that indicate a general approach to materials and specific patterns relating to different materials. Here are suggestions for what to include in such a summary:

1. How the child uses the various materials—paint, clay, blocks, etc.—over a period of time, in persistent or changing ways

   How the child comes to use the material generally (on his/her own initiative, on the suggestion of the teacher or another child, through imitation of other children)

   Coordination (physical ability to carry out techniques)

   Techniques (Include the stage of development—manipulative, exploratory, representational—in relation to child's age and background of experience. For example, painting dots, rolling clay, or piling cubes are techniques that can be early steps in the use of new materials, typical techniques of an age group, or excessively simple usage of material by a child who has the age and background for more complex approaches.)

How the child works (concentration and care used; exploratory; competently, skillfully, intensively, carelessly, tentatively, distractible, in different ways).

Language or sound accompaniments.

Mannerisms.

Products (creativity, imagination, originality shown).

Attention span (in general, and in relation to specific materials and activities).

Materials chosen by the child for dramatic play and how they are used.

Whether or not the child completes what he/she starts.

Adult role and child's response. (Indicate rules, limitations, participation, what is permitted, and how child accepts all these.)

2. How the child seems to feel about the materials.

Number, variety, frequency of materials and activities enjoyed, used, and avoided. (Include changing and static interest.)

General attitudes—enthusiastic, eager, confident, matter-of-fact, cautious, etc. (Include attitude toward new as well as familiar materials.)

Importance of given areas to the child—interest, intensity of pleasure, preoccupation, fears, avoidance, resistance.

Specific materials in relation to which the child apparently feels satisfaction, frustration, self-confidence, inadequacy, etc.

How the child reacts to failure, to success. (What constitutes failure or success? What is the level of aspiration?)

3. How the child's use of line, color, and form compares with what most children in the group seem to be doing.

4. Child-adult relationship revealed via materials (independence—dependence).

5. Special problems: distress over breakage, avoidance of messiness, concentration on only one material or idea, inability to concentrate and enjoy.

Following are examples of two children's overall use of materials.

The various items from the records, when brought together in a summary of persistent or changing patterns, are easily written up as a sketch of a youngster's use of materials. In time this sketch becomes part of the end-of-the-year record of the child.

RECORDS OF OVERALL RESPONSE TO MATERIALS

Lee, age four-and-one-half:

Lee's work with creative materials has been largely teacher-initiated. Before he begins any activity he usually spends some time watching the other children. Then, when he apparently feels sure of himself, he begins. His attention span is adequate to complete the activity. He works deliberately and quietly, absorbed and interested in the task at hand. It is quite evident that this is real work. His work is neat and carefully done. When he abandons this approach to materials he seems worried, and seeks reassurance from the teacher that this untidiness is accepted comfortably by her. He verbalizes as he works, a running commentary to teacher, children, or no one. He shows pride in accomplishment and again often seeks approval from the teacher. His work with clay is delightful and imaginative and he seems to feel more freedom here than in the use of other media.

Iris, age three:

Materials most used by Iris are sand, mud, crayons, easel paints, finger paints, and water. Just recently she has begun to use the clay to make cakes with cooky cutters or make imprints with any article handy. At first her attitude toward materials was one of indifference, but now she is interested in what she is making and comes to show it to the teachers or children. Paste on her hands at first annoyed her so that she did not want to use it. Today she was pasting and I was delighted to see a paste smear in her hair, and Iris concentrating intently on her creation.

When a new material was introduced she looked at it but did not attempt to play with it. Recently we received train and track, musical bells, new dishes, and started a new project of covering our rug chest. She wanted to be part of each group, except dishes, and went from one thing to another as fast as she could. This was so unusual that we almost gasped in surprise. The part that gave us the biggest thrill was this morning when two children were taken upstairs to cover the chest. Iris went to the toilet and on the way back noticed what was going on. Going up to a big five-year-old she said, "Give me hammer" in a demanding voice. Teacher said she could have a turn next. Stamping foot, trying to pull hammer from Lucy's hand, she replied, "Now, I want it right now." Not receiving it instantly, she came down to tell the other teacher her trouble. She did get a turn and then went to the musical bells. While there are still materials she has not touched, such as blocks, setting table with dishes, cars, she is adding to her play more materials each day. Outside equipment is now, and has been from the beginning, used without fear of falling. Every piece of equipment has been used by her, and with good control of muscles, expression and movement of body indicating extreme satisfaction. The swing is the one place where she always hums and sings.

4

RECORDING CHILDREN'S BEHAVIOR WITH ONE ANOTHER

HOW CHILDREN LEARN TO SOCIALIZE

It is perhaps hard to believe, but nevertheless true, that young children at first look at one another as they do at objects and materials —as something to touch, to smell, and maybe to taste! So much is this so that a little two-year-old pours sand on another child's head and then stares in amazement at his distress, or calmly pushes someone down the stairs if she is in the way, or pokes a finger into a youngster's eye to see what makes it shine. This sounds like the cruelest savagery but it is really nothing more than evidence for the fact that there is a time in the life of human beings when they do not understand that other people have feelings like their own. As a matter of fact, there is even a time when human beings do not understand that they themselves are separate, individual people, capable of independent feeling and action. The consciousness of self, of being somebody, comes gradually. Paradoxically, one must have awareness of this selfness, this being, before one can even suspect that other living creatures feel pain and pleasure.

Feelings and Know-how

The early years are the time when attitudes toward people are laid down in the character structure of the child, and the techniques for getting along in our culture are more or less painfully learned. As teachers, we have to be aware of three things about children's social development:

- A child's attitudes toward people

49

(affection, love, trust, suspicion, hate, etc.)
- The strength of a child's feelings
  (deep, casual, indifferent)
- How much and what kind of know-how a child has in getting
  along with others
  (Do you get a doll by asking for it, stealing it, or grabbing it?)

In this sense, a child may feel warm and loving to all humanity, but show it crudely, perhaps by hugging those who do not want hugging at the moment. Or a child may be jealous or resentful, but knowing that hugging is approved by adults but hitting is not, may hug to hurt. By the time children come to school, there has already been a complex background of experience shaping their attitudes and techniques. They are, however, still very much in the process of learning (as we are too) and quite receptive to our efforts to help them feel wholesome attitudes and practice constructive techniques.

A Child Becomes Aware of Self

Babies at birth are completely unconcerned about other human beings. They become conscious of others in relation to the fulfillment of their own needs and wants, which means, quite naturally, from a self-centered point of view. This is neither wrong nor unnatural. It is, however, the base from which future behavior will develop, sooner for some, later for others.

At the time that children start to speak of themselves as "I" instead of in the third person ("Baby wants a drink"), they are still examining other children with curiosity and interest but without comprehension. Not until children feel themselves persons (know their names, their sex, their likes and dislikes, and something of where they belong) can they look at others and sense "They feel even as I feel." It is natural to the growth of a young child, therefore, to be in a state of progression from nonidentification with others toward increasing capacity for sympathy and understanding. Before one can guide a child in social relationships, one must know how far along that child is on the road to maturity.

How Far Is Far?

A brief look at a pair of two-year-olds and a pair of three-year-olds reveals clear differences in their social maturity.

Two-year-old Natasha and the teacher have been playing together with a Snoopy Jack-in-the-Box on the floor. Cory has been playing hide-and-seek in a nearby closet with some of the other children. Suddenly Cory's attention is caught by Natasha's happily saying, "Bye-bye, Snoopy," as she pushes the toy back into the box, and he reaches out to grab the toy with a look of envy in his eyes. Natasha, startled, whines, "No." Hesitantly she reaches out toward the Snoopy while gazing pleadingly at the teacher. The teacher explains to Cory that Natasha does not want to share the toy just now, maybe later. Cory looks angrily at the teacher and then leans viciously against Natasha, attempting to bite her but biting the Jack-in-the-Box instead. He breaks into a frustrated sob, then, after some comforting by the teacher, wanders off to find another toy to play with.

A group of three-year-olds were sitting on the floor in music class while the music teacher was playing her guitar and singing "There was an old woman . . ." The children were instructed to clap their hands and sing along if they knew the song. Melissa and Daniel were sitting next to one another, each focused on the music teacher. Both of them clapped and joined in singing many times. At one point Melissa sang words that were different from the teacher's and Daniel's. He quickly switched his focus to Melissa and stopped clapping and singing. He leaned over, looked squarely into Melissa's face and announced matter-of-factly, "Stupid!" Melissa stopped singing and clapping and looked at Daniel quizzically but said nothing. Daniel once more proclaimed Melissa "stupid" but not before he was almost on top of her with his voice and body. By this time, neither one was focused on anything but each other's eyes, waiting to see who would make the first move. Suddenly Melissa smiled, happily repeated "Stupid!" to Daniel and fell on the floor laughing. Daniel caught her infectious laugh as he fell on the floor, having fun with the word stupid. Very soon they were both just laughing together and the word stupid was no longer heard. By the time the music teacher finished the song, both children were sitting up and clapping along with one another and with the teacher.

When teachers first see them at school, children have not had too much time as yet for maturing. They behave with one another only as they know how within their limits. They may long to please but still do unto each other only as they know how rather than as we think they should. Even as we show them better techniques for getting along with one another, we must accept without condemnation the inadequate techniques they already have. This does not mean that all and any behavior is permitted to go on without an effort to direct it. To do that would be a real disservice to children because they are dependent on us for cues to what is socially acceptable. It does mean, however, that we may not expect of children behavior they neither know about nor are capable of performing. So often what we judge to be naughty is due to sheer ignorance.

By the time we reach adulthood we have already incorporated into our personalities the morality and ethics of our culture. Young children, however, are still somewhat uninitiated and much of what they do is meaningful to them only in the purely personal terms of how they feel about what's happening and not in the objective sense of what is right or wrong. Understanding and accepting children's anger, jealousy, rivalry, fear, ambition, and anxiety establish an atmosphere of acceptance in which they can grow into socially necessary and morally desirable behavior without losing their self-respect and dignity as human beings.

We cannot close the gap between adulthood and childhood by trying to behave like children ourselves. But we can use our imagination and feel with children so that we see what is important to them from the limits of their experience as well as from the breadth of ours.

DO WE REALLY SEE WHAT IS GOING ON?

It is inevitable that teachers will apply their own yardsticks of social right and wrong to children's behavior, and it is good for children to learn from people who have convictions. But we adults have to be reasonably certain that our expectations fit the capacities of the children. We feel sure about what is right and wrong because we learned our lessons well in childhood. It may happen, however, that our "intuitive" knowledge is contradicted by thoughtful child study, because what we learned as children we learned uncritically and without understanding. Many of the attitudes we consider "natural" and "right" as adults were learned this way. Earlier in this manual, biases and prejudices that influence interpretations of behavior were discussed. They influence what we see, too, as anyone can testify who has listened to the conflicting testimony of eyewitnesses to an accident. Biases and prejudices are not necessarily negative or undesirable. But observation and, it follows, interpretations of children's behavior are more likely to be accurate when we know what our particular biases happen to be.

Seeing a child rejected by his peers is for some of us clearly a call to come to the child's defense, and in we move to demand humane behavior from a little tyrant. For others of us a physical tussle between youngsters is unnerving and perhaps a little frightening. Again we hear the call to action and with feelings of righteousness mete out justice "impartially." For still others the "show-off," the "bossy type," the "hog," the "poor sport," the "sneak," etc., are children whose behavior does something to us, impelling us to stop them somehow. And stop them we do, not always because it is necessarily right or in the children's best interests, but because we need to quiet the disturbance inside ourselves. We have feelings, too. And when children's behavior makes us uncomfortable, we do something to ease the discomfort if we possibly can.

How sure can we be that our techniques for handling antisocial or asocial behavior are the most helpful ones when we ourselves feel personally involved in this way? How sure are we that we are seeing all there is in a situation, and not only the obvious, the dramatic, or that which is personally important?

Do we assume that all smiles mean pleasure and all tears pain? That boisterous, noisy fighting can hurt more than quiet, calculated avoidance? Do we really see what is going on?

What, for example, is happening to the two who are smiling at each other on the swings? Is this a budding friendship of two shy ones or a budding plot of two rascally ones? Just what is going on between the two who hug a corner and engage in endless conversations? Are they seeking each other out for support or for stimulation? Can we always be sure what and who started a fight? Is every fight bad?

We need to ask ourselves whether every child in the group has a friend and whether all the friendships are profitable to those concerned. Do some children need special help from adults in getting along with others? Are there some for whom the best adult guidance is a "hands off" policy?

We must learn to look at children without preconceptions of what they "ought" to be doing, if we want to see what they *are* doing.

The following observation records a scene that is quite commonplace among six- and seven-year-olds. It shows behavior that can be very upsetting to some teachers. Yet the recorder does not reveal a single bit of her own attitudes. She just describes what she has seen and heard, quite objectively.

Seven little girls sit busily drawing at a round table, the center of activity in the empty room. Spying the group, Eva scampers over and seats herself comfortably on a chair. Meanwhile, Koko has been displaying the contents of a plastic doctor's bag that she has brought to school. She hovers about the circle speaking and gesticulating importantly. Calling out in a stentorian voice meant to arrest all activity, she offers, "Who wants some gum?" Eva asks politely and cajolingly, "Can I have some?" Koko answers in a stern, firm manner, "Only my best friends." Instantly a chorus of voices pledge in unison eternal friendship with Koko, Eva among them with her lilting "I'm your best friend."

Koko then commands, "Just raise your hands and you'll get some." All obey unquestioningly, enjoying the game, as Koko walks around distributing wads of white tissue which serve as gum. Eva's eyes sparkle with excitement as she rocks in her chair from side to side. "Now everybody close their eyes." Eva sits upright, her eyes barely closed as if in a trance, eyelashes trembling slightly. She claps both hands over her eyes, opens her mouth slightly, and waits expectantly. Disappointed, she opens her eyes and begins to mold a bit of clay, declaring in a confident, conspiratorial tone of voice to Koko, "Anyway, I don't have to close them because I already know, right? I don't have to because I already know it, right? Right, Koko? I don't have to. Yeah, because I already know the trick, right?"

Koko whispers to Alexis. Interjecting, Eva says, "But I'm going to your birthday, Alexis." Koko turns to Eva and says persuasively, "Don't go to her birthday. You can hold Leo (her baby brother)." Completely dissuaded, Eva croons, "Oh. Leo's so cute." Koko, looking satisfied, strolls off.

We can assume that any good teacher would make a note to herself to watch Koko and Eva more closely and to find the appropriate time and place when she could be helpful to each in a more effective way than if she had interfered at this point. The teacher *as a teacher* is given to action; the teacher *as an observer* must record as though not involved. These are separate parts of a teacher's task, both necessary and not to be confused with each other!

Children Are Different from One Another

Some children follow a consistent pattern toward all other children. They are pleasant and sweet-tempered with all comers, always welcoming and accepting and equally gracious with everyone. An opposite kind of consistency is present in the child who is always suspicious, always hostile, a "lone wolf." How many such completely one-dimensional personalities are there in the group? Not many. We might say that such people, big or little, seem to have something inside them that keeps them one way all the time, regardless of what is happening outside themselves. But most children, like most adults, react to a number of things. One might be the behavior and expectations of the other fellow. A second might be the irritability of coming down with mumps or measles. A third might be the abundance or scarcity of something a child wants. And so on.

Many situations can affect children's reactions to one another. The presence or absence of certain teachers or children, or a long spell indoors with no chance for physical activity, would be such a situation. Or, on occasion, normally unaggressive children can become aggressive under the cover of group protection or when they feel unjustly deprived. Some children learn quite early whom they can push with impunity and whom to follow with regard. Most children seem to have a sixth sense about the children who are unable to defend themselves.

In other words, reactions to people are many-sided, especially while children are still learning the techniques of getting along with others, as is true in the early years. It is no surprise, therefore, that the healthy, normal youngster may show contradictory reactions. If we would guide children to good, successful interpersonal adjustment, we have to be sure that we know what their reactions to others actually are.

DETAILS TO LOOK FOR IN OBSERVING A CHILD'S BEHAVIOR WITH OTHER CHILDREN

Every teacher picks up a lot of useful information out of the corner of her eye as she goes about her busy day. She knows that a combination of Pamela and Naomi is sure to end up in mischief; that once started on cowboy play, Juan, Sean, and Evan will keep at it for the whole outdoor period; that Kay Kay will probably wander again today as she has since coming to school: and so on.

Is that enough? *Who approached whom* in the Pamela–Naomi combination? Who started the cowboy idea? Who leads? Who follows? How do the children make contact with one another?

Some children approach others with certainty and sure-footedness. "Let's play," they say forthrightly, and play it is. Others come along with less assurance. "May I play?" they ask timidly, or hesitantly, or uncertainly. Some children walk up to others and stand speechless, waiting for acceptance and admission to the golden realm. And some wait for no introduction, but direct the activity immediately. "You be my passenger. I'm the driver."

Here are two children whose approaches differ considerably from each other.

It was midmorning, and the class had just come out into the play-ground. The yard is filled with a wide variety of climbing and swing-ing equipment. Matthew headed straight for the large, wooden climber in one corner of the yard. On the way, he picked up a short wooden board that the children place at various levels on the climber. The jungle gym itself is about four feet by eight in area and about seven feet high, open at the center except for two "fireman poles" that run from top to bottom.

Matthew places his board carefully on a high level, climbs up the side of the gym, and perches on a corner of the board. Three other children have followed him and climbed onto surrounding bars. He watches the others arrive and seat themselves, and then firmly and quietly proclaims, "I'm Superdog and I need some food!" Gary re-sponds, "Hi, Superdoggie," and Matthew begins to make dog-like sounds of "Rufff, rufff." He reaches for a nearby pole and slides to the ground. His movements are smooth and easy, and he is smiling when he gets to the bottom, at which time he turns and climbs right back up to his perch.

The children have been on the play-roof for about twenty minutes. Most have settled into some game or activity. Carlo is standing alone on the tree house. He gazes longingly at the sandbox, where a group of children are involved in making cakes.

"Kelly, Kelly, Kelly," chants Carlo softly as he begins to climb down skillfully from the treehouse. He wastes no time, though he manages to get himself down without mishap.

"Kelly, Kelly, Kelly." He sings her name as he gallops across the roof, his face glowing with excitement, his hand swinging freely at his side.Kelly sits comfortably in the sand, her attention on her cake, her back propped up against the side of the sandbox. She seems oblivious of the almost imperceptible chanting of her name. Carlo leaps over the side of the sandbox, his arms and legs swinging in the air, and flops down beside Kelly. "Are you spitting in the sand?" Carlo asks cheerfully. He leans toward her as he asks.

Kelly, who has been looking intently at her cake, turns quickly as if startled to find Carlo's face about an inch from hers. "No!" she yells adamantly. "I have not. I'm making a cake."

"Oh," replies Carlo, a little disappointed. Kelly begins to fiddle with her sock, shaking the sand off with jerky, somewhat angry movements.

Carlo watches intently. He squats there perfectly still. Kelly demands in a loud, shrill voice, "Let me see your sock, Carlo."

Carlo grins sheepishly, pushes his leg out in front of him, grabs his pants leg, and tugs it up to his knee to reveal his sock. "There," he exclaims victoriously.

Kelly inspects his sock closely. Carlo holds his pants leg up with both his hands and watches Kelly. "Oh, you don't have them," she states emphatically, a note of disappointment in her voice.

Carlo sits still, his eyes glowing with expectation, his body leaning toward Kelly. He drops the pants leg down. It sticks on the top of his sock. Kelly turns her head and her attention back to the sand and her cake. She begins to pat her cake.

Carlo watches her, then slowly gets up and, still looking intently at Kelly, climbs out of the sandbox and ambles over to the teacher.

Who Approached Whom? How Did the Child Do It?

Who approached whom? Is it that way all the time? Are there some children who always have to be asked and some who never ask? Are children different with different members of the group, asking some and not others, accepting some and not others?

- How did the child approach the other?
  Was he bold and demanding?
  Was she friendly and assuring?
  Was he frightened and expectant of rebuff?
- How was the approach made?
  Did she touch or push?
  Did he caress the other child?
  Did she gesture at the other child in some way?
- Or did the teacher get the whole thing started?

As children approach each other, they may be casual, relaxed, and at ease; they may be friendly or hostile, confident, or afraid. They may have the right words or still be relying on body contact. *Their approach will show both their attitude and their know-how.*

How Does a Child Do What He/She Does?

We get the quality of a child's approach to other children by the quality of the voice, the rhythm and tempo of the speech, the facial expression, and the body movements. They are all there in one integrated response. We react to this total response, of course, but in recording it is necessary to articulate quite consciously the nonverbal clues that will eventually help us determine a child's feelings.

We have talked before of the difference between *what* a child does and *how* he or she does it. It is perhaps more important to see how children behave socially than how they use materials, because adults are far likelier to take sides and do something when children are working out their social relationships than when they are exploring materials. To see the meaning of the experience to the child, we must be sure to see how that child does what he or she actually does. The action alone is not enough. See how Juana's mood changes are revealed in this record.

> Juana had a wig on; she was the "mother." Glenda and Robert followed her, saying, "Mommy, Mommy." She pretended to be annoyed and said, "Hey!" very loudly. She turned to the children and shook each very briskly. She walked away, they followed; the action was repeated many times. They all smiled during this play. At one point Juana shook Glenda so hard that Glenda fell down and began to cry. Juana walked away. As she passed a table, she saw plastic Legos; she picked up a few very casually. She began constructing and sat down, getting more involved in the activity. Roger and Glenda began tickling her wig. Juana took it off. They tickled her head. She told them loudly to stop. They continued. Juana began to cry, with tears in her eyes, but not audibly. She complained to the teacher, who told Glenda and Roger to leave her. She went back to the Legos. Glenda tried to grab the wig; Juana put it firmly between her legs and got involved in her Legos again. Maria, sitting next to her, grabbed the wig. Juana grabbed it back. Maria began to cry. Juana worked at the Legos without looking at Maria, who continued crying. After a while, Juana said to Maria, "Mira, una máquina." (Look, a machine), and showed her what she was making. Maria's crying stopped. Juana said, "Quieres hacer este?" (Do you want to make this?) Maria responded pleadingly, "No, quiero eso," (No, I want that), pointing to the wig. Juana said cheerfully, "O.K.," and gave it to her, putting it on Maria's head and smiling broadly.

BODY POSITIONS AND MOVEMENT

Perhaps it is hard for us to pin down and record significant body positions and movements in children because as adults we have become so circumscribed in our own movements that we cannot feel the meaning of theirs in their own bodies. We do not sprawl on the floor easily any more; we don't give way to laughter by flinging our legs over our heads; we don't fall easily; we prefer sitting to running. In short, we have ceased to use our own bodies with the freedom and abandon of children. Consequently, we do not look at jumping or climbing youngsters and tingle in our own muscles with their exhilaration in stretching limbs. Yet body expression is personality expression. One's body is oneself. One uses one's body as one feels.

Even if Janine, in the next record, had not said a word to her father, we would know how uncertain she was about getting into the swing of things from her body movement and gestures.

Janine arrived, holding her father's hand tightly, her thin body curved in an S-shape, her hand gently rubbing her father's sleeve. In a soft, anxious voice, she whispered, "I don't want you to go." Then she put her index finger into her mouth and sucked on it wistfully while her father put his arm on her shoulder and urged her to take several steps forward. Janine dragged both feet forward hesitantly, still sucking her finger, and put one hand up, resting it on the door frame. Her father rubbed his hands together cheerfully and said gaily, "Well, I'm off," and left Janine still leaning indecisively on the door frame. Mousily she moved to the chair next to Andrew only four steps from the door and stood with both hands resting on the back of the chair, watching him write his name. Abruptly, she plopped into the chair and a moment later stood up again. With a sudden burst of energy she stepped over to the crayon box. She picked up a crayon and purposefully and quickly wrote her name, her tongue sticking out between her lips. Still no greeting passed between the children, Andrew being involved in decorating his sign.

Just as quickly as she had started, Janine finished her name, did not decorate it, and slunk over to the rug by the book stand, shoulders drooping, head slightly hanging down. She flopped loosely onto the rug, reached casually for a book, and gazed absently at it, methodically turning page after page. She looked up as another child sat down with a book. She stared at the child. Except for her eyes, she was motionless, with her big toe occasionally wiggling in her sandal.

In the process of relating to each other, children so often strike first and ask later, or grow rigid with fear but say nothing, or stand with head low and voice mute. The tilt of the head, the use of the hands, body stances, amount of body activity, bodily contacts (touch, shove, push, pat, buck), all are means of communicating.

Trust and fear, self-confidence and inadequacy, all find expression in bodily posture. So do restlessness, irritability, composure, and serenity. We know this to be true from experience. We must include the details of body movement in our records.

QUALITY OF VOICE

This is an integral part of communication. As children speak, their emotional state will be revealed in their voice.

- Is it strident, soft, querulous, screechy, flat, pleading?
- Is it lilting, whining, demanding, loud, strained, forceful, quivery?

" 'Give it to me,' he growled" is hardly the same expression of feeling as " 'Give it to me,' he whined petulantly." "I want that," can be said angrily, hungrily, wistfully, urgently, teasingly, or happily. It makes a difference to know with which kind of voice a child makes a comment or asks a question.

TEMPO AND RHYTHM

These qualities of a child's speech tell us something about the tempo and rhythm of that child. He may drawl and move in unhurried fashion; or her words may tumble in unending floods of ideas and feeling. Slowness or speed may simply be the result of the organization of the child's nervous system (as it usually is), but it may be the result of anxiety, too. Children slow up when they are afraid of saying the "wrong" thing. They hurry when they are afraid they won't be listened to.

Fast, slow, moderate—these refer to *tempo*. Rhythm is something else again. Rhythm is smoothness, jerkiness, or hesitancy. The rhythm of speech can be staccato, cadenced, flowing. Combining tempo and rhythm, we find that a child's speech can be fast and smooth or fast and jerky, slow and even or slow and hesitant. Rhythm and tempo together characterize the quality of the speech.

Six-year-old Jules adapted his needs to meet the needs of the occasion. Neither Jules nor Rick were at all ready for rest at the scheduled hour.

> As the boys' eyes met across their mats, they broke into wide grins that exposed the many empty spaces where their baby teeth had once been.
>
> "Oh good-eee," chirped Jules, looking at Rick. He raised himself from the waist and clapped his hands. "Give me six to pick up

sticks," he chanted rhythmically, stretching out his left hand, palm upward. Rick, understanding the ritual, slapped Jules's palm, and a wide grin sprawled over the bottom half of his face.

The teacher approached in businesslike fashion. "Do you two think you can manage yourselves?" she asked crisply.

"Yeah, we can do it," Rick quickly asserted.

Jules confirmed with, "Sure—er—no problem at all," giving the sentence a bit of a lilt as he spoke it.

The teacher left, but soon laughter was heard again, and she approached a second time.

Jules was spouting dramatically: "And-d I to-o-old the m-a-n to be of-f (giggle). And then the sp-oo-ky-ee cat (giggle) me-e-owed . . . (giggle) . . . He la-aa-anded like Sprunky-eee . . ." Lots of giggling. Jules sang and laughed and sang again at a high pitch, his eyes dancing as wildly as his words. Without saying a word, the teacher motioned Jules to carry his mat to another spot.

FACIAL EXPRESSION

This accompanies "quality" in speech. We expect smiling eyes with laughter, a droopy mouth with tears. Here are some of the descriptive terms we can use:

Eyes can be solemn, glaring, flashing, tearful, smiling, sleepy, bright, shiny, dull, sparkling, etc.

Mouth can be drooping, smiling, pouting, quivering, laughing, puckered, drawn, lips curled over teeth, etc.

Smile can be wholehearted, uncertain, full, wistful, furtive, reluctant, shy, open, dimpled, and half.

Of course not all details appear in every record. For one thing, children do not use their entire battery of possible shades of expression every time they react to life. For another, no human recorder could see enough or write fast enough to get everything onto a piece of paper. But the more details you can record that point to what is happening inside a child as he or she makes contact, the more accurate and expressive will be the picture that emerges.

Vanessa shaded her eyes with her hands, frowned, and stared across the yard at Lillian. Her under lip jutted forward in a pout and her brows furrowed deeper than ever. Suddenly she swung her hands into fists at her side, stamped her foot and exploded. "Hey!" She ran across the yard and grabbed Lillian by the arm. Her head punctuated every word as she screamed into Lillian's face, "Who told you to take my umbrella out of my locker?"

Elisa slithered silently against the wall, slowly edging her way from the clothing lockers to the clay table. She stood still some two feet away, sober and unsmiling, eyes darting from side to side as she followed the conversation being tossed around the table. Norman looked up and saw Elisa. "Hi," he grinned. "Hi, Lisey." Still standing immobile, Elisa crinkled her face into a warm, open smile. Her eyes alive, shining, she chirped, "Hi, Normie."

Approaching someone is only part of the relationship. After that, the other person's response or lack of response determines further action. What does the other child do and say? How does that child do it? The record above about Elisa, though short, is a clear-cut illustration of how behavior is affected by other persons' responses.

What Does the Child Say? How Does the Other Child Respond?

Speech may not reveal everything, but it tells a good deal. Record the actual words as far as possible and not just the sense of what a child says.

"Hey, Pete, let's put the big one here."
"Naw, it'll fall off."
"No it won't, no it won't."
"O. K." (good-naturedly).
"Push that one back a little.'
No answer.
"Hey!" (sharply) "Push that one back."

Does it take longer to write the actual dialogue than to write a paragraph about dialogue? The conversation above could be written about as follows:

Lucas told Pete where to put the blocks. Pete was pretty agreeable. When Pete didn't answer, Lucas shouted at him.

The first is raw material. It is flavorful and authentic and, more important, uninterpreted. The second may be accurate as to interpretation, but it involves the teacher's appraisal of the situation. Should she be wrong, there is no going back to check.

In the following record, both the dialogue and the quality of the voice form a very important part of the children's interaction.

Pilar and Ann are building together. Pilar puts a large cardboard cylinder in the house:

PILAR: We need this. (She accidentally knocks over the blocks of another nearby structure.)

ANN: Why are you doing that? That's not our house.

PILAR: (has begun using the knocked-over blocks, switches gear, and starts rebuilding the toppled building): I'm fixing it up.

ANN: How was it? Do you know?

PILAR: (matter-of-factly): We'll just put it back. (She finishes and stands up. She has previously been sitting on her haunches in a scrunched up but apparently comfortable position in which she moved about easily. She watches the goings-on in the dramatic play area inquisitively and then stoops down again. She speaks to the wooden doll in a chastising tone.) How did you get out of here? (She puts the doll on the bed, speaking firmly.) You go to bed. (She begins talking in a stream-of-consciousness style while Ann sits nearby.) And the woman (meaning the little doll, which she is holding) is the "figeroa," right? . . . You know what a "figeroa" is? (Ann does not respond so Pilar continues.) The woman go out to a "figeroa" and dance now. (She sings.) Doo-doo-doo-doo-doo-doo. (She moves the doll to make it dance, going up and down a clear aisle in the block area, walking on haunches as before.)

ANN: (bringing over a male doll): Man's gonna dance too.

PILAR: (with furrowed brow, her eyes bright, and a hint of authority in her voice): Wait, I'm gonna tell you something. We're gonna sing together. (And they do, making up words to their songs.)

What Happens Next?

After a contact is made, then what does a child do? Is there a sigh of relief and a quiet settling down to blissful submission? Is there a staccato-like bidding for supremacy of ideas and position? Or is there a purr of contentment as alternatives are weighed with other children? Do the children carry on conversation? Play the same thing separately? If the contact ends without going on into dramatic play, tell how it ends and what the child does immediately after. Subsequent behavior may reflect feelings about the contact.

Here are two boys reacting very differently to an event that was disturbing.

It was the middle of block building in the first grade, and the children were working on their buildings. Hank, however, was very upset, having just been involved in a very emotional, yelling, fist-swinging altercation that was broken up by the teacher. Seething, Hank stomped away from the block area, but on his way he accidentally brushed against part of Christopher's building, causing some damage to it. Christopher became upset, and his face started to wrinkle as if he might cry. Then, as if having second thoughts, he raised his head and hurried over to Hank on all fours. He shook his fist menacingly in front of Hank's face, but not too closely. Hank was by now sitting in a chair in the meeting area, his face tense, silently fuming and staring in the direction of the blackboard. He was obviously still troubled by his previous altercation and could only blankly acknowledge Chris's anger. Chris looked into Hank's face, saw how upset he was, then turned, and edged his way back on all fours to make repairs on his building.

RESUMÉ OF DETAILS OF A SINGLE EPISODE

Taken all together, the significant aspects of a record of a child making a contact with another child might fall into some such general outline as the following.

1. Setting:
   Where does the contact take place?
   What were the children doing before the contact was made?
2. How is the contact made?
   What does the child who initiated the contact do? What does he say?
   Did the teacher get the whole thing started? How?
   How does the child do what she does?
   Body positions and movement
   Quality of voice
   Tempo and rhythm of speech
   Facial expression
   How does the other child respond? What does the other child say?
3. What happens next?
4. How does the contact end?

Patterns of Behavior

Out of such details as those above, perceived in many episodes, there will emerge *patterns of behavior,* or the characteristic way in which a child is likely to respond in the daily relations with children. Over a period of a school year, *changing* patterns indicate growth or regression. We can organize these patterns of behavior by clustering items from the single episodes around such categories as the following:

1. Evidence of interest in children:
    Direct evidence would be the number of children played with; or a child's request for help in entering play situations; or positive approaches to children.
    Indirect evidence would be staring at others or watching them; imitating; attempting to attract attention from children by various means.
2. How contacts are made:
    Does the child move toward others or against them?
        (initially or always)
    How does he move?
        (confidently, tentatively, pleadingly, timidly, aggressively, etc.)
    Do others move toward him, away from him, or against him?
        (initially or always)
    How does she react to the behavior of others?
        (to their affection, invitation to play, criticism, suggestions and ideas, aggressions, etc.)
    What does she do?
        (withdraws, enters play, rejects, tolerates, defies, aggresses, complains to adults, etc.)
    How does she do it?
        (shyly, confidently, eagerly, with curiosity and interest, crying, angrily, happily, fearfully, etc.)
    What methods does he use in making contacts?
        (speech, attack, with ideas, with things, enters situation directly, threatens, bribes, uses others to gang up, asks adults for help, etc.)
3. How does he behave with children?
    To what extent can he make his wishes, desires, irritations, annoyances, ideas, etc., understood?
    To what extent is she able to share equipment, props, materials?
    To what extent is he able to await his turn?
    What are the more usual causes of clashes with others?
        (possessions, ideas, unprovoked attacks, etc.)
    How does she handle conflicts?
        What does she do?
        (runs to teacher, cries, fights back, reasons, jokes, etc.)

How does she do it?
> (tearfully, righteously, sobbing, angrily, indignantly,
> etc.)

To what extent is she aware of others' rights and needs?
How realistic are his demands for his own rights?
How does she protect her rights?
To what extent does he seek help from other children?
> (how, under what circumstances, from whom)

To what extent is she able to help others?
> (how, when, and whom)

To what extent does she contribute ideas, suggestions?
Does he accept other people's ideas, suggestions?
What seem to be the child's defense mechanisms?

4. What seem to be the child's feelings about other children?
> (likes, fears, envies, etc.)
>
> Special friends
> > (How many and who; nature of interrelationships)

5. Special problems or trends
> > (impatience with others; allowing or encouraging ex-
> > ploitation by others; excessive hitting, temper, or
> > withdrawal; lack of speech; other physical handicaps;
> > excessive dependence on teacher; different cultural back-
> > ground from group's; etc.)

6. Evidences of growth
> Comparison of earlier and later behavior indicating more
> mature level

GROUP MEMBERSHIP

If children learn to get along with each other within a school situation they inevitably begin to develop a sense of the meaning of the
large group along with their more intimate excursions into two-
somes. But becoming a member of a group is a challenging task.

Every group develops a dynamic of its own, and groups of young
children do the same. Once the children's first period of adjustment
is over, they begin not only to seek their own place within the
group's emerging structure but to recognize the places held by others as well. See, for example, how Paul, a six-year-old, was already
wise to the hierarchy within his group.

Richard and Larry were playing a board game at table 3 with Paul and Tom standing by and watching, when George, the acknowledged leader among the boys, arrived, late. George sat down at table 2. Richard, with no outward sign that he was aware of George's arrival, said to Tom (who was just watching the game), "Tom, how would you like to play my man in the game? It's a very lucky seat." Paul, the other observer at table 3, turned to the teacher and said, "All the boys like George and all the girls like Heather." The teacher asked Paul what made him think so. He replied, "Look. See how all the boys stay near George?"

Paul then decided he would take Richard's place, at which Richard announced, to no one in particular, "I have to do something." Larry, his erstwhile partner in the game, remembered he had something to do too and stood up, saying to the teacher, "I'm very sorry."

Both Richard and Larry then made a "casual" beeline for Table 2 Paul gave the teacher a significant look and declared, "See, I told you so."

In addition, then, to observing a child in relation to individual others, one would want to know how the child is faring within the larger, total group.

- Where does the child fit in relation to entire group?
- Does she play with none, one, many, both sexes?
  Is he an established member of group; is he making his way; is he a lone player?
  How does she act toward new children entering the group?
- What is the child's position within the group?
  (leader, follower, instigator, disrupter, clown, uses group to hide etc.)
- What status does the child have?
  Is the child chosen by others, e.g., in games?
  How frequently is the child chosen by others? repulsed?
- Is the child accepted? a "fringer"? a scapegoat?

Summing up the generalizations that seem reasonable in light of the patterns that emerge out of the wealth of detail, we bring into focus an image of how a very much alive, vibrant child reacts in one important area of living. On the basis of such evidence we shall eventually be able to form hypotheses and plan for action. Judgment will have been based on objective data. Generalizations about two children's relationships with others follow.

SUMMARY OF A CHILD'S BEHAVIOR
WITH OTHER CHILDREN

Jimmy, age four:

Jimmy has always shown a great interest in the other children and their activities. He used to stand watching them at their work a great deal. But if they looked his way, he would turn away and drop his head. He made no effort to contact anyone. At first the children ignored him pretty much. It was not until he began to help me serve juice that they even seemed aware of him at all.

The two children who seemed to fascinate Jimmy most were Lenny and Marilyn. Both four-year-olds, they are quick, active children, hopping from one thing to another. Good friends, they laugh and sing all day. Jimmy began to follow them around after being at school about two months. He would laugh at their antics until they began to use him as their special audience. Some time later they began to draw him into their play, giving him the role of baby or dog or anything else which they themselves preferred not to be. Jimmy, not being aggressive, fell into these roles and played them to the limit, delighted at being included.

The other children now seem to accept Jimmy as Lenny and Marilyn's friend and apparently like him. Although he never initiates play, we notice that he is not always willing to play baby any more. He seems to avoid rough-and-tumble, stepping aside if he sees it near him. He rarely joins in a group, but will now play with two or three children he knows well.

Lee, age four-and-one-half:

With his peers Lee shows a pattern of caution, observing them closely before he joins them. It has just been during the past few weeks that he has taken part in singing and rhythmic group activities. He seems to derive great satisfaction from this type of activity, asking, "Are we going to play the Jingle Bell game today?" etc. If sufficiently absorbed in a certain task, he ignores others in his immediate vicinity completely. He is friendly with most children, but tends to seek out one particular child to play with. This child changes on a day-to-day or week-to-week basis. When a third child enters (in my notes, it seems always to be Michael), he feels very insecure, covering his feelings of hostility with a sulky withdrawal, seldom with an overt act of aggression. (This week I did see him pounce unexpectedly upon Michael's back and wrestle him to the floor with much triumphant laughter on his part and complete bewilderment on Michael's.) Although Lee talks a great deal, he seems to be talking at the children most times, not with them. They all delight in listening to his tall stories. He has a good sense of humor and his hearty laugh can be heard throughout the room. He often uses laughter as a release from tension.

Just lately Lee has shown signs of approaching readiness to take aggressive action (e.g., wrestling Michael and Greg). His mother reported that he has told her proudly at home, "I had a big fight and I made that kid almost cry." Actually it was a very little fight, but its importance to Lee in his self-picture is very evident.

5

RECORDING CHILDREN'S BEHAVIOR IN DRAMATIC PLAY

DRAMATIC (or symbolic) play often springs from children's contacts with one another, but it also occurs when children play alone. Whether the child plays alone or with others, there are many aspects to be considered. These can best be understood if we recognize that children project themselves into their play and work out problems both of intellectual comprehension ("Is steering a bus different from steering a plane?") and of emotional complexity ("I want what I want now, but if I say so, Rashid may go away"). Mostly, dramatic play is fun, and deeply satisfying fun at that. But it is also the children's way of exploring the meaning of activities and relationships in the grown-up world. It is, of course, learning to get along with other children, to share and bargain, to compare and evaluate, to compete and cooperate, to give and take. At the same time, the magic of "make-believe" allows children to work out their wishes, aspirations, fears, and other childhood fantasies. All this they do by playing a part, *a role* (persig play), or by making objects—real or imaginary—act as if they were animals, persons, superheroes, etc. (obsig play).* Both the roles they take and the

---

Persig and *obsig* are neologisms devised not only for the purpose of brevity and clarity, but also because there is no commonly used word for play in which objects are made to act like people, animals, etc. See Virginia Stern, "The Symbolic Play of Lower-Class and Middle-Class Children: Mixed Messages from the Literature," in *Current Topics in Early Childhood Education*, vol. 4, ed. Lilian G. Katz (Norwood, N.J.: Ablex, 1982).

content of the play with these symbolic objects are compounded of bits from the real world and pieces from inside themselves. Bits and pieces do not always make a logical whole in the eyes of an adult, and that is perhaps why children's play often seems inconsequential, irrational, or delightfully fluid and without boundaries to adult perceptions.

But play has logic to children, and the strongest evidence of this is the amount of dramatic play that goes on all through childhood. Even children who hardly know each other slip into the world of imagination together, understanding each other hardly at all in our sense, but speaking the language of dramatic play.

Listen to these two children working things out individually and together as their imaginations meet, diverge, meet, and develop together.

Willie and Tracy, four-and-one-half:
Willie was building with the large cardboard blocks and using one of the child-size trucks in his construction. As he carefully placed the blocks in rectangular formation around the truck, he began howling with a high-pitched "Oh-Ooh!" that sounded like the siren of a police car. Tracy came over and got on the truck, and she and Willie rode over to the nearby playhouse and went in.

Willie began tapping a rhythm on a drum, with a stick in each hand. "Give me one," Tracy asked playfully, pointing to the sticks. "I have to practice somethin'," Willie replied in a spirit of concentration. After a few more taps, he gave the sticks to her and announced with an air of having come to a conclusion, "I'm finished." He got up to leave and stepped out of the house.

Tracy poked her head out and caught Willie's eye. "I have to go to do my work. How should I go?" she asked expectantly. Willie was busy pushing the truck over a mat that prevented its movement, and didn't answer.

They both then got on the truck, and Willie drove it over to the area where he had been building with the cardboard blocks. "At last we have a new garage," he declared proudly as the truck rolled into the enclosure which he had constructed earlier.

"This is my *house*," Tracy cried gleefully.

"This is the *garage*," Willie countered.

"So where can I sleep then?" queried Tracy with a note of concern in her voice.

"In my room. You'll sleep with me," Willie replied firmly. "We must go," he commanded.

Tracy walked quickly over to the housekeeping corner. "Honey, don't leave," Willie urged in a manly voice. Then he drove the truck around to the library corner, where he picked up two pillows, and drove back to the playhouse. Tracy returned to the housekeeping corner carrying a small blanket and pillow. "I got the blanket," she said cheerfully.

"You can lie on it if you want to," said Willie with an air of unconcern. They both went into the house.

"Let me sleep this way," Tracy said lying down on the pillow.

"I have to practice somethin'," said Willie as he tapped the drum with two rhythm sticks.

"Who's wakin' me up?" Tracy complained, sounding annoyed.

"I'm practicin' somethin'," said Willie, defending his activity.

"Honey, could you sleep?" pleaded Tracy. Willie put down the drum and sticks, and, sounding tired and weary, said, "I'll do this tomorrow." He lay down next to Tracy with his head on the pillow too.

Suddenly he shouted angrily, "Who' wakin' me up?" He popped his head out the door to observe some other children who were playing on the jungle gym nearby. "They are big boys. They can stay up," he said in a tone of responsibility. "Just ignore them. Go to sleep," he said to Tracy fondly. For a moment they just looked at each other as they lay quietly together.

RECORDS OF DRAMATIC PLAY
Many of the same features are recorded for persig and obsig play:

Features to Be Recorded in Both Persig and Obsig Play
- How the play gets started:
     Does the child initiate it? The teacher? Another child?
     Does the child join the ongoing play of another child or group
          of children?
- The setting (the block corner, housekeeping corner, out-doors, etc.)
- The course of action, or sequence of events
- All the child's comments and verbal interaction *about* the play; for example:
     What is happening ("The car is going into the garage.")
     The roles each child should take ("You be the mommy. I'll
          be the daddy.")
- What other participants in the play say and do
- How the play ends

Since the content of the play and/or the child's role is often ambiguous, all actions and remarks should be recorded whether or not they are meaningful, at the time, to the recorder, as in the following short record:

David (age three) picks up a figure of a man and lies down on the floor, cradling his own head on one arm. He moves the figure about and says, "Mailman, mailman, boom-da-boom-da-boom."

The *content* of both kinds of play may come from the real world or from television or stories.

- Ideas from the tangible world of reality may come from:
  The people they know or have seen—father, mother, baby, sister, pilot, astronaut, bus driver, storekeeper, fire fighter, police officer, beauty parlor operator, etc.
  Inanimate objects—train, airplane, truck, car, doll, etc.
- Ideas may come from television or stories.

By reproducing aspects of the real world that they have experienced, or long to experience, children try to fix in their minds the properties, processes, and relationships of what they have encountered. Observations of dramatic play can be used by teachers to assess how well children understand what they are experiencing. Such information furnishes a base for planning experiences that can increase and/or clarify children's conceptions of the real world.

Whether the play's content is related to the real world or to fantasy, it may be used by children to work out their feelings—their fears, wishes, aspirations—and as a means of solving their developmental and emotional problems. Teachers can learn from dramatic play the emotional meanings attached to the content: how the child perceives the important people in her life or how she wishes they would be; the feelings the child is unwilling or afraid to express overtly in daily behavior.

There are also aspects that are peculiar to each kind of play. Let us look at the details that relate to each kind of play.

CHILDREN TAKE ON ROLES (PERSIG PLAY)
The Role Itself, Its Content
In persig play, the role the child takes is usually related to the general content of the play. Thus, the role may come from the real

world or from television or stories. In these roles, children include
that which to their minds and limited experience is the meaningful
quality and *character* of the person or thing. And how accurately
children pinpoint the essence of train, plane, animal, or parent in
terms of outstanding action, sound, or feeling value! It takes them
longer to see and understand technical details, parts of a whole,
ramifications, complexity, variety, etc. We must be careful, however, not to jump to conclusions. Fantasy is a very important part
of children's play, and a child may be sitting on what looks like a
train and not give us a hint as to whether he or she is the engineer,
the train itself, a passenger, or the cargo.

What to Record

The details to be recorded relate both to the content of the role
and how the role is played. They include:

- All *symbolic* actions taken by the child in his role (Tracy picks up
  a very small plastic baby bottle, gets a doll, and sits down.
  She puts the bottle to the doll's mouth and holds it there for a moment.
  She gets up and puts the doll down and the bottle on the
  shelf. *She gets a doll bib and pretends to iron it.* When she finishes,
  she takes the bib and puts it on the doll.)
- The language spoken by the child in his role (as mother, conductor, Superman, etc.)
- Onomatopoetic sounds uttered by the child (as a cow, she *moos*;
  as a train, she makes engine or whistle sounds; etc.)
- Accessories used by the child (a conductor's hat, a firefighter's
  coat, a man's or woman's hat, etc.)
- The child's facial expression, body movements, tone of voice,
  etc., which give the role its emotional quality (e.g., a *nurtur-
  ing* or *punitive* mother, a *timid* or *aggressive* child)
- Any *symbolic* objects the child uses while playing (a block building
  on which the child sits, a long unit block used as a gun, etc.)

Records of dramatic play show the level of the child's understanding and comprehension, as well as the content of the role and
how the role is played.

Four-year-old Alfred went straight to the blocks when he came to
the nursery. There were only two other children at school at the time,
both at the clay table. Alfred started to build what looked like a train.
He set five blocks in a long row on the floor. At one end he put two

blocks on top of each other and sat on them. Danny had just come in and walked over to Alfred.

Danny: "Is that a bridge?"

Alfred: "No, it's a train."

"Where's it going?" Danny asked.

"To New York," replied Alfred. "I'm the engineer. I build big trains."

"I'm conductor. I drive the train," boasted Danny.

Alfred (impatiently): "No, no. I'm the engineer. I made it."

Danny: "What can I do?"

Alfred replied, "You collect the tickets."

"What tickets?" asked Danny.

Alfred: "The ones the passengers give you. . . . (out loud) Who wants a ride on the train? . . . All abo-a-rd . . . All ab-o-oard. Train going. Woo . . . woo . . . It goes so fast."

Harry came into the room and ran over to the train.

Harry: "I want to get on." He got another block from the shelf and put it on the middle of the train. He picked up a very small block from the floor and held it to his mouth as he would a telephone and yelled, "Hello, hello. What's wrong with you? We're leaving and we gotta have food. Bring hundreds of boxes. . . . Right away, you hear?" He slammed the telephone down.

Alfred: "We got a flat. I'll fix it. Got to fix it now." With swaggering pretentiousness he removed one of the blocks from the line and turned it upside down and replaced it. Then he got back on the two blocks.

Mitchell came over and got on the train.

Alfred: "Get off, get off. It's my train. . . . (demandingly) *Go Away.*"

He gave Mitchell a push to get him off. Mitchell attempted to get on again, and again Alfred pushed him off. The teacher complimented Alfred on his train and suggested that he allow other children to share it with him. Alfred made no response, but did nothing when Mitchell got on again and sat behind him.

Alfred: "No gas, no gas. Hey, Mitch, no gas. Ha, Ha! Now no gas. First flat tire, now no gas."

Danny took the block which Harry had used as a telephone and called on it. "Hey, you. Bring gas. Train needs gas. Ha! Ha! Hurry up, you dope."

Alfred: "All off! It's lunch time. Let's get some food. Follow me. I'll show you, men."

We can deduce what Alfred knows about trains from his train play (that they are long, that the engineer sits in the front of the train, that trains have passengers, that the conductor collects tickets, etc.). His confusion of trains with automobiles (the "flat" that must be fixed, the train needs "gas") are also portrayed vividly in his play.

In the following record, the source of the content is television. Frankie plays alone, for the most part. His occasional contacts with other children are short-lived.

As Frankie gets to the door of the yard, his face broadens into a wide, happy grin, and he races down the steps into the yard. He shouts delightedly, "The monsters!" and begins jumping on one foot and then the other while his arms flap wildly in every direction. He shouts to some nearby children, "Come on!" and begins to race around the playground boundary with his arms waving exuberantly and a wide smile on his face. Two or three of his classmates follow his path and copy his gestures.

Frankie then walks over to a large, circular wooden spool, climbs up effortlessly, and sits down on it cross-legged. He sits for just a few seconds, then stands up and leaps off, making flying gestures with his arms. He seems quite excited and delighted with these movements, since there is a broad smile on his face and his joyous shouts ring out.

He runs around the yard again and leaps on the wooden spool. He stays a few seconds and shouts forcefully, "I'm getting outa here," and leaps off again. He turns around and jumps up again. He neither looks at nor talks to the other children on the spool. He seems preoccupied with his own movements at this point.

He jumps off again and runs wildly around the yard with fast, strong movements and his arms swinging from side to side. He runs back to the spool, sees Monte, and acknowledges him with a nod. Monte gets up (he was sitting next to Frankie), kneels behind him, and begins to massage his shoulders. Frankie starts to move his body up and down (he is sitting cross-legged), and one arm is outstretched and moving rhythmically in the air. He has a look of concentration on his face, and his movements look as if he is imitating a horse-and-buggy rider.

He stops abruptly and leaps up. He shouts, "We're playing Tarzan!" and he beats his chest shouting, "Ah-a, ah-a, ah-a." He then yells, "Now I'm Spiderman!" and leaps off the spool and races off. He runs over to the basketball net and begins to climb one of the poles. Using the brick wall in front of him as support for his feet, he extends his arms up the pole, first one hand and then the other, pulling his body up with each reach. He gets to the top and slides down, holding the pole with his hands.

Christa comes over and demands, "Let me try." He turns to her and shouts excitedly, "Try and catch me." He races off with Christa chasing him. He again runs around the perimeter of the yard and back to the basketball pole. He climbs again, making loud, grunting sounds as he pulls himself up. On reaching the top, he yells, "Watch out!" and slides down. He runs over to a group of children and shouts at them, "Bulls." He runs around the yard yelling, "The bulls! The bulls! The bulls!" while putting two fingers on his head to imitate a bull's horns.

He runs up to Vivian and announces, "I'm Batman." He clenches his fist and begins making imaginary hits on her body. She stands there watching him calmly while he begins to bob around like a fighter. She says matter-of-factly, "I'm the mother," and Frankie turns and runs off without acknowledging her statement.

True to his stage of development, Frankie picks out the more obvious aspects and imitates these. He jumps, climbs, "flies," and hits—but there is little comprehensible content. The swift changes from one role to another are indicative of his inability to play out in a differentiated and coherent fashion what he has seen on television.

Emotional Investment in the Role

As children play a dramatic part with real-life content, such as, doctor, mother, baby, captain, they may give the part an emotional tone that is deeply personal.

- They may play the role in terms of their feelings and attitudes toward other children.

    (Even though a child is storekeeper, mother, or firefighter, he/she might be domineering, bossy, timid, conscientious, kind, forceful, subservient, tyrannical, protective, etc.)
- They may act out areas of feeling not otherwise revealed, e.g.,

    How they think people feel toward each other

    (The doctor may be kind, brusque, or scolding; mothers and fathers may be kind, brusque, or scolding.)

    How they wish people would behave toward them

    (A father is understanding, forceful, positive, kind, a friend, etc.; a sibling is a giving, helping person, a pal, etc.)

    How they would express themselves if it were permissible

    (He plays the baby so he can pretend he is protected and dependent; she becomes a tiger so she can growl with impunity; he plays father so he can dominate, etc.)

Any of these attitudes could be consistently held in any kind of play. A child would then always be tyrannical or always kind, or always meek, whether father, mother, captain, police officer, uncle, or aunt. But it is just as likely that attitudes will change with the role as with different play companions. A child could be subservient to a big, strong playmate, but high-handed with a small one, a bossy doctor but a gentle father. We have to observe a child at dramatic play more than once and with many children to see which behavior is characteristic of his/her relations with others.

When children play superhuman/magical roles, they can fulfill certain emotional needs more satisfactorily than in roles with real-life content. These needs, however, are very limited:

- The need or desire to be powerful, more than human—a need that is common to young children because of their powerlessness.

    (As Superman, they can fly, exhibit superhuman strength.)
- The need to be aggressive

    (As the Incredible Hulk, they can be aggressive in order to right wrongs, protect the weak.)

CHILDREN PLAY WITH SYMBOLIC OBJECTS (OBSIG PLAY)

What to Record

In obsig play, the details to be recorded relate to the content of play. They constitute actions that are slightly different from those in persig play.

- The symbolic actions that the child makes a symbolic object (real or imaginary) perform (e.g., moving a small car, or object representing a car, on a road of blocks; pushing a long line of interlocking blocks representing a train on block "tracks"; "flying" a wedgie or small figure of a man, representing Superman, through the air, etc.)
- The words the child speaks *for* symbolic objects that represent a person, character in a story, or superhero (e.g., Jim, speaking for a "child" wedgie in a high, squeaky voice, "O.K., then I'll get my fadder." And Tom, speaking for his "man" wedgie, also in a high, squeaky voice, "But I *am* your fadder.")

- The quality of voice used by the child when speaking for a symbolic object (as in the above example)

As in persig play, you also record onomatopoetic sounds (a train whistle, motor sounds), other symbolic objects used in the play, and comments, if any, that a child makes about what symbolic objects represent, what is happening in the play, etc.

In obsig play, ideas come from the same sources as do the ideas for roles.

- The content can be inspired by inanimate objects in the real world (train, airplane, boat, car, spaceship, doll, etc.).
- Real people can be the inspiration (conductor, engineer, storekeeper, astronaut, mother, father, etc.).
- The idea can have its source in television characters (Batman, Superman) or stories.

In the following record the content comes from real life. It is simple repetitive play.

Lawrence (age 4:10) is in the block corner. He takes the Tinkertoys and puts some together in the shape of an airplane. Holding it in the center, he zooms it through the air, making motor noises. He "flies" it to the book corner then back to the block corner.

He says to Johnny, who is watching, "I making a airplane." Then he goes over to the teacher, saying, "See, airplane." The teacher admires it, and he leaves her and goes to the book area where he zooms the airplane around.

Johnny, who also has an airplane, joins him and they both zoom their planes around, making motor noises. Lawrence lies on the floor and "flies" the plane around over his body, rolling as he does so. He puts the plane on the floor and, with a slowly accelerating noise, has it take off and zoom and then land. He then goes around the room, zooming his plane and making motor noises. He has the plane touch table tops, as he passes, and go up in the air again, making a louder noise when the plane goes higher in the air.

The teacher says it is time to go out. Lawrence puts the Tinkertoy plane in the box and lines up with the other children.

Here, two four-year-old boys engage in Superman play together. They both contribute ideas to the play.

Ben and Alan, each holding a small rubber figure of a man, go to the housekeeping corner, where there is an old television set. The set

is a large old table model with an open back. The front, of course, is
the glass screen and there are two holes where the knobs once were.
Ben now gets behind the set, lying on the floor, and begins to push his
figure through the round hole that once held a knob.

ALAN (who is in front of the set): Good, Ben. O.K. Now here's a trap.
    (He then pushes his figure in.)
BEN: That's a good trap. Now we'll pretend that they got out.
ALAN: O.K. Now pretend he got in a truck and got locked up and
    then he still got away.
BEN: Now he gets out. He gets away.
ALAN (talking for his figure): Superman, come and play.
BEN (talking for his figure): I'm coming. I'm out of my trap.
    (Ben then pushes his figure into the hole and Alan takes it.)
BEN (stands and shouts): Eeeeeek, give it back.
    (Alan hands it back and Ben gets right back down on the floor.)
ALAN: That's fun. Let's do it again.
BEN: No.
    (Both boys leave and go over to the tool bench.)

ASSESSING THE CONTENT (PERSIG AND OBSIG)

The source of the content that inspires children's play seems to
make a difference in the way they are able to adapt the content to
their make-believe. Real-life experiences of actions and processes
they can reproduce seem in general to lead to better developed,
more sustained, and more productive play than poorly perceived or
confusing experiences. The former allow the children and the
teacher to extend the children's knowledge with additional information and/or clarification.

This record of Wanda making popcorn suggests that she had spent
a considerable amount of time observing how popcorn is made.

Wanda was standing at the kitchen table and slowly looked down
at the bowl of fruit on the table. She continued to look at it for awhile
and studied the contents of the bowl intently. She turned around
quickly, heavily using her whole body to propel herself, and grabbed
a large frying pan from the "stove." She spun back to the table
forcefully, and carefully and noisily, with a thud, plopped the pan on
the table. In a loud, firm voice she said, "Cooling," as she held the
handle and looked quizzically into the empty pan. She did not look at
the girls, who were busy with their own housekeeping activities. She
began gently to shake the pan back and forth on the table top. Her
face was expressionless while she seemed seriously involved in this
activity. She moved her body closer to the table and quickly changed

the intensity of her shaking from the gentle and slow rhythm to a swift and energetic one, creating a bristling, forceful sound. Loudly she said, "Popcorn in the big pot." Upon hearing this, Helen, Audry, and Sasha came quickly to look. Wanda held the handle while the other girls dipped their fingers into the pan and put the pretend popcorn in their mouths. "Yum," they said gleefully. In the meantime, three boys joined the girls. At once, and eagerly, they also pretended to taste the popcorn. Wanda continued to hold the handle and smiled as the children tasted. Her smile was soft and she glanced into each child's face as each tasted with glee. The pace quickened as the children reached into the pan faster and faster to gobble up the popcorn.

Television sources, on the other hand, generally lead to simplistic play about superheroes whose few major activities are endlessly repeated and rarely developed imaginatively. Here is José (age 5) playing he is Bionic Man.

When José finished sanding his piece of wood, he said something about "bionic" and moved, with his elbows back, his head down, his knees high, in a sort of slow-motion effect, across the room. He then came back, moving the same way, and went to the doll corner, where he declared he was bionic. He started to play-fight with Fernando, who complained. He picked up a toaster and moved it to a doll house (near the window), then back to the doll corner, and, with the same bionic walk, brought a can to the house. He left the house and, still walking like the Bionic Man, went over to the rocking horse, stood up in the stirrups, then sat and rode gently, looking around. Although José's pace was slow, he leaned very far forward and back on the horse, occasionally saying, "bionic."

When the teacher said it was time to stop playing, José got off the horse and went over to the rug.

SOCIAL ASPECTS OF DRAMATIC PLAY

When two or more children engage in dramatic play together, they express not only what they know about the world, their fears, wishes, and aspirations, but also their social attitudes, techniques, and relationships.

Children's Reactions to One Another

Children test and modify the effectiveness of their social attitudes and techniques via the response of others. Position, status, and acceptance within a group depend to some extent on an individual child's actions. But they are affected also by the willingness of other children to see an individual in terms suitable to his or her own self-concept, wishes, needs, and wants. The teacher who would help a child achieve more mature social behavior must know the impact of children on each other in two ways: objectively (this is what happened), and in the subjective meaning to the youngster involved (what that child thought happened).

- Which children react? To whom?
- What do they do? How do they do it?
- What do they say? How do they say it?
- Do they fit in with others' plans, use others, resist others, follow them under protest, etc.?
- Does a child's desire for status, prestige, affection, or attention interfere with the progress of the play situation?
- What is a child's general tone at play—amiable, hostile, creating dissension?

Jan is dressed up in a long skirt and a hat from the dress-up corner. She is moving pots on the stove while Aaron uses a wooden iron on the tablecloth. Aaron says, "Pretend this is an eating table."

Jan does not reply but keeps on cooking. Aaron ignores the lack of response. He leaves the iron and gets another hat from the dress-up corner. He says, "Look what I brought you, Mother. Does it look nice?" He gives the hat to Jan and takes the old one. Jan puts the new hat on her head but says nothing; she continues her cooking.

Aaron gets an apron and puts it on. Jan turns to him and says reprovingly, "No. That's a girl's suit." Aaron takes it off and Jan puts it on over the long skirt.

He gets another apron, a full-sized one with a bib. He asks, looking for approval, "Is this a boy's?" Jan nods. Aaron persists, "Is this the head?" Jan says agreeably, "Yeah." She helps him put it on and fixes it efficiently, adjusting the length so that Aaron doesn't trip.

She picks up a flashlight and tries to turn it on. "Turn on the light," she says. The flash does not work, and she puts it down after several attempts. Aaron and Jan stand side by side and pretend to cook. They talk quietly about what they are doing as if giving themselves directions.

Sometimes they address each other more directly and seem to expect a reply. For example, "You lay the table, right?" Eddie comes up and says, smiling, "Is this a real house?" Aaron replies, "Would you like to be visitors coming to the house?"

Eddie: "O.K." Donnie joins him and they formally approach, already immersed in the action. They knock at an imaginary door.

Aaron says as he opens the door, "This is a restaurant." Jan nods her confirmation. Donnie and Eddie come in and sit at the table.

Eddie calls out imperiously, "Service! Service!" Jan comes over and says, "O.K."

Eddie: "I want my dinner. What's for dinner?"

Jan goes back to the stove and calls over her shoulder crisply, "Hot dogs."

Eddie: "O.K. Hot dogs with mushrooms."

Jan continues cooking and Aaron joins her, moving pots and pans. Eddie and Danny get bored and leave.

Jan makes coffee in the coffee pot. Aaron takes the kettle and comments, "This is the coffee." Jan contradicts him. "No, that's the tea."

Aaron: "You'd better hurry up. Here's more customers."

This time the customers are imaginary. They lay the table together. Jan says, "The yellow cups are for coffee, the other ones are for tea."

Eddie returns and seems to want to join the game. Aaron pushes him away roughly. "You're not playing. You can't play." Eddie persists and Aaron pushes him away again.

Meanwhile, Jan gets up, goes into the corner, and spins around and around, watching the motion of her long skirt and feeling the motion with her palms. She just might be deliberately avoiding the confrontation between Aaron and Eddie.

As soon as Eddie gives up and leaves, both Aaron and Jan return to the game. They continue play acting with a great deal of cooperation.

In this record, Jan's attitude toward Aaron changes as the play proceeds. At first she ignores him, then disapproves of some of his actions, and finally becomes cooperative and more amiable. Aaron, who obviously is very anxious to play with Jan, accepts her reproofs at first, but persists, and comes into his own as an equal partner in the play as Jan's attitude changes.

A Child's Position in Relation to the Others Playing

As the members of a group interact, they tend to find spots for themselves in the group's hierarchy and structure. Some children are leaders, some followers, some peacemakers, and some moralists representing the adult point of view. Some children barely fit into the group as legitimate members at all.

A child's position in the group may be obvious or may be subtly concealed and disguised. A child who seems to be a cooperator may just be a slavey in disguise. Eagerness to be accepted or anxiety about what he has to offer may lead him to a fairly thorough denial of his right to a genuinely cooperative position. The child who is noisiest in a group may seem to be the leader and yet the real direction may be coming from a quiet youngster who controls the play by force of ideas.

Position in the group is one of the important components of inter-relating. For one youngster leadership may be so important that she will resort to any trick she can think up to reach her goal. For another there may be quiet contentment in not being challenged. Position has two faces—how the adult sees a child's position in the group, and how the child sees and feels about it.

> Position could be boss, constructive leader, cooperative member, "fringer," compromiser, etc.
>
> Position can be maintained by bullying, force of ideas, persuasion, reasoning, coaxing, bribing, silence, force, etc.

In this record, the child's position in the group, his feelings about maintaining that position, and the reactions of others seem quite clear.

> Several little groups of youngsters were scattered through the wooded area of the play yard, some digging, some filling cans, some using a rock for the dinner table in their imaginary home. Peter and cohorts had used cans to collect items for dinner, then to gather maple syrup (sap) from the trees. Peter left his cans by a tree and came swinging past Denise's rock.
>
> Peter announced: "I'm going to get my fishing cast and go out in the boat. Mama (addressing Denise), will you row the boat for me while I'm fishing?" Peter did not wait for an answer but continued on his quest for his fishing rod. From far away he called, "Come on, Mama!"
>
> Denise was adamant. "I need to make the lunch at home on the stove!"
>
> Peter found a long rod-like pole and returning, paused again by Denise. "Come on, Mama. Now you be careful making that lunch." He strode toward his boat rock. "Come on, Mama. Come on, we have to go. You have to row . . . That's the boat house and you come with me."
>
> Denise kept on with her lunch-making, but called after Peter, "Goodbye!"
>
> Peter was now back on his rock, his fishing rod stowed aboard. He stood there holding onto a tree branch, looking across the woods to Denise and calling. Impatience at being balked was beginning to creep into his tone. "Come on! You have to row for me."
>
> Denise: "You go on. I can't do it."
>
> Peter, screaming: "Come on! *You have to do it!*" With each word he

beat the branch with a short stick for emphasis and to give vent to his feelings, since he couldn't beat Denise but would probably have liked to rush over and do so.

Denise, in a disgruntled, placating voice, "All right. Let me finish the onions. Bring the children. Come on, Louise." She and her companion moved over to the boat.

Peter now had Stephen, Leslie, Robert, Denise, and Louise on the rock-boat. He was using a stick for an oar. Then he saw Nancy and Julie busy digging. (New fields to conquer!) "Come on, sisters (to Nancy and Julie). Will you row for us, sisters?" They came easily. But soon Julie was in tears. Denise was slapping her hands hard for dumping dirt from her can and getting the boat dirty.

"Stop that, Denise!" Peter commanded. Julie got off the boat, spirits wounded, head bent.

Louise edged in next to Peter on the rock. "That's where Mama's going to sit. Now get out." He pushed her away so Denise could come.

Then Denise took up Peter's long stick. "Stop! That's my fishing cast," he told her. Denise got off the boat, found herself a long fishing rod, and returned.

Peter, to Leslie: "Brother, will you row?" Leslie refused.

Peter, looking around: "Well, who's going to row?" Spying Denise with her own fishing rod: "Mama, you row. We only want one fishing cast. Look! I caught a big one (a leaf at the end of his stick). *Listen*, who's going to row? (To Denise) Mama, you go over there and fish over there. It's the nicest place on the boat. Now, man (to Leslie), row with this stick."

Having at last made someone row, he turned to his fishing.

Peter obviously wants to be the boss, but seldom succeeds. He uses several methods to attain his aim—verbal insistence, persistence, and, occasionally, force. His manner provokes considerable resistance from the others.

SUMMARY OF A CHILD'S BEHAVIOR DURING DRAMATIC PLAY

Records of a child involved in dramatic play would not only include evidence about the following aspects of his play behavior, but also reflect any changes in behavior over a period of time.

- Is obsig or persig play more predominant?
- To what extent is the content of the play concerned with real-life or fantasy activities?
- What are the usual specific contents of the play?
    (train, airplane, family, Superman, monsters, etc.)

- What roles does the child usually take in persig play?
  (driver, father, mother, baby, animal, superhero, train, etc.)
- Does the child tend to play alone or with others?
- When playing with others, does the child usually take on a different role from the others (e.g., he is the bus driver and the others are passengers)?
- When playing alone, does a particular content (e.g., playing house, putting out fires) or role (driver of a vehicle or superhero) predominate?

Records of play in which other children are involved would also shed light on the child's mode of interacting with others.

- In playing roles, what *position* does the child take in relation to others?
  (Although playing such roles as mother, baby, or storekeeper, the *position* is that of boss, subordinate, leader, cooperator, moralist, scapegoat, etc.)
- Does she always assume one position or is it only in relation to certain personalities, i.e., is she always the boss or only with the timid children (younger ones, older, boys, girls, aggressive children, etc.)?
- How is the child's position maintained?
  (By the enticement of ideas, rationalizing, talking excessively, reasoning, humor, verbal or physical aggression, threats, bribery, voicing protest, acting helpless, etc.)

As you complete the recording, be sure to indicate how the play ends. How the child terminates play if playing alone, or leaves a group when playing with others, has as many implications as how the child begins play or enters the play of others.

- Does the child leave for some other activity?
- If playing with others, does the other child (or children) leave first?
- Does the teacher interrupt the play?
  (for juice, pick-up, etc.)
- Does it develop into some other kind of play?
- How long did the child's participation last?
- What or who seems responsible for the ending?
- How do the children disperse?
- What is the feeling tone?
  (happy, guilty, despairing, belligerent, contented, etc.)

6

THE CHILD'S RELATIONSHIPS WITH ADULTS AND IN ADULT-DIRECTED ACTIVITIES

CHILDREN ARE BORN helpless, and for a long time they remain largely dependent on adults. Yet, to reach mature adulthood, they must somehow make the transition to relative independence. This they accomplish in many steps and stages, sometimes obviously and dramatically, sometimes with quiet ease. The struggle for independence is not waged without qualms and fears. While they are breaking the bonds, children continue to need adults, not only for physical sustenance, affection, and understanding but for moral support in this drive to independence.

From the adults who are most important in the early years, their parents, children learn many things. Their concepts of people and what to expect of them and their concepts of themselves and what they may and may not do are shaped by their daily contacts with these significant adults. Children believe that all adults are like the ones they first knew best until long years of experience beyond early childhood teach them to recognize differences. They assume that what adults tell them about themselves is true, unless other people later teach them otherwise. Consequently, when a child enters school for the first time, his or her behavior with teachers will in large measure reflect home experience and indicate how far along the road to independence and a positive or negative self-concept the child has gone.

RECORDING A CHILD'S INTERACTION
WITH AN ADULT

Observation of a child's relationship with adults as we see it revealed at school can tell us whether the child feels that adults are to be trusted, or viewed with suspicion; whether they are to be exploited for one's own ends, hated fiercely, or avoided. We can tell, too, whether the child believes it is possible to run the gamut of human feeling from best to worst, break adult taboos of right and wrong, and still remain loved; or whether it is necessary to carefully refrain from doing anything that will offend adult standards and thus bring about a loss of adult love.

The details of the adult-child relationship will, in many instances, be an incidental part of the situations dealt with up to now, i.e., the child's functioning during routines, with materials, or in relation to children. In addition, however, there are special adult-child contacts, as all teachers know, because they themselves are involved.

There is the time a child grabs one's hand and squeezes it, or catapults out of the doorway and forcefully leaps onto us by way of morning greeting; there is the quiet moment of confidence when a child brings something precious for inspection or holds up a wet nose to be wiped; there is the imperious demand for attention, the teasing, and the shared laughter. Every day brings new relationships with the individuals who make up the group. Every child feels special in the eyes of the teacher and makes individual, "special" contacts with her. (If a child does not, it is worthy of note.)

Details to Look for in Recording a Child's Contact with an Adult
● Setting in which the episode takes place
● Who makes the contact?
  If the child makes the contact:
    Is it purposeful?
    (child asks for help, asks for materials, shows products, asks for comfort when hurt—actual or imagined, seeks help at routines, asks to be played with, etc.; bestows affection or asks for it; asks help in social relationships, ideas)
    Is it indirectly purposeful?
    (child seeks attention by excessive talking, by a stream of presents, by provocative activity done deliberately with awareness that it is not acceptable, such as screaming, dangerous climbing, breakage, hiding things, etc.)

If the teacher makes the contact, what is her purpose?
(to give assistance with materials or equipment, settle a dispute, enter the play, make suggestions or requests, give directions or orders, give comfort following injury or insult, offer props, etc.)
What attitude and feeling are revealed by the child as evidenced by voice, tempo of speech, facial expression, body positions and movement, body contacts?
● Dialogue (direct quotes)
● Sequence of events
Include what adult does and says.
Indicate child's responses, both verbal and bodily.
● How does the contact end?
● What does the child do immediately after?

Patterns of Behavior
These are two children who reveal different approaches to a teacher.

Sharon, very blond, pale complexion, blue eyes, flat pug nose, and mouth slightly open, arrives at school each morning with her mother. She walks up the path expressionless, almost dragging her legs. Looking around slowly, she heads toward the teacher. The teacher calls, "Hi, Sharon!" but does not receive a response. She calls again, "Hi, Sharon!" and this time receives a faint smile. Sharon maneuvers toward the swings, where one child is already swinging. Sharon wraps herself around the pole and waits. The other child, paying no attention to Sharon, gets off, and Sharon, still moving slowly, eases herself on and begins to pump. Once again she has a slight smile. After a few minutes, she begins to play in the mud, working seriously by herself. She looks up blankly and sees another child bring his finished mud cake to the teacher. The teacher tastes enthusiastically. Still staring, Sharon slowly stands up, and walks over to the teacher, carrying the mud pie carefully. Holding the dish, she stands motionless and speechless for several moments. Then, not saying a word, she turns and sluggishly moves away.

Picking-up time and teacher is cleaning tables. Martha comes over "I can count to ten," she offers confidentially. "I'd like to hear you," says the teacher, scrubbing away. Hopping on one foot, Martha slowly and accurately counts from one to ten, holding her arms out all the time to help her keep balance. She gives the teacher a smile, all front teeth and crinkled eyes, jumps on two feet and runs off.

Teachers Observe Themselves

Young children need adults but they must also gradually loosen the ties. Teachers must be able to observe the relationship in which they are themselves involved with enough dispassionate interest to see the child's dependency needs with objectivity and see the denial of dependence with realistic and unbiased appraisal. It is perhaps easier to do this if we ask ourselves about a relationship with a child, "Do I enhance or detract from this child's sense of personal powers?" It is hard to be oneself and the impartial observer at the same time. Our professional selves (objective and educated) must become one with our personal selves (subjective and emotionally involved).

THE CHILD IN TEACHER-DIRECTED GROUP ACTIVITIES

The special relationship each child may experience with a teacher of necessity exists within a group structure. This means that the one-to-one contacts give way regularly to experiences in which a child must share the teacher with many other children. This sharing takes place in informal situations, as when a child must wait a turn to be helped, and in more formally planned activities, such as music time, a group story, or a trip.

How grown up must a child be to enjoy sharing a common experience with friends? It's one thing to be yourself and get along with others at your own speed. It's another to become an anonymous someone and be moved with a group as an integrated part of it! A child wonders whether to listen for an adult's directions and try to please her or him, or to listen to the cues the children give and seek to be acceptable to them. For most young children, the group situation offers challenges toward adjustment. The one-to-one relationship is still very meaningful, and individuals vary in the degree to which they can function comfortably outside close and intimate adult-child interaction. Children's responses when the group is directed as a group may therefore be quite different from their responses when the teacher speaks to each one directly or alone.

For one thing, in teacher-directed group activities, the teacher often speaks to any one child only by inference, because she speaks to all the children at once in a group. (This is often the reason young children do not respond to requests given to the group as a whole for cleanup, dressing, etc.) For another, the obvious and compelling competition for the teacher's attention may affect a child's feelings about a group activity. If a child is more concerned about the teacher's favor than about the story, for example, he may respond to the most appealing tale by squirming and wriggling, meanwhile pushing and edging toward the beloved adult.

Or, a child's very ability to perform may be affected by the overwhelming presence of nonindulgent peers, because comparisons are all too often offered by them, and this is not always easy to tolerate. The group situation established by the teacher (i.e., everybody will do the same thing) may therefore be a challenge to a child that is quite different from the looser group situation in which individual behavior is more closely related to a child's own desires and wants and not as immediately bound by peer involvement. Behavior in a teacher-directed activity may thus have its own meaning to a child, quite unrelated to the intent of the teacher.

Any school activity may be reminiscent to a child of experience outside of school, and this will influence behavior in the group too. For example, if listening to a story at home is enjoyed as much for snuggling next to an adult as for the story itself, how well can a youngster listen at school, removed from physical contact with the teacher and sharing her with a lot of other youngsters? Or, if a child has been struggling secretly to conquer skipping, or jumping with two feet, or hopping, she may not yet be able to prance unselfconsciously at rhythms with her better coordinated peers. And it is easy to understand the panic some children undergo as they start across the floor and feel themselves swamped by the stampede of galloping bodies all around them!

Details to Look for in Recording a Child's Reactions to Group Activity

In observing a child at any teacher-organized activity, we look for the general child-to-group and child-to-adult relationships as well as to the specifics of the activity.

- What is a child's initial reaction to the announcement that the group activity is about to begin?
    Positive (eager, joyful, ready to discontinue previous activity immediately)
    Negative (continues with previous activity, dawdles, refuses,

complains, runs away, etc.)
    Accepting (compliant, goes along in matter-of-fact way, etc.)
- What is the sequence of events?
    (the contents of the rhythms period; walking to a trip site;
    nature and length of the story read; directions given for a
    project; etc.)
- What part is played by the adult?
    (shows children how to move; keeps children from bumping
    into each other; plays an instrument; reads aloud; etc.)
- How does the child react to sharing the adult with other children
    or with other adults, as when the teacher is helping other chil-
    dren; is talking to another teacher or to a parent; is directing
    the entire group in an activity such as a story, game, trip,
    rhythms, an explanation, etc.?
    (child accepts easily, ignores, interrupts and demands atten-
    tion, sulks, cries, has tantrums, waits for adult to return,
    awaits turn patiently but not resignedly)
- What does the child do if he/she participates?
    How does the child do it?
    (responds with body movement, facial expression, speech; is
    swift, impulsive; interested, involved; etc.)
- What does the child do if he/she does not participate?
    (observes group, disrupts, clings to teacher, turns back on
    group, does something else, runs out of room, etc.)
- How does the child respond to adult directions?
    (blankly, agreeably, happily, reluctantly, petulantly, tearfully,
    angrily)

Since a child's participation in a teacher-directed activity may
also reveal a child's level of interest and functioning in the activity
itself, recording the details of the child's involvement gives us additional data by which to measure the effect of the relationship with
the teacher and the children. A child who can cope with feelings
about adults, children, and an activity in a reasonable balance is
clearly one who has integrated the several areas of relating. Many
children are still working at achieving this balance. Four-year-old
Mollie, in the next record, is clearly one such child.

It is 9:30 A.M. and the kindergarten is having music. The music
teacher sits before the group while the two regular teachers sit with
the children. Mollie sits near the music teacher. The children have

been singing a song about animals and are discussing what kind of sound a turkey makes. Mollie looks around at the children, and her face lights up in a bright, full smile. Her body is in constant motion, switching rapidly from one position to another. She makes hand motions; the contact is made.

Focusing on the music teacher now, she listens to the questions, her eyes darting around the circle of children, her mouth working, her brow slightly knit.

She moves to sit next to the teacher on the opposite side, then returns to the original spot next to John. The music teacher is telling a story. Mollie looks around at the other children, then looks pertly at the music teacher, listening carefully. She plays with her dress, turns to watch another child who is making a scratching sound, and turns her attention back to the music teacher.

Her face is alive, interested; sometimes she seems to slip off into her own world, then comes back. She is extremely attentive to the other children. She listens to their verbal responses and watches carefully, although she says nothing in response to questions directed to the group.

The children are taking parts to act out the story. Andy is a frog. Mollie says, "I wanna be a frog too." She becomes very involved in being a frog, joyfully jumping around. She continues being a frog after the time for the frog part is finished.

The music teacher begins singing "My Little Rooster." Mollie watches the children intently as they choose animals and make the sounds. Mollie doesn't sing. She wiggles over to Andy, whispers, then to Adele. A child chooses "donkey," and the music teacher sings "bray" for the sound the donkey makes. Mollie screws her face into a puzzled expression and says, "No, hee-haw," quietly but audibly.

Her expression shifts rapidly and constantly. She raises her hand. The music teacher calls on her immediately. "Mollie, what's yours?" Mollie giggles, says something inaudible. The children start guessing her animal. She says clearly, "Peacock." She listens intently as the verse is sung about the peacock. Then her concentration breaks and she makes contact with Ruth Ann.

Summary of a Child's Relationships with Adults

A summary of a child's relationships with adults can be drawn from many areas of school living, such as casual adult-child contacts throughout the day (what the child says and does); the relationship at routines and while using materials and equipment; through the roles (and the meaning given to them) adopted during dramatic play; and the child's behavior during teacher-directed activities.

1. How frequently does the child make contact with the adult and in what situations?
   (routines; coming for approval, help in conflicts, with materials, ideas, etc.; to give or get affection, be comforted; express hostility; involve adult in play, seek attention, directly or indirectly; group activities, etc.)
   Is there a special quality in contacts with adults?
   (whining, demanding, trusting, coy, timid, belligerent, clinging, openly hostile, matter-of-fact, warmhearted, reserved, etc.)
   What are the child's special mechanisms for gaining attention?
   (excessive talking; tattling; showing clothes, toys, products, bruises; bringing presents; telling about family; sidling up and touching, hanging on, etc.)

2. How does child react when the teacher is a *giving* person?
   When she offers affection:
   child returns it, looks uncomfortable, squirms, seems startled, stiffens up, becomes effusive and gushy, rejects offering, etc.
   When she offers help:
   child accepts it as a right, becomes clingy and helpless, brushes it away, becomes angry, discusses, becomes interested in procedures, etc.
   When she offers suggestions:
   child follows through reluctantly, eagerly; ignores; is grateful; follows through mechanically; rejects; discusses; questions; etc.

The summary of a child's total response to the teacher as a *giving* person would indicate:

Dependence on this adult (and possibly all adults)
Rejection of this adult (and possibly all adults)
Ability to meet adults on equal terms, both to accept and reject the adults' overtures as appropriate

3. How does child react when the teacher is a controlling, inhibiting person, curtailing child's actions and feelings?
   When limits are set down, such as group rules and/or personal denial:

child defies openly; resists passively by lingering, slowing up, remaining at another task; etc.; accepts with over-seriousness; accepts with no emotional investment; accepts with a verbalization of the reason; accepts and repeats instructions with parrot-like insistence.

When criticism is given:

child cries; pouts; accepts cheerfully; shows interest; becomes belligerent; sulks; etc.

The summary of a child's total responses to the adult as an authority figure would show the child as someone who

Always does as told, to whom following adult direction seems more important than his/her own ideas, who has a consistent pattern of subordination to adult wishes—who is compliant, or

Resists authority by any one of a number of patterns, by defiance, questioning, or indifference, or

Finds a balance between carrying out her/his own independent ideas and wishes and accepting reasonable restrictions.

4. Evidences of growing independence from adults, as seen in routines, use of materials, relationships with other children, identification with other children rather than with adults (perhaps even against adults)

5. Direct verbal expressions

6. Special problems:

Overdependence

Excessive insistence on independence

Fear of new adults

Persistent hostility to adults

Excessive displays toward adults, including strangers

Records of Children's Behavior with Adults

The first two months José was at school, he seemed to need a lot of reassurance from the teacher that he was doing the right thing. He seldom talked, but would raise his eyes questioningly, as if to say, "Is this all right?" With a nod and a smile from her, he would take paper and crayon, or some other material, and proceed to work. But again and again he would seek the teacher out with his eyes. After finishing any work, he would always walk slowly and proudly to the teacher and say, "See, it's for my mommy!" Since he often wandered out into the hall leading into the kitchen, the teacher asked him one day if he would like to accompany her to get the juice. He nodded enthusiastically and walked faster than usual down the hall and into the kitchen. There he struck up the beginning of his friendship with the cook. He remarked to her after a few minutes of observation, "I like it here. What are we going to eat?" After that, José accompanied the teacher into the kitchen every morning, and he would talk to the cook as the juice was being prepared.

José seems drawn to any visiting adults and will always edge his way slowly and cautiously to their side, usually displaying something he has made for approval and appreciation. For a long time he just smiled and dropped his head if spoken to. But by now he has gained enough courage to tell his name and age if asked. He is very happy if they praise his work and lingers near until they leave.

At the beginning of the year it was evident that Amanda was embarrassed by any attention shown her by adults, except in the routine of help with clothing or toilet. She showed this by her posture, gestures, voice, facial expression, and jerky movement of her body. Next came her bid for attention by loud and excessive talking, laughing, antics, climbing performances, and pretended inability to dress herself (this last in spite of the fact that in the beginning she never needed help with dressing with the exception of placing a garment into proper position). At present she is still behaving in this attention-demanding way, but not as frequently as she has. She comes to show us her dresses (she usually wears slacks), asks to pass out items when need arises. She also seeks help in toileting. Help is not actually needed, but she apparently wants the presence of the teacher in the room.

7

CLUES TO COGNITIVE FUNCTIONING: STAGE-RELATED STYLE

HOW DO WE recognize that a child is a learning child? And just as important, how do we determine that a child is having difficulties understanding what the world and reality are all about?

HOW DO CHILDREN LEARN?

As in the nonintellectual areas of functioning, we concern ourselves here too with the *what* and the *how: what* does a child know; *how* does the child go about the business of learning?

Piaget's studies have made us realize that children work hard and steadily at finding meaning in everything they encounter. They continuously shape a reality that makes sense to them out of their interactions with the people, places, and things of their everyday lives. Naturally, their understanding is limited by their egocentric interpretations of everything they encounter; yet unless they are restricted by adults to learning only what adults want them to learn, they tend to explore freely and happily in a variety of directions. They need to learn from adults, of course, but they do not feel constrained to focus only on adult-directed paths unless parents and teachers misunderstand the motivating force of childhood curiosity and insist on repressing it.

Thus, the capacity to learn feeds, and blooms, on curiosity, that human birthright that goes into action the day a child is born. Read the following description of a baby less than one month old and see how early curiosity appears:

This was on the twenty-fifth day, toward evening, when the baby was lying on her mother's knee by the fire in a condition of high well-being and content, gazing at her grandmother's face with an expression of attention. I came and sat down close by, leaning over the baby, so that my face must have come within the direct range of her vision. At that she turned her eyes and gazed at it with the same appearance of attention, and even of some effort, shown by a slight tension of brows and lips, then turned her eyes back to her grandmother's face, and again to mine, and so several times. The last time she seemed to catch sight of my shoulder on which a high light struck from the lamp, and not only moved her eyes, but threw her head far back to see it better, and gazed for some time with a new expression on her face—"a sort of dim and rudimentary eagerness," says my note. She no longer stared, but really looked.*

The same intense curiosity in exploring the environment normally continues all through childhood. Here is how it looks in a nursery school classroom:

> Robin quietly approaches the art table. She stands curiously watching three other children who are busy sanding the wood of a stool the children are making together. The teacher asks Robin if she would like to sand and she nods her head. She pulls over an empty chair and settles down without a sound. Her eyes are focused on the children's hands and she seems to be mesmerized with the back and forth rhythm of the hands. Her right hand slowly reaches for a piece of sandpaper, her eyes and fingers simultaneously study the paper, and with a contented smile she begins sanding in a back and forth motion. She works away, staring intently at her wood. After a few minutes she stops, stares, and in a voice filled with wonder and delight, bursts out, "Look at the dirt!"

Here it is again in a self-directed activity of two first graders at school:

> It's early in the morning, and six-year-old Ariella is the first child in the room. After wandering around aimlessly for a few minutes, she asks if she may hold the male garter snake, Stinker. She gets permission and takes the snake out of the tank with the teacher's help. Suddenly Ariella looks up and asks curiously, "What's that on his tail?" Holding the snake with one hand, she gently strokes his tail with the other. The snake coils itself into a complicated knot on her

---

*M. Shinn, *Biography of a Baby* (Boston: Houghton Mifflin, 1900 as quoted in Lois B. Murphy and Associates, *The Widening World of Childhood* (New York: Basic Books, 1962), p. 194.

hand. She remarks, half to herself, "Look at his shape," and continues to stroke it and watch it. Then she begins to shift her weight back and forth excitedly as she watches the snake's gymnastics. She looks down at the snake and softly croons its name, drawing out the syllables, "Stinn . . ker." She does this several times.

Mary Ann comes over holding the female snake, Diamonds. She says to Ariella, "Under here she's really cold." Mary Ann lifts up the snake and peers at its underside. Ariella glances over at Diamonds quickly, and Mary Ann walks away to play with the snake on the rug.

Listening to What Children Say

The most direct and obvious way to find out what children know is to listen closely to what they say. The following children are all under six.

Hilary comments during a class discussion, "After 14 is my favorite number; it's 15. That's the floor I live on."

Noah arrives at school and heads straight for Philip. One fist is tightly closed, but when Noah gets to Philip, he opens his hand and shows him its contents. "What is it?" Philip asks. "It's not an 'it'," answers Noah. "It's a seed. If you plant it you get more."

A teacher threading needles for children staves off pressure for help by asking, "Why can't I do more than one at a time?"
Says Charles, "Because you only have one pair of hands."
Esther, suddenly animated, bursts out, "A squid could do anything."
"Why could a squid?" the teacher asks.
"Because he has eight legs," Esther replies.

Nelson falls back on his head, gets up, and says quickly, "See, I'm O.K. I'm bionic."

Nicole says at meeting time, "I'm flying to Worcester tonight. It's a very short flight." To which Owen adds, "Well, I've flown to Boston, and Boston is near Worcester."

Such different things children get to know and understand without being formally taught. Listening to them closely, one also finds out what a child does *not* know or misunderstands or misinterprets.

As the teacher counts heads in the three-year-old group, she chants, "One, two, three, four, five," She is interrupted by Victor, who says seriously as she taps his head on the five, "No, I'm three."

A teacher asks three-year-old Todd about the picture on his polo shirt. Todd's face lights up and he tells her in one long breath, "That's King Kong who's playing at your neighborhood movie."

At the collage table, Josy and Meryl, both four, are cutting and gluing. Josy looks up and says, "Me and my brother has the most money in the whole wide world. . . . We have a hundred."

Tanya, almost five, pipes up, "We have a hundred million. That's less than a thousand, you know."

Josy states firmly, "And we get allowances. I get a dime and my brother gets a quarter. *So there,*" she adds firmly.

Tanya responds, "I get allowance of a penny a week . . . when I take the baby downstairs."

Three five- and six-year-old boys building helicopters, cannon, and motorcycles out of blocks have the following conversation while playing:

DAVID: The war is between the Germans and the Americans.
HARLEY: The war is between the Eskimos and the Americans.
NOEL: South America is against America.

Do all these children know what they are saying? Or are they trying out words that sound important to them?

Language and Learning in Early Childhood

Children love to talk, and as soon as they begin the mastery of language, they use it steadily, increasing in skill all the time. Through listening to what children say to each other and to adults, teachers can learn not only what they know or misunderstand, but what their thinking is like. During the early years, children's involvement in the *process of thinking* is of greater, more far-reaching effect than whether they know a great many right answers to adult questions. According to Jean Carew, who did extensive observations of intellectual growth in toddlers, "Wrong answers after a struggle are indicative of intellectual development; clumsy execution is as acceptable as smooth."* The process by which children arrive at conclusions is thus more significant, at this stage, than the answers, valuable as these are.

Children's language, while important, is not, however, the only clue to their thinking processes and understanding. For some children it is not even the major clue. So much of young children's

---

*Jean V. Carew, Itty Chan, and Christine Halfar, *Observing Intelligence in Young Children* (Englewood Cliffs, N. J.: Prentice-Hall, 1976), p. 11.

thinking is done with their bodies that it is possible, in many instances, to deduce the thinking process directly from their behavior. One can easily see curiosity in their eyes and faces; exploration and experimentation in their active hands; concentration and attention in their postures and expressions; persistence and involvement in the continuity with which they pursue their tasks. By the same token, one can also see when they are distracted or are making random, empty gestures that lead nowhere. Learning is an active process in early childhood, and it is through a child's activity that one can see quite clearly the presence or absence of investment, struggle, purposefulness, and organization, all elements of thinking. Observe this three-and-one-half-year-old child who does not speak English too well.

> Eneida walks to the table, where the teacher has set down two cartons of milk, four paper cups in a stack, and a serving dish with peanut-butter cracker sandwiches. Without a word, Eneida takes a milk carton and opens it with deliberation. "Look," she says, smiling with pride. (She was shown how to open a milk carton without touching the part that becomes the spout, and she has done it well.)
>
> Eneida separates the paper cups. Silently she counts the four cups with her eyes, not pointing, and then with her eyes counts the three children at the table. She gets up and puts one of the cups back on the cart. Cheryl sits down next to Eneida, and Eneida, smiling, says, "Wait," and goes to the cart to get a cup for her.

Is there any question that this child is thinking and reasoning? Here is another record, also of some three-year-olds, who are struggling with a different kind of intellectual task, that of perceiving the relationship of parts to a whole. They are putting a puzzle together. Here, too, the evidence of their thinking is in their activity rather than in their speech.

> Abigail sat by herself working intently on a puzzle. After quickly placing the most obvious pieces, she began to struggle with the rest. She tried one, then another, a slight grimace passing across her face after each failure. The teacher suggested Darcy could help because she knew that puzzle well.
>
> Darcy sat on one side of the puzzle, Abigail on the other. Neither said a word. Darcy picked up a piece, trying it in several places before she found a fit. "Goes there," she said softly, more to herself than to Abigail. Abigail sat back watching carefully, with a puzzle piece in each hand. She watched with interest as Darcy placed another piece.

Then Abigail leaned forward and tried to put a piece in. "It goes there," she stated with authority to Darcy. "No-o-o!" Darcy argued as she grabbed the piece out of the spot and fitted in another piece. Abigail sat back looking a little surprised but seemed resigned to letting Darcy have her way. They finished the puzzle together, taking turns placing pieces. The only verbal communication was an occasional "There," or "It goes here."

As they finished, Abigail patted the puzzle, grinned, and proudly called out, "It's done, Miss Behan." She then turned the puzzle upside down and started doing it again, working intently and silently.

In a quite different situation, Janet is also intently absorbed in what she is doing. Is she learning anything? How is she going about the process of learning?

At the water table, Janet poured water through a funnel into a tall bottle. She did this very contentedly—slowly, in rhythm. She noticed water trickling from a small hole in the bottle; she said. "Peepee," and continued pouring water into the bottle. She stopped and just watched the water stream out. She then took a water wheel and poured water into it very quickly with a shovel, picked up another bottle, filled it, and poured the whole contents onto the wheel. This made the wheel turn very quickly for a long time. Smiling, she said, to no one in particular, "Wee . . . wee . . ." She then became interested in the sponge, putting it under water, slowly squeezing it downward, then releasing it again and again, with her whole body going up and down as she did this.

This child is methodical and systematic in her efforts. From an intellectual point of view, she is gaining something. In exploring the properties of water, she has made a connection between the stream of water and the more familiar, personal stream that flows from her body. She has learned how to act quickly and apply pressure to keep a water wheel turning. She has also gained knowledge about the properties of a sponge. Throughout, she was strengthening a bodily sense of rhythm that pervaded all her observation, exploration, and experimentation.

COGNITIVE STYLE IS RELATED TO STAGE OF DEVELOPMENT

Curiosity about the environment, the desire to explore new situations and places, the need to manipulate and experiment with new objects and materials—these are the natural ways of childhood.

They are the key elements in learning and as important as the ability to remember what one has learned. So basic to humanity are these characteristics that they do not have to be taught to children anywhere.

As a result of this biological need to find out, all peoples everywhere seem to have tackled certain common aspects of physical and social reality and given them form and meaning. Among these are the phenomena of matter, number, space, weight, time, perspective, volume, distance, and morality.

It was Piaget's studies of children that made people realize that in every society every child pursues the search for physical and social meaning all over again as a way of understanding the world. It is not possible to know how much understanding of such phenomena a given child has developed by using standardized tests. The conceptualization that marks true mental growth is not *quantitative*—as sheer accumulation of facts is—but *qualitative*. Growth in capacity to understand creates a basic, organic change in a child's way of perceiving. Such change, being qualitative, is not measurable by quantitative means. It is therefore necessary for teachers to know what the important processes of mental growth are in early childhood so as to document them. This means looking for, and finding, the evidence that a child is thinking and therefore developing intellectually. *What* a child knows (i. e., information) can also be documented by good observation (see Chapter 10).

The *style* of children's learning—their *cognitive style*—is affected by two influences. One of these develops sequentially, the other does not. The sequential development in cognitive style is related to the growth that occurs as a result of maturation *and* experience. (Either alone does not work well.) The nonsequential element is the personal, idiosyncratic way in which an individual functions all through life, although possibly with modifications caused by self-learning and/or the guidance of others.

Each of these influences on cognitive style can be looked at separately, although in reality they function together (along with feelings), because children always act as whole beings.

Stage-Related Cognitive Style in Early Childhood

In Piaget's terms, a child's style of learning in early childhood can be *pre-operational* or *concrete-operational*. Both terms refer to specific ways of thinking.

1. Pre-operational

Children at this stage believe mainly what appears to be obvious to their senses. They are literal; they think in concrete terms. Piaget calls them "perception-bound."

> "Pennies can't make a dime," says the pre-operational child. "A dime is smaller."

Pre-operational children look at life from an egocentric point of view. That is, they cannot see things from another person's perspective. They give personal meaning to objects, people, and events. This is why these two three-year-olds sitting near each other can achieve equality on totally nonlogical terms:

> First Child (banging a can): Only *one* can play.
> Second Child: No, *two.*
> First Child: Only *one* can play.
> Second Child: No, *two.*
> First Child: I'm older than you.
> Second Child: I'm going to a birthday.
> First Child: We're both as tall as each other.

Pre-operational children cannot understand the difference between alive and inanimate, and they project life onto that which is inanimate.

> Caroline walked into the room cuddling a teddy bear.
> Teacher, smiling, "Is that a new teddy bear?"
> "No," Caroline laughed.
> "He never came to school before. Why not?" the teacher asked.
> "He's afraid to go to school. His name is Ted. He's two."

Pre-operational thinking is fixed on one attribute or characteristic at a time. It is not possible for the children to deal with several aspects of objects or events at the same time.

> Oliver's mother told him that she was going to teach mornings in the primary division of his nursery school. Oliver was very upset and kept asking her, "Will you still be my mother?"

> Axel, a German child, was in attendance in a kindergarten class for a month and learned much English. Several weeks after he left, a little black girl joined the class. (There was one lighter, brown-skinned child there already.) The children walked around the child, sizing her up. Finally, Rachel asked, "Can you talk English?" The child spoke up, assuring every one that she could. "Oh, then you're not different," Rachel said, and all agreed.

2. CONSERVATION

Between the pre-operational stage and the next one, the concrete-operational, there is a transition period during which the pre-operational child shakes loose from the earlier rigidities. The child begins to understand that a characteristic that cannot be seen may nevertheless exist, that unseen characteristics remain part of an object even when that object undergoes an outward change in appearance. Conservation allows a child to realize, for example, that a wooden airplane painted silver to look like metal is not actually metal but really still wood; that a chunk of clay transformed first into a long, slithery snake, then into a series of small balls, into one large ball, and finally into a person is still the same quantity of clay throughout. Children who are just approaching this level of understanding—that is, that the abstract characteristic does not change although the object's appearance does—at first make contradictory judgments about the existence of the abstract characteristic (number, length, volume, distance, etc.). Once children have made the transition, or, in Piaget's term, have achieved *conservation,* they speak with certainty about what they know to be true despite what their eyes see. They are no longer perception-bound.

Here are three examples from Piaget's own records that show the steps through which children develop conservation. In all three, fluid and glasses are used in the interviews. The interviewer was interested in discovering the extent to which a child understood that a quantity of liquid remains the same regardless of the shape or number of containers it is in. The glasses are designated A1, A2, A3, A4; B1, B2, B3, B4; and C1, C2, C3, C4 (see illustration on the following page). The interviews begin with the children's identifying names and ages, given in years and months. The child's responses to the interviewer's questions and instructions are given in italics.*

STEP I: ABSENCE OF CONSERVATION (At this stage the child ignores the quantity of liquid, but is impressed by the number of containers.)

SIM (5:0). She was shown A1 and A2 half full. There's the same amount in the glasses, isn't there?—(She verified it) *Yes.*—Look, Renée, who has the lemonade, pours it out like this. (Pouring A1 into B1

---

and B2, which were thus about 3/5 full). Have you both still the same
amount to drink?—*No. Renée has more because she has two glasses*—What
could you do to have the same amount?—*Pour mine into two glasses.*
(She poured A2 into B3 and B4.)—Have you got the same now?(She
looked for a long time at the 4 glasses) *Yes.*—Now Madeline (herself)

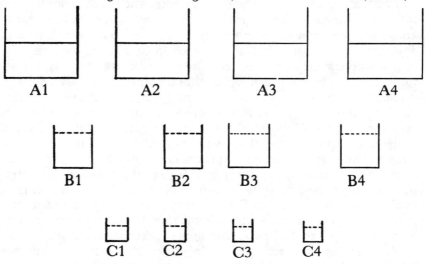

is going to pour her two glasses into three (B3 and B4 into C1, C2,
and C3). Are they the same now?—*No.*—Who has more to drink?—
Madeline, because she has three glasses.

STEP II: INTERMEDIARY REACTIONS (At this stage the child sometimes
perceives accurately and sometimes is confused.)

EDI (6:4): Is there the same in these two glasses A1 and A2?—*Yes.*
—Your mummy says to you: Instead of giving your milk in this glass
(A1), I give it to you in these two (B1 and B2), one in the morning
and one at night. (It is poured out.) Where will you have the most to
drink, here (A2) or there (B1 + B2)?—*It's the same.*—That's right.
Now, instead of giving it to you in these two (B1 and B2), she gives
it to you in three (pouring A2 into C1, C2, and C3), one in the morning, one at lunch-time and one at night. Is it the same in two as in the
three, or not?—*It is the same in 3 as in 2 . . . No, in 3 there's more.*—
Why?—. . .—(B1 And B2 were poured back into A1.) And if you pour
the three (C1 + C2 + C3) back into that one (A2) how far up will
it come?—(He pointed to a level higher than that in A1.)—And if we
pour these 3 into 4 glasses (doing so into C1 + C2 + C3 + C4, with
a consequent lowering of the level) and then pour it all back into the

big one (A2), how far up will it come?—(He pointed to a still higher level.)—And with 5?—(He showed a still higher level.)—And with 6? —*There wouldn't be enough room in the glass.*

STEP III: NECESSARY CONSERVATION (At this stage the child retains the constancy of quantity despite the overt changes.)

BERT (7:2): The orangeade (A1, 2/3 full) is for Jacqueline, the lemonade (A2, ½ full) is for you. Who has more?—*Jacqueline*—You pour yours (A2) into these two (B1 and B2, which were then full). Who has more?—*It's still Jacqueline*—Why?—*Because she has more.*— And if you pour this (B1) into those (C1 + C2)?—*It's still Jacqueline, because she has a lot.*—Every change produced the same result: *It's Jacqueline, because I saw before that she had more.*—Then A3, equal to A4, was poured into C1 + C2: *It's still the same, because I saw before in the other glass that it was the same.*—But how can it still be the same?—*You empty it and put it back into the others.*

3. CONCRETE-OPERATIONAL THINKING

After children have grasped the notion that objects and events may have characteristics that are not necessarily apparent to the senses of sight, hearing, touch, smell, or taste but that nevertheless *do* exist, they become less dependent on their senses and therefore less egocentric; they can deal with *some* nonconcrete reality. For example, having learned by experience that many things which *look* very different from each other can all be warm, they can now grasp the existence of an abstraction, the concept of *warmth;* knowing that light and dark are not always related to their own getting up and going to bed, they can grasp the concept that light and darkness have objective existence; knowing that the same numerical symbol, for instance, 4, can be used to measure age (4 years old), time (4 o'clock), place (4th floor), weight (4 pounds), quantity (4 wheels on a car), and so on, children can now grasp the concept of *number* as an abstraction that has a meaning of its own. Number is no longer perceived as an integral part of a child, a building, a car, or a television set; it has an existence of its own. Once children grasp this, they can understand and develop relations with numbers, play around with parts of the whole, and reverse relationships within the whole. They grow ready to deal with a wide variety of abstract concepts—*provided these are perceivable in connection with some concrete base of action.* For example, while using a scale to balance out various items of different size and weight (a hammer, six pencils, a bag of corks, a small stapler, a large cardboard box, etc.), children are now able to recognize that size and weight do not have a necessary relationship to each other. They could not understand this concept if it were taught them by words alone, and it is not possible to grasp at the pre-operational level at all. Children who conserve, however, can understand many relationships of an abstract nature *if they discover them through concrete experience.*

Patrick and Joshua (sixes) are playing Rig-A-Jig. Patrick hums quietly. "You know what, Miss R? I found out something new about Rig-A-Jig. Look!" He puts two pieces together.
TEACHER: What did you discover?
PATRICK (excitedly): That you can fit the pieces together like this. I discovered this and I didn't even know I was doing it.

The two Piagetian stages and the transition between them (conservation) occur in sequence, generally across the range of the early childhood years. Conservation occurs developmentally in children sometime between four and eight, most often between five and seven, with the greater likelihood of its occurring closer to seven than to five. The pre-operational child is likely to be over two and under eight; the concrete-operational child functions in concrete-operational style from about age six to eleven or twelve. Age, obviously is not the decisive factor. Yet, by and large, preschool children are pre-operational and elementary children are concrete-operational in thinking style.

It is not only possible, but even likely, given the nature of growth, for a preschool child to be generally pre-operational, in transition toward conservation, and thinking in a concrete-operational way in a particular matter of much experience, all at the same time. The *stage* is determined by the more preponderant, and therefore more consistent, style of thinking.

How Can We Know a Child's Cognitive Style?

Children's cognitive style can be observed while they are using play materials, are involved in drawing pictures, are writing or dictating stories, doing specific academic activities, experimenting, discussing, etc. Teachers who are observant will look for the following kinds of evidence:

• Does the child make generalizations from examining and using specific materials? (E. g.: "The clay gets too mushy from too much water." "If you press too hard on the crayon, it breaks.")

- Does the child rely totally or partially on the use of concrete objects or experiences to understand ideas and to learn? (E. g., in choosing a block to fit a certain space, needs to see a picture in order to understand a description.)
- How accurate is the child's understanding when concrete materials are absent? Is the child confused? Does the child "catch on" after a while?
- Is the child's understanding of an event limited markedly by personal investment, or can the child "see" an issue in its own terms? For example, when a child bumps accidentally into another child's building or drops another child's crayon or pours juice so that it overflows onto another child's lap, does the victimized child recognize that this was an accident? Or does this child assume that the action was deliberate?
- Can the children be logical?

The teacher approaches Timothy, who has built two towers. She asks about the road going between them.
TEACHER: Where does the road go?
TIMOTHY: I don't know.
HENRY (building nearby): Then why did you build it?

Phoebe and Valerie had built a "two-room house" in the gym connected to Benjamin's and Tommy's house. Benjamin was wearing a hard hat and was attempting to carry one of the small chairs into his house.
"How can I get in there?" he puzzled. The opening for a door was not wide enough, although the blocks were only up to his waist. Phoebe glanced over and suggested, "Take your hat off. Hold it (the chair) over your head."
Benjamin shook his head, but Tommy picked up the chair for Benjamin, held it high over his head, and carried it into the building.

- Does the child see part-to-whole relationships? In what contexts? Which are missed?

Marcy (almost three), helping the teacher clear the table, gathered pieces of a puzzle together and put them in their places in their box. When all the pieces were in, she stuck her finger in the one empty space left and announced gravely, "We missed a piece there. There's one piece missing there." The teacher found the missing piece mixed in with another puzzle and gave it to Marcy, who pushed the last piece in and shrieked, "I did it!" jumping up and down in her seat.

- Does the child think that breaking up a cracker, a piece of clay, or a crayon gives him more?
- Does the child see sequence? In what situations, content, or experiences? Which are missed?
- Does the child understand causal relationships? Which ones? Which are confusing?
- What criterion does the child use as the basis for grouping objects? Is it interest? function? theme? color? any other? (E. g., loading same-shape blocks before putting away; putting color forms, paint brushes, crayons, or pegs into their appropriate containers; categorizing children as older and younger; etc.)
- Does the child use more than one criterion for grouping or categorizing? For example, does she know her brother as a brother *and* a boy? As a child categorizes materials and play objects, do the categories change along the way or remain stable?
- Play, art work, writing, movement are all symbols for experience. In what way does the child use symbols? conventionally? freely? uniquely? often? seldom? (For example, does the child adapt materials for props in dramatic play? Does the child use letters to make up or figure out words?)
- Can the child sometimes "play" with abstract ideas? Which ones? How are they used?
- Does the child form and express concepts? What sorts?

Teachers can, if they like, try some of the Piagetian conservation tasks with individual children. This would not be to *judge* them (Piaget never passed judgment on children; he assumed they were all in the process of growing), but to help decide whether or not a child is ready for some kind of abstract learning (for example, phonics), which is more likely to be learned successfully when a child is at the more appropriate cognitive step. In the following example, the task concerns conservation of volume. Its three questions give a child the opportunity to predict, make a judgment, and explain the phenomenon under observation.

On the table, have two glasses of identical shape and size filled with liquid to look like lemonade or orangeade. Have ready a third glass of another size and shape (tall and thin or low and flat).

Ask about the filled glasses, "Is there just as much to drink in both glasses?" If the child doubts that they are equal, suggest, "We'll make them the same" (by adding or pouring off liquid).

When the child is satisfied that the two glasses contain equal amounts, ask the prediction question, "Suppose I pour one of these into this (the third) glass, will there be just as much to drink in each glass?"

After the child's prediction, actually pour the contents of one of the glasses into the third glass while the child looks on. Ask (judgment question), "Is there as much to drink in this glass as in the other one?" Then ask (explanation question), "Why is that?"

Exactly the same procedure can be used to test for the conservation of mass, weight, or number. Thus, to test for the conservation of mass, use two equal balls of clay. Ask, "Do both balls have just as much clay?" Then, "Suppose I roll one of the balls into a hot dog, do I have as much?" And so on.

For number conservation have checker pieces or color cubes in two piles and then string one of them out.

If you like, you can score each conservation response 1 and all non-conservation responses 0, so you can analyze the responses and know the child's state of conserving. For example,

Prediction question_____

Judgment question_____

Explanation question_____

A cautionary note: Do not try to *teach* children the processes of thinking! This has been tried and does not work. A richly interesting, stimulating, and warm school environment is what will do it, given time.

8

CLUES TO COGNITIVE FUNCTIONING: INDIVIDUAL STYLE

QUITE SEPARATE FROM stage-related style, although often difficult to differentiate in young children, is the unique individual style that emerges because children have differing temperaments and personalities. The inborn differences in temperament show up at birth, and interwoven with them thereafter are the differing experiences after birth. Both affect a child's cognitive style.

IDIOSYNCRATIC COGNITIVE STYLE REFLECTS TEMPERAMENT AND CULTURE

Inborn temperament has to do with such things as the *pace* of development, *adaptability, moodiness, intensity of response,* etc. For example, as to *pace:* some children seem not to be progressing, and then growth emerges dramatically; others grow steadily, with regularity and evenness. *Adaptability* means that some children make easy adjustments to new experiences; others are more cautious. Temperament shows up in cognitive style as impulsive or reflective reactions to stimuli; as dependence on external stimuli or being tuned in more to inner stimuli; as persistence or impatience; in degrees of being playful and imaginative; or in the strength of enduring in the face of difficulty.

Life experience seems to influence such aspects of learning as feelings about failing (is it a spur or a dampener to a child?) and standards for self (are they too high, too low, or realistic?). Either temperament or experience or a combination of both are responsible for a child's ability to cope with ambiguity and uncertainty, to control impulses, to take chances, and to separate relevant from irrelevant clues.

Yet age is a factor in all these things too. How, then, can one ever be sure about what causes one child to think more clearly and effectively than another? The same contradictory characteristics appear in high and low I.Q. children! It is perhaps wisest that teachers concern themselves with recognizing where each child is in the development of intellectual processes so as to be able to support growth in each child without worrying excessively about why individual children are not all growing in the same way. Of course, there are inherent differences in capacity, but except for the extremes (retardation and genius), they are not too significant for the early childhood teacher.

How Do We Know a Child Is Learning?

The evidence teachers should look for as signs of cognitive functioning would flow from the following:

● Is the child actively involved in learning or is the child passive? How would you describe the child in this record?

> Brian, three-and-one-half, spent an hour experimenting with Scotch tape and masking tape. He put it on his head; put it on a piece of paper and colored the paper (discovering that there was nothing on that part of the paper when he pulled the tape off); cut the paper with a scissors and taped the two pieces together; put the tape on his finger as a bandage; felt the stickiness; tasted it; taped his mouth; covered his eyes.

● Does the child show curiosity? About what? How often does he/she show it? In what way? How does the child go about satisfying his/her curiosity? Does the child experiment? Is the search persistent?

● Does the child ask questions? What kinds? Does the questioning seem to come out of a desire to find answers or to develop relationships? Do the questions make sense? Do the answers lead to action?

● During a story, does a child ask questions about what is in the pictures or why a character does something? Or on a trip, about the things she sees or hears, about the people, etc.? Or about what is happening around him—in the classroom or outside—e.g., what a truck is delivering or a worker repairing?

• Is the child an adventurous learner or restricted? Is she willing to take chances? Or does he, *must* he, do things the "right" way? For example, when painting, does the child always use the same kind of stroke, or try new ones. e.g., swirling lines, dotting with hard and soft motions, etc.? Does she enjoy mixing colors and creating new ones? During rhythms, story or group discussion, does he contribute anything that is unique and idiosyncratic?

In the following records, the first child, five-year-old Kevin, was very controlled in his use of the paints and apparently felt compelled to turn his painting into something useful and logical, if unimaginative.

Kevin took his smock off a nearby hook. The teacher helped him put it on, and he quickly buttoned up the front. He stepped up to the easel and looked behind it, where he found a pencil hanging by a string. Holding the pencil lightly, he leaned forward. His left arm rested on top of the easel. His right arm hardly moved as with his left hand he meticulously wrote the letters of his name in the upper-left corner. He wrote slowly with his eyes steadfastly fixed upon his task. When he finished writing his name, he carefully picked up a brush loaded with blue paint. Gradually he proceeded to move the brush across the middle of the page. He continued with this punctilious method, using only one other color, red. After carefully adding a few more horizontal and vertical lines, he stood back and made a forceful announcement: "I'm finished." He continued to study the painting. In a pleasant voice he said, "How do your like it? It's a game." He then picked up a crayon and began to draw inside the rectangles of the grid which he had painted. Slowly he drew small circles, carefully writing numbers inside of each.

"This is a ten," he said casually, never taking his eyes off the work. He drew several more circles and put a number in each one. He stepped back and studied for a moment. "This is where you stop," he said decisively. Turning to the teacher, his eyes full of accomplishment, he asked, "How is it?"

Five-year-old Dean was painting one color at a time too, but when he noticed two children mixing their colors, he was inspired to try to do the same.

Dean, watching Debbie and Edwin: "I don't like to mix my paints."

Edwin: "We do, because we make different colors, and you don't."

Dean then slid his painting away from the tray and toward the center of the table, saying, "Sometimes I mix mine, like now I'm gonna mix my red with my blue." As he said this, he carefully picked up a paint dish with his thumb and index finger. He tipped it slightly to pour a tiny bit into another paint dish. He grabbed a brush and with big swishes stirred the two colors, splashing some out of the dish. He began to rock from side to side and chant "Stir, stir, stir," as he stirred with strokes much too big for the dish. Another child spoke to him excitedly.

Michelle: "Now it's purple! I think it's gonna make pink." (She squeals.)

Dean, speaking slowly and emphatically: "It's not that purple." He stopped stirring and rocking, dropped the brush on the tray, and began to pour the red into the yellow. He was precise in his movements.

Dean, pouring: "Now we're gonna make . . ." (His voice trailed off as he poured.) "Then see what we get." He grabbed the nearest brush and began to stir in short, fast strokes. He exclaimed, "I'm getting orange!"

Debby, across the table, said smugly, "So we already got orange."

Dean didn't focus on Debby but began to mix two more colors. His movements were quick and jerky, his eyes were wide open and gleaming, and he had a big grin on his face.

- Does the child start the activity with a plan and lose it along the way? What happened to Chad in this next episode?

The children's outdoor playtime is over. The teacher has called for the leader and door-holders to line up. Chad, who is playing near the door, transforms himself into a locomotive. Holding his tight fists in front of his body, he pushes one hand forward sharply and along with the motion whispers "Choo." Drawing the other hand back and thrusting the first hand forward, he continues, "Choo—choo—choo —choo." His steps are short and skid along the ground. Suddenly, with a twirl and a flourish, he waves his arm and announces, *"Batman!"* The children have gathered, and he then begins stomping with one boot on a rock. As he stomps, he says loudly to the on-lookers, "I'm Steve Austin. I'm getting more superpowers . . . Watch." He jumps and stomps on the rock. Turning to Jessica and retaining his composure, he says authoritatively, "We're lining up now, O.K.?"

Jessica, who has made a dash for the last turn on the fire engine, wheels it over to Chad. They both begin running around the engine, making clicking sounds and pinching the air directly above the engine. Chad explains to a bewildered crowd of onlookers, "I'll lock up the fire engine now." He stops suddenly, turns sharply, and swinging his mittens, which are secured to his coat, marches to the end of the line.

- Does the child make an effort to understand what is going on? to master a skill? to solve a problem?
- Is the child easily sidetracked? Is she easily distracted by other children? by noises? by arrivals and departures, etc.?
- Does the child go through a series of steps in developing a product or an idea? Does he act hastily?
- Does the child show persistence in exploring? in manipulating? in trial-and-error approaches? Or does she jump from one thing to another?
- How does the child start an attack on a problem? by saying "I can't, or "I don't understand it"? by examining the situation and arriving at a thought-out action? by eliminating extraneous factors? by picking a solution out of the air? by impulsively jumping in? by testing each possibility in turn in some kind of order? by selecting the important cues? Does the child have difficulty knowing what to do first?
- Are there indications of persistence in working on a task? Or does the child concentrate on finding an answer and learning facts? Are the facts important to the child to know? Or is the process of finding out itself exciting enough?
- Which details, and how much, can the child remember of a story that has been read many times over or of an experience in or out of school? Or, when games are played in which each child has a turn to guess what object or objects of a number of objects displayed have been taken away, does the child remember the missing items? Is the child aware of who is absent? who came back to school?

Attention span, persistence, concentration, and distractibility can be inferred from almost any activity in which a child engages.

During quiet time Yael works with rubber bands and board. She stares at the board with a look of concentration as she makes a series of three squares with rubber bands. She works confidently and at a quick but methodical pace. She seems to have a preconceived pattern in her head, as she doesn't hesitate with placement of the rubber bands.

Her mouth is slightly opened. She stretches the rubber bands when they are too tight to reach the nails. Occasionally she is distracted by noises in the room and looks over her shoulder to see what is happening and then returns to her board. Each time she selects a rubber band, she looks into the box and carefully chooses one. When the bands are too large, she makes them go around four nails instead of two.

She stares at the board, then selects another rubber band, this time a longer one, and stretches it from one end of the board to the other. When it doesn't fit, she makes a sound, "ts," with her lips as if she were annoyed. She makes another small square. The next band drops to the floor, and she bends down and picks it up with ease.

"I'm all finished," she says with a smile when the pattern looks complete, and she pushes her hair behind her ear. She carefully removes the rubber bands but has some problems getting them around the nails, and she pulls at them. She smiles at the board, and then at me when she is quite finished.

It is important for the teacher to be aware of the degree to which a child is able to persist despite difficulties and frustrations and to ignore distracting environmental stimuli. It is important to observe these in relation to many activities and at different times. For example, a child may spend a half hour on a swing but only ten minutes building with blocks on one day. On other days the time spans may be quite different. For records of all activities in which a child engages, if the time at which the activity begins and ends is noted, the assessment will be easier and more objective.

Other questions follow that one might have in mind as one observes intellectual involvement:

- Does the child have a variety of responses to questions or does she tend to stick to one answer?
- Is the child relaxed or anxious in academic situations? Does he work steadily? withdraw? whine? bite nails? attack problems cheerfully?
- How does a child respond to academic challenge? eagerly? indifferently? seriously? fearfully?

Learning Is Both Affective and Cognitive

Here are several children involved in academic work. See how differently they respond emotionally and socially as well as cognitively.

The assignment was to copy different numbers of different shapes from the board and color them the designated colors. Tiffany was coloring quietly and seemed to be concentrating quite hard, as her eyes were fixed on her paper and she was curling her bottom lip over her teeth with her mouth open slightly. She finished coloring a group of circles and then looked up at the board, giving it a long, hard look. Then she looked at her paper. She nodded her head in surprise with her eyes and mouth wide open. She carefully erased something on her paper, then counted the circles on her paper, whispering aloud and touching each one as she counted it. But she seemed still to be unsure, for she stood up and looked carefully at Samora's paper. She erased something on Samora's paper and then something on her own. Still standing and with a serious expression on her face, she touched one area of Samora's paper and commented, "This side—more better." She helped Samora by erasing and writing on her paper, then turned and scurried to the blackboard with a quizzical look on her face. She counted the shapes, touching each one. Her knitted brow suggested intense concentration. She scurried back to her seat and counted the shapes on her own paper, on Samora's, and on those of other children at her table. After counting the shapes on the paper of the girl across from her, she sat down slowly, turned to Samora, and said, "She got ten and I got ten."

The teacher's aide came to the table and complimented Samora on her work. Tiffany stared at them. Billy came over and announced, "I always get mine right." Tiffany boasted haughtily, "I always get mine right too—and it's not crooked like yours."

Ms. J. reminds Bryant that he needs to work on his math. Slowly he drags himself to the shelves, bypassing the math folders, and pulls out the Cuisenaire rods. He hauls the rod tray to an unoccupied table as if it weighed a thousand pounds. Barely lifting the tray, he slides it to the middle of the table, then drops into an empty seat, and stares at the rods.

Bryant turns to watch someone walk by, then returns to staring at the rods. He drops one hand limply into the tray and sifts the rods through his fingers. Finally, he pulls out three orange rods and places them on the table. He picks out a few more orange rods and a few blue ones. He starts stacking them neatly on top of one another. Then, scooting closer to the edge of the chair and using both hands, he begins to arrange the rods vertically and horizontally to form a very interesting geometric structure. Thoughtfully he begins to test and balance the rods in a purposeful effort to arrange them to his satisfaction. Now his tongue appears, pointing toward his nose. Slowly it begins to move from one corner of his mouth to the other as he concentrates on placing the yellow rods diagonally across the blues.

Alexander bounces over and wiggles into the chair next to Bryant. He starts talking a mile a minute as he begins replicating a building out of rods that he built last year. They talk about forts and cannon. Alexander demonstrates a cannon's blast with a loud "Pooooouush!"

Bryant brings his attention back to his own structure and becomes intently involved in his project once again. He looks only at his creation and does not become involved with Alexander or Anthony. He says something to himself about the rods, and then, for no apparent reason, the top layer topples over. His eyes and mouth open wide in shock. "Oh-h-h-h," he whines sadly as he bends over to pick up the fallen rods from the floor. As he returns to an upright position, he clenches his fists and thrusts them downward to show his frustration.

Laura walks by and accidentally bumps into the table. "Oops, sorry," she says as half of Bryant's creation crumbles and falls. A long drawn out "Oooooo" pierces the air as Bryant's shoulders go up and his hands make an ineffective attempt to catch the pieces. His face is red and crumpled with anger but slowly turns to pink as he begins once more to rebuild. Eventually his face regains its natural color and composure. He has invested quite a bit of time and quite a bit of himself in this activity, so now, when only one rod falls, he gets frustrated and lets out a painful "Ooooh!"

Now the structure is complete, and Bryant looks proudly at his structure. When anyone gets too close or even breathes on it, he puts his hands up as if to catch it.

The teacher informs everyone that it is time to come to a short meeting and that all the children must clean up their work materials. Bryant is reluctant to disassemble his creation, but he finally does, very slowly and painfully.

Some additional clues to cognitive functioning lie in answers to the following:

- What is the child interested in? What gives him/her satisfaction? What is frustrating?
- To what is the child typically indifferent?
- Does the child seem to feel competent as a learner?

Most of the questions in the cognitive realm will be answered in records that show a child in the typical actions of the day. It is not necessary to ask children how they think or to set up special tasks for them. Thinking skills are used and strengthened by the children —and best observed by teachers—in the everyday situations of life that demand them. And that is just about everywhere.

HOW MUCH DOES A CHILD KNOW?

There are certain kinds of information about the world and self that most children with average opportunities seem to learn on their own, and it is reasonable to expect a young child to have the beginnings of information in many of the areas indicated below. Naturally, age makes a difference in the accumulation of knowledge; so does opportunity (including the role of helpful adults), and so do individual interests and readiness for certain kinds of information. To some extent, however, knowledge gathered by children is an indicator of curiosity as well as of memory. But misconceptions abound in childhood, even in the most knowledgeable children, so teachers need to be sensitive to how accurate—or how confused—children's information is within the limitations imposed by their stage of development. Be careful not to be misled by an easy flow of words children could be repeating but could not possibly understand. And do not use the suggested questions as a list of what every child *should* know.

• What does the child know about the body?
   Can children name the parts of their bodies? Which parts?
   Do they know what different body parts can do?
   Do they know whether they are boys or girls?
• What does a child know about his/her family?
   Does the child know who is in his/her immediate family? extended family? his/her relation to them?
   Does the child understand the meaning of the words daughter, son, sister, brother, and their relationship to self, mother, father?
• What does the child know about work roles?
   Do children know what their fathers and mothers work at?
   Do they know what storekeepers, police officers, garbage collectors, coin booth agents, garage mechanics, etc. actually do?

A glimmer of the difference between the reality of adult work and the preparatory nature of child's play appears in this four-year-old's astute comment:

Watching his parents painting the kitchen, Danny asked several times if he could paint too and they said no. Finally, he said pensively, "Grown-ups have lots of things, and kids have just one thing, right?" "What do you mean, one thing?" his mother asked. "Grown-ups have lots of things," he said, "and kids just have toys."

Four-year-old Deborah, who had visited her father's law office, described his work as follows: "He just sits there and gives out pencils and paper clips when the people need them." In the same vein, when Mark brought some records to school, he explained to the teacher, "My uncle gave them to me when he opened his store. He sells records, money, and children."

Lawyers and selling are difficult concepts for four-year-olds.

- Knowledge of observable, concrete, mechanical processes.
  What makes a car go? Is it the parent? gas? the steering wheel? the engine?
  What makes electric lights go on and off? Is it the switch? wires in the wall?
  What makes water flow in a sink? Is it turning on the faucet? Is it the pipes below?
- Knowledge of natural processes of birth, growth, death, the sources of food, etc.
  Where do babies come from?
  What does a flower, a fish, or a child need in order to grow? For example, when Shari, age four, says, "The plant needs water to grow and then it will open by magic," what is she clear about, and what does she mean by magic?
  Do children have an idea of what happens when a flower or a person dies? where eggs come from? oranges? milk? cheese? tuna fish? bacon?
- Knowledge of animals—domestic, wild, prehistoric, imaginary.

At first children generalize from the one animal they know, and all four-legged creatures could be dogs, cows, or whatever. In time they differentiate one animal from another.

Do they know the names of common domestic animals?
Do they know anything about the lifestyles and habits of common domestic animals?
Are they able to recognize pictures or models of wild or prehistoric animals?
Do they know which are alive now and which lived long ago?
Do they recognize the difference between imaginary and real animals?
Do they make up imaginary animals?

- Knowledge from specialized experience.

Many children from impoverished families, or those who have different cultural backgrounds from those of typical American middle-class children, may have information that is quite different from the usual because their experiences are different. They may know about different kinds of food, about techniques of gathering fruit from trees, about what happens in hospital clinics or welfare offices, about how to go to the supermarket and back alone, or even about what happens at racetracks and in a church of a small sect. This knowledge is as valid an indicator that a child is learning as any other kind of information, provided it is understood by the teacher.

How Do Teachers Find Out What Children Know?

Children's knowledge about themselves in relation to their families, about what they like and what they feel, is likely to be verbalized mainly in intimate situations—alone with the teacher, in conversations with other children, or in discussions focused on family life and relationships. It is tempting to ask young children personal questions, but this is not fair and to an extent an invasion of privacy. However, when children trust adults, they will speak of what is important to them. Evidence of the child's knowledge of the world and self will probably come mostly from remarks made by the child; from questions the child asks during trips and subsequent group discussions; from responses to stories read by the teacher or to a book a child is looking at alone; from questions or remarks during cooking or science experiments; while building with blocks, etc. Records of these activities are likely to be a more valid indicator of what a child knows than what he or she does during dramatic play, although information is revealed there too. But during dramatic play the child's feelings and needs often dominate what is said and done. Fantasy mingles with reality as children work away at resolving issues related to their wishes, fears, aggressions, and ambitions in self-created, imaginary situations. During dramatic play children may move a car up the side of a building, or put cows in the bedroom with the baby, although they may recognize, if asked, that such things do not really happen. For this reason, teachers need to be very wary of hastening to correct inaccuracies revealed during dramatic play, unless they are very sure the child is not deliberately ignoring the logic of reality in favor of a psychological need.

As has been indicated, actual information is as much the result of opportunity to experience as of readiness to learn. All too often, the information a child has is unfamiliar to a teacher who does not know the context in which it is valid, and it is therefore underestimated. However, every child, within any context, can and does reveal the capacity for thought in a number of processes that reveal a mind at work. For example, a five-year-old child in a slum neighborhood school worked away at a fairly intricate puzzle showing a steam shovel at work while men were setting dynamite. The child worked through trial and error, and then his perception improved visibly as he sought matching shapes. He completed the puzzle in good time, but when asked about the picture, he shrugged his shoulders and said, "I dunno." The capacity to do a puzzle showed a good mind. The lack of knowledge showed inadequate exposure. The two must not be confused.

It is not in the children's best interest to consider the rote accumulation of information as the goal of intellectual development. Knowledge of facts is by no means the only or even the best indication of a mind at work, although it is one. Especially among children whose lives were begun in one kind of environment and for whom school represents a very different one, it is important to place greater stress on how they approach learning than on what, at their very young ages, they already know. But this truth is valid for all children; a good attitude toward learning will carry them through life much more effectively than specific information learned earlier rather than later.

9

OBSERVING CHILDREN DEVELOP
THE POWER TO THINK

THE CHARACTERISTICS THAT influence the *level* or *style* of a child's cognitive functioning are *curiosity,* the tendency to *explore* or *experiment* with the environment, *attention span, persistence, concentration/distractibility,* and *memory.* The records a teacher takes of a child's behavior at play, when a new material or piece of equipment is introduced, while on a trip to a place never before visited, or when a strange person enters the classroom will be helpful in indicating whether the child is interested in or curious about new objects, places, and people or is indifferent, apathetic, or even fearful. As indicated in Chapter 3, exploratory, experimental, and creative approaches can also be discerned in the way a child uses materials. Observing closely in many kinds of situations, one can see a number of thought processes developing.

CHILDREN'S THOUGHT PROCESSES THAT INDICATE INTELLECTUAL DEVELOPMENT

Forming Generalizations

Out of their experimentation, exploration, and varied experiences, children form generalizations, which are for them true discoveries because they are based on their own observations. This process can begin early in babyhood and never really ceases.

For several days after a heavy snowfall, two-year-old Mike spent a good part of the outdoor playtime gleefully throwing snowballs against a wall of the school building. Finally he went to the teacher and said, "Snow breaks into little pieces."

Uncovering principles is a major occupation of learning children. It is most effective when children come to conclusions on their own. Teaching them to repeat a principle by rote verbally does not have the same effect.

Ability to Differentiate

Children's generalizations enable them in time to make comparisons among objects, people, or events. Using all their senses, they learn to differentiate:

- Between themselves and others—
  Does a child speak of himself/herself in the third person or as I, me, mine?
- Among members of the family—
  Does a child know who are the members of his/her family?
  Does she know the names of each member? their kinship names, i.e., father, grandmother, etc.? which are older, which younger? which male, which female?
- Between animate and inanimate—
  Does a child know whether a stone, a bug, a tree is alive?
- Between fantasy and reality—
  Does the child know whether Superman is real?
  When the child is playing fireman, does she know that she really isn't a fireman?
  When a child says that he visited his grandma in Puerto Rico yesterday, does he know that he really didn't?
- Between appearance and function—
  Does the child know that the toy airplane cannot fly as airplanes do on television?

Ability to Perceive Similarities and Differences

Two four-year-olds are fingering their short pony tails and braids in the manner of older children.

ALEXANDRA: Mine is longer.

KAREN: No, the same.

(They come closer and touch each other's hair.)

ALEXANDRA: I have more hair.

Mattie comes up to the teacher, stretches her arms, rotates them, and says, "My arm is darker than the inside because my father is dark and my mother is light."

Ability to Draw Anologies

Franklin, who has had a fracture, remarks knowingly at lunchtime, "Peeling a banana is like taking a cast off."

Ability to Perceive Cause and Effect

It is easier for children to understand causality in physical phenomena than to understand it in social relations, where their feelings are so involved. It is important to listen for the causes children attribute to specific events and phenomena as a way of assessing what they do and do not understand and what they are confused about. Even their errors reveal their struggle to understand, as in these records, where there is groping for cause, but the clarity is affected by different levels of egocentricity.

Two-year-olds
Ellen hits John and John cries. Ellen asks her teacher, "Why John crying?"

Four-year-olds
JOEL: I'm the sunshine. I'm going up in the sky and stay there.
STEVE: Won't you ever come down?
JOEL: The sun doesn't shine all the time. When it gets dark, I'll come down.
TEACHER: What makes it get dark?
JOEL: The moon makes it get dark.
ALAN: Oh, no. God makes it get dark.

Six-year-olds
Nicholas asks Seth, "Why did you stick your tongue out at me on the playground?"
Seth, still a little angry, replies: "Just because Mr. C. said I knocked Gabe's building down, and he made me sit alone."
They both walk over to their lunch boxes, and Nicholas says in a very serious tone, "I still don't like that, Seth."

Some of this understanding, or lack of it, is a matter of age. But a good deal is due to experience (or lack of experience) with the specific phenomenon or event. A four- to six-year-old may say that the food she eats stays in her stomach, and after she has eaten a lot of food, her stomach will get fat and there will be a baby in her stomach. At this stage of development, a child is aware that there is a cause for the presence of the baby, but she attributes the wrong cause for the effect, selecting as the cause a personally experienced happening.

Time Orientation

Children learn to use the words *when, soon, later, remember, last, next week, next year* before they can fully conceptualize the meaning of time. They incorporate the words in their play as well as in their communication with others, using them correctly in context on the whole but missing out on the more remote, abstract concept of what time is.

"And every day I go to work, all right?" says Angelo in the housekeeping corner.

"In two weeks is Christmas," says Cynthia, although it is actually a month away.

And a four-year-old who was told the birds were migrating because the seasons were changing, agreed heartily. "Yes," he said. "The birds will fly north in the summer and south in the winter, and time will fly."

How well do children understand time? *Now* is more convincing than *tomorrow* and far more concrete than *yesterday*.

Chris, four, arrived in school after an absence and burst into the room exuberantly, shouting, "I'm here!"
"Were you sick?" the teacher asked.
"No," Chris answered, "in 'Mont (Vermont)."
"Did you get back yesterday?" asked the teacher.
"No," answered Chris, "tomorrow, in three weeks."

Time is an elusive concept, and even as late as five, children can show both their beginning grasp of it and their resistance to accepting its structure over their egocentric wishes, as the following record of two five-year-olds shows.

STEWART (to Ronnie): You're always hitting me. I'm not playing with you any more.
RONNIE: Are you sorry when you hit me?
STEWART: Yes, but I'm not playing space creatures with you.
RONNIE (pleading): But you said yesterday you'd play space creatures with me, and that's today.
STEWART (turning away from Ronnie): I didn't mean today. This isn't the tomorrow I meant. I meant another tomorrow.

A sense of time begins with a sense of order and sequence.

- Do the children know the usual daily schedules? E. g., do they know they go outdoors to play first; do they remember that they have a snack before a story?
- Do they know on which days of the week they stay home and on which days they go to school? Do they know the days of the week? the order of the seasons—spring after winter, etc.?
- Do they know whether a five-year-old is younger than a six-year-old?

Ability to Classify

Children reveal their ability to classify in informal as well as formal situations. Often they combine the two, as five-year-old Jackson did with classroom material deliberately designed to encourage classification.

Jackson has just walked over to the shelf and taken a box divided into three compartments, each containing circles, squares, and triangles of varying size. He quietly places the box on his table and removes the lid, using both hands. He places the lid under the box.

He removes the circles first, looks up, and says, "Hamburgers." He looks around for Bobby, spots him at a nearby table, and says playfully, "Bobby, want some hamburgers?" He then arranges the circles in a sequential order from largest to smallest across the table. He then looks up, makes eye contact with the teacher, points, and says, "Largest, smallest." His voice is loud and animated. He seems pleased with himself and his work. A huge smile appears on his face.

He rearranges the circles and says, "A snowman." He is aware of other activities in the room, since he leaves his work and walks over to Bobby to see what he is making.

When Jackson returns to his table, he pauses for a few seconds and then announces, "I want to make a car. I've got to try and do a car." As he slowly removes the squares, he looks over at Tiernan, who has the same materials. They begin chatting excitedly about monsters, and when the conversation ends, Jackson hums contentedly as he arranges the squares in various patterns. First he arranges them in a sequence from largest to smallest, proceeding from left to right. Then he takes the triangles out and places them above the squares, again in sequential order of size. He observes that two are missing and looks over at Tiernan's table. He sees that Tiernan's set is complete and asks the teacher where the missing triangles are. She tells him she doesn't know, and he comments ruefully, "Probably lost." He has difficulty picking the pieces up and experiments with many gestures of his fingers. Finally he slides the pieces off the edge of the table one at a time and places them in the box, again from largest to smallest.

The ability to classify is likely to develop from recognition of concrete qualities that are observable through the senses to abstract ones that must be conceptualized. Color, shape, and size can be seen and are easier to learn about and to categorize than something nonconcrete like direction or theme. All classification, however, depends on the perception of similarities and differences. When there has been a good deal of concrete experience in perceiving similarity and difference (which need not be formal to be effective), children will attempt to classify at a simple level of abstraction when they are about seven. Thus, a child who tried to place a newcomer to the classroom into a recently grasped understanding of group membership, asked, "What are you? Christmas, Chanukah, or Vegetarian?" The facts may have been distorted, but the thinking process was on target. (Note: it is easier to correct facts than to change processes.)

Perceiving Patterns

The ability to perceive patterns (visually, tactually, or aurally) is a basic underpinning for learning to read.* See how differently the following two six-year-old children respond to the opportunity to form patterns out of colored pegs. Darren, who is having trouble perceiving possible patterns, is also having trouble getting pegs into holes. Both difficulties could well have a common source in poor coordination because of slow neurological development. Gideon, the same age, proceeds smoothly in both regards.

At quiet time, Gideon and Darren are working with pegs' and peg boards. They are talking to each other and sharing pegs, although they have separate boards. Gideon, smiling and relaxed, is making colored patterns with his pegs with ease. Darren has some difficulty getting pegs into holes and sits rather tensely. He has four yellow pegs on his board; other pegs are in a jumble on the rug.

Says Darren in a lecturing tone, half to himself, "You can't take all one color."

---

*For an excellent discussion of this, see Katrina de Hirsch, *Predicting Reading Failure* (New York: Harper & Row, 1972).

Gideon, concentrating on his peg board, replies matter-of-factly, "But I had all the blues."

Silence follows while Darren tries to sort the pegs on the rug according to color. Gideon looks up from his board and states with quiet authority, "You don't separate them according to colors."

With a look of some frustration and irritation, Darren replies, "O. K. Take all the blues," and he tosses some blue pegs on the floor near Gideon. He frowns slightly but looks more helpless than angry.

Very patiently and in a conciliatory tone, Gideon says, "Here, you take the blues—take the ones you want," and goes back to concentrating on his board.

Darren's shoulders relax, and he says, picking up on Gideon's tone, "I'll take the yellows, and you take the blues."

Apparently annoyed by being interrupted again, Gideon frowns and says, "Hey, you don't separate into colors."

Darren seems embarrassed at not knowing Gideon's rules, then looks defiantly at him and says conclusively, "That's what I'm doing —you take all the blues."

Gideon, back working at his board, replies quietly, "I don't want to."

Silence. Darren now has five yellow pegs on his board; Gideon has an elaborate color pattern in progress, with half to two-thirds completed. Darren, frowning slightly and with tension in his body, seems disturbed but is also concentrating on trying to get a peg into a hole. Gideon is totally involved in his pattern and begins to sing and hum quietly. He finishes a section and looks to Darren helpfully, saying, "Here's some red and orange for you. I don't use all of these at once."

Darren responds irritatedly, "Well then, how can I make mine?" He glares at Gideon, who looks at him in surprise and says confidently, "Ask someone to help do it with you."

Darren takes some pegs very close to Gideon's leg on the floor. Gideon cries angrily, "Don't steal."

Darren, defensively, "I'm not stealing."

Gideon, in a lecturing tone, "Don't steal." At this, Darren's face turns red, and he lunges forward and grabs pegs off Gideon's board, destroying his pattern and sending pegs flying.

Gideon bursts into tears and wails. The teacher quickly intervenes.

If one did not see Darren's awkwardness, one would not recognize that his frustration requires help.

Understanding Spatial Relationships

A child's sensitivity to pattern and awareness of space are readily observed during rhythms.

- Does the child respond with bodily movements or instruments to the rhythm of the music being played, the drum beat, or the teacher's clapping?
- Does the child maintain an individual rhythm at variance with the rhythm being played?
- How does the child use space? (sweeps the room, stays in one spot, likes to jump, etc.)
- Does the child move with, or against, others? Does he/she seem confused as to which way to go?

When a child doing a jigsaw puzzle tries every piece in order to find out which fits, it is clear the she/he is working by trial and error and is not yet able to perceive either visually or tactually the relationship between a space and the corresponding shape of the piece of the puzzle. By the same token, the child who holds a piece while her/his eyes roam over the puzzle and then places the piece accurately shows grasp of spatial relationships that marks a different level of development. Many of the materials and equipment that children use will demand awareness of spatial relationships, and teachers can be thinking of a number of questions as they observe children at play with puzzles or blocks.

- Does the child recognize that a space between two block buildings is large enough for the truck to get through? that a double-unit block will just bridge the space between two upright blocks?
- Does the child know how to get from the classroom to the kitchen? how to get to school from home?
- In solving spatial, construction, and other physical problems, does the child manipulate the objects involved? For example:
    In order to determine how to place a "Stop" sign in the road Luis has built so that it could be seen from the road, he first placed it on one side, apparently realized that it was not visible there, and then placed it on the other side of the road, where it was visible.
- Does the child experiment with blocks of different sizes to fill a space?

Three-year-old Vicki pulls two double-unit blocks from the shelf and takes them into the building area, which is marked off by a strip of tape. She places the blocks on end, about two feet apart. She stands back to look at them for a moment, then goes back to the shelf and selects a flat double unit. She tries to lay this across the first two, but they are too far apart. She carefully moves one block toward the other and again tries to lay the flat block across. It just barely reaches, and she smiles, her upper lip tucking under slightly.

She returns to the shelf for two more double units and places one next to each of the first two. Then she lays another flat block across, so that she has a "bridge" two units wide.

Vicki stands back to survey her work. She appears satisfied so far, but her eyes are still set in an expression of intense concentration. Now she begins to bring unit blocks, piling them two at a time under the "bridge" almost exactly. She makes a pile of thirteen units, which comes within about eight inches of the top of the bridge.

● Are children aware of space relationships in drawing?

Shannon and Keisha, both seven, are carefully sketching a face on the class pumpkin preparatory to carving it. Shannon decides she will do the eyes and nose and Keisha can do the mouth. They agree. Shannon begins to design her part, carefully sketching the eyes first and then the nose. She checks the placement and appropriate size of the nose. As she finishes, she says to Keisha, "Make a mouth that goes with what I do." After a few minutes of laughing and giggling, Keisha suggests they cut out the parts they have drawn. Shannon notices Keisha's mouth drawing and says, "You should have made it a little smaller, but my nose is too fat too."

Capacity for Symbolic Representation

Symbolic representation is a human capacity with which all except some brain-damaged children are endowed. Its development proceeds in fairly sequential fashion, and it becomes the base for continued learning, since it makes it possible to learn from the experience of others, thus leading to a broadening of one's horizons. The presence of symbolic representation in a child's repertoire of activity indicates intellectual functioning; yet its most likely appearance in early childhood is not in writing or reading but in dramatic play and in the use of materials. Although speech is a form of symbolic behavior, it serves in a secondary way to reinforce young children's learning rather than as a primary, instigating vehicle of thought.

Symbolic representation may take many forms. It appears at two basic levels:

1.   The ability to *recognize* that one thing, for example, a picture of a cup, stands for another, the cup itself; or a doll stands for a baby and a toy car for a real one.

2.   The ability to create symbols—to *make* one thing stand for another. Children create symbols in dramatic play (the child himself represents a father; a block is used as a pretend hammer), in block building (a line of blocks represents a road, a line of chairs a train), in painting, drawing, clay, etc.

The capacity first to recognize the role of symbols and then to create one's own is the essential underpinning for the use of *social symbol systems*, such as words, numbers, letters of the alphabet, and the innumerable symbols we have to learn, such as traffic lights and signs, mathematical and scientific symbols, etc. Children who do not develop symbolic representation in their play and use of materials tend to have difficulty learning to read because the basic awareness of the function of symbols is likely to be missing. Children may be able to *recognize* and *identify* symbols, *but not be able to use them in ever fresh situations*, which is the key to further learning.

How do these levels of symbolic representation look?

> Tricia is slowly pushing Holly in the carriage around the play yard. She seems to be a mother pushing her baby. She stops the carriage and bends down to pick up a small wooden wheel. She hands it to Holly and says, "Here's a doughnut." She continues to push the carriage and occasionally stops to supply her baby with more doughnuts and cookies. She pulls the carriage backward, using two steady hands, and controls the movement of the carriage competently. From the anchor of the carriage, she keeps an eye on all of the play on the terrace. Annie and Joy walk up to her and ask, "May I play?" "No," says Tricia. "We're going shopping and then we are going home."
>
> Tricia pulls the carriage behind her with one hand, leaning forward against the strain of the load. She reaches into David's wagon and snatches an imaginary ice cream cone (much to David's surprise), licks it, and tosses him a pretend coin in payment. She continues to push the carriage until she gets to the climber. She lets go of the handle, reaches for the rope on the climber, and starts to climb up. Holly screams, "I want my mommy." Tricia acknowledges her by looking down at her. "Wait, baby. I'm right here."

In this record of dramatic play, Tricia not only indicates that she *recognizes that one thing stands for another* (that the doll carriage represents a baby carriage), but also *creates symbols* (the little wooden wheel stands for a doughnut, she herself represents a mother). She also creates symbols by her actions (licking an imaginary ice cream cone, tossing an imaginary coin to David).

Here is an example of the *creation of symbols* in a child's painting:

Raoul begins to paint from the bottom of his paper in slow, steady, upward strokes. He puts his brush in his cup of water and rinses it, carefully allowing the excess water to drip off by pressing the brush against the side of the cup. He continues to use more green on his figure, slowly adding more lines. Finally he says, "I made a cactus," and he points to his picture, which does look like a cactus. He then rinses his brush and rubs it in the yellow. He adds this to the cactus. His lips are pursed and his face taut. Jeremy tells him he has made a Venus's-flytrap. Raoul leaps up and says, "Let me see." Jeremy points to his painting, and Raoul asks, "Where's the bug?" Jeremy tells him he hasn't put it in yet. Raoul returns to his seat and carefully twirls his brush in the orange paint. He begins slowly to paint something above his cactus. As he is doing this he comments, "Mighty Mouse is flying." He finishes and gets up and asks Jeremy earnestly, "Where's the bug?" Jeremy points to it, and Raoul appears satisfied as he returns to his seat.

He rinses his brush, and as he looks at the water, he shouts, "My water turned green. Before it was purple." Some hairs of the brush stick to his paper, and he uses his thumb and index finger carefully to remove them. He adds more color to his paper and says confidently, "This is my Venus's-flytrap." He then paints another figure carefully and says, "This is the butter plant." The teacher asks does he mean butterwort and he says, "Oh yeah, butterwort." (The day before the teacher had shown the children pictures of plants that eat insects.)

Raoul rinses his brush and again observes the change in color exclaiming, "Look! It keeps turning colors." He begins slowly to add more paint to his paper and says as he makes his strokes, "Now I'm gonna make me a bird." He dips his brush to clean it and swirls it in the brown. He slowly outlines a bird on a leaf. He exclaims, "Look! There's a bug, and the plant's eating it." He invites Jeremy to come and look. Jeremy gets up and comes to Raoul's side. Raoul points to his painting and says, "The plant's eating it. Look at this Venus's-flytrap. Look at that (pointing to some red color). It's juice from the bug." He points to the bug and says animatedly, "That's the bug," and he begins to paint another one.

He then tells Jeremy confidently, "I'll tell you how to make Gamra."

The teacher asks, "What?"

Raoul answers calmly, "The monster." He slowly paints a large figure in the top right-hand corner. He says, "That's Gamra," then adds, "That's blood from the monster," pointing to some red lines he has just added. Raoul then takes some black and carefully outlines Gamra. He says, "This is his shell."

Jeremy says quickly, "He needs a head."
Raoul indignantly replies, "This is his head."

Children's Use of Materials Indicates Levels of Symbolic Representation

Each of the materials commonly in use in early childhood programs is a good source for observing a child's level of symbolic representation. Each has a consistent sequence that follows a child's age and development, provided the material has been available throughout the appropriate time span. If not, and an older child comes to the material for the first time, the child is likely to race through all the earlier stages to reach his/her own stage fairly quickly. The point at which a child seems to be stabilizing can be considered the current level.

Symbolic representation depends upon a technical level of competence in the use of the material. Since the two are tied to each other, an inadequate level of competence may indicate inadequate experience in developing modes of use that support growth in symbolizing capacity. For example, what evidence of growth in symbolization can we observe in children's use of blocks?

SEQUENCE OF SYMBOLIZATION IN BLOCK BUILDING

Children evolve four basic patterns in block building, *tower, row, bridge*, and *enclosure*. These develop in stages. Complex buildings are adaptations of these four patterns. As generally perceived, the stages are as follows.

STAGE I: Children make rows, horizontal and vertical.

STAGE II: Children bridge two blocks in a two-step sequence.

1. By setting up a vertical block and trying to place a horizontal one on that, then adding a second vertical parallel to the first.
2. By setting up two parallel vertical blocks and bridging them with a third.

STAGE III: Enclosures made with four blocks.

STAGE IV: Decorations on unnamed buildings (improvements of shapes).

STAGE V: Naming buildings relevant to their function, e.g., house, garage, firehouse.

STAGE VI: Reproduction or symbolic rendition of actual structures, e.g., Sear's Tower, spaceship, zoo, etc.

- What are the space problems a child is attempting to solve? Bridging? Enclosure? Repetition? Decoration? Symbolic representation?
- Does the child plan ahead? Are plans carried out? Are there changes in intentions?
- Does the child name the building?
- Can the child predict what will happen with certain placements?
- Can the child reconstruct the building after it has been taken or broken down?
- Is the child's work person-centered (he sits in the building) or object-centered (she manipulates the use of the building from outside it)?

EVIDENCE OF GROWTH IN SYMBOLIZATION IN DRAMATIC PLAY

There are developmental changes in children's dramatic play also. Unfortunately, these changes have received little attention from researchers. In addition, although there is occasional agreement by two or more researchers about a specific developmental change, there is contradictory evidence about others. But teachers who review records of children's dramatic play taken during a school year, or have taught children of different ages, will be aware that changes take place; that, as children get older, their play becomes more complex, more elaborated.

Here are some examples of changes that a teacher might become aware of:

- The number of symbolic actions that are different from each other, within a play episode, increases; that is, the play becomes more differentiated.
- The child expresses the emotional quality of a role (through actions, language, facial expressions, or body movements) more frequently.
- The play tends to become more coherent, better organized.
- Children tend to play together, instead of alone.
- When two or more children play together, they are more likely to play different roles instead of all playing the same one.

These tendencies can be observed although there usually is a range from simple to more elaborated play in the records of each child.

10

RECORDING CHILDREN'S DEVELOPING LANGUAGE

ALL CHILDREN EVERYWHERE who are in contact with speaking adults learn to speak unless they have a physical disability. Because no one teaches children to speak, this spontaneous and exciting development seems nothing short of a miracle. What is more, children learn right off in babyhood that language is for communication, not repetition. They pick up the grammar and syntax of the language they hear completely by themselves and use it creatively to say what they need to say.

During much of children's play, language is an accompaniment to action, a means of thinking out loud, an aid to defining action and organization plans. "We're going to make an airport," "I'm gonna put icing on the cake," "A parking garage has to have more than one floor," "I need another block." These are the kinds of things children say as they play.

Their language can also be descriptive of the *quality* of an action, as when it becomes onomatopoeic and an endless "gr . . . gr . . . grrr . . ." accompanies the gesture of the make-believe tiger or the make-believe car. That, too, helps to pin down understanding.

Language offers many clues to children's cognitive level, not only to the obvious things, like accretion of information or the evidence of confusion, but to less obvious though equally important indicators of cognitive development. For example, when children say what they will do and show ability to imagine *before* doing, they are revealing a beginning time sense and an awareness of sequence; when they differentiate as to the degree and kind of detail included

137

in their play, they are showing development in perception.

On the whole, children tend not to use language well for expressing feeling or examining ideas. Their egocentricity prevents the distancing for that and keeps them close to the immediacy of action. It is not accidental that in vocabulary lists showing levels of usage, the word *laugh* appears before *humor* and the word *grandfather* appears before *grandchild*.

Like all growth that is developmental, the interaction of environmental support and individual differences in aptitude may bring children of the same age to different levels of language facility. It is important, therefore, to be aware of the elements of language that give children the full power they need to express anything, and to observe what use the children make of the language they do use.

TO WHAT END DOES A CHILD USE LANGUAGE?

- Does a child use language for social purposes? to express wants and needs? to share pleasures? to complain? to demand, plead, beseech, cajole, or control?
- Is the child's language directed more to adults or to children, or is it equally distributed?
- Is the child able to communicate well enough to get through the normal activities of the day?

These three-year-olds are struggling to develop relationships, and it is quite a feat to put their needs into verbal terms. A year earlier they could not have done it.

Kristen and Jill are sitting in the small barrel very close to each other, their bodies touching. Their knees are bent, and they are crouching in the small space. They nuzzle up closer together and casually touch heads. They stay in this position for a while without saying a word. Kristen pulls her head away, moves closer to Jill, and gently kisses her on the cheek. Jill lowers her head slightly, Kristen lifts her arm and puts it gently around Jill's shoulder. Their heads touch. Suddenly a loud voice comes from the barrel. "Are you my friend? Are you my friend?" It is Kristen. She continues to ask the question in a moderately loud and clear voice. She raises herself up onto her knees and brings her head close to Jill's face. Jill sits with one arm resting on the side of the barrel and looks away from Kristen.

Kristen urgently asks again, "Are you my friend?" Jill turns her head further away. Kristen puckers her lips and looking at the teacher says, "I want Jill to be my friend, but she won't listen to me."

"That's a problem," the teacher says sympathetically. Kristen continues to look at the teacher and puckers her mouth. The teacher approaches the girls and tries to make eye contact with Jill, but Jill continues to look away. The teacher says to Jill, "Jill, Kristen is asking you a question, and you need to answer her." Jill continues to look away. The teacher looks at Kristen and suggests she ask Jill again.

Kristen: "Jill, are you my friend?" Without looking at her, Jill replies in a whining voice, "No, I don't want to." She seems to be forcefully pushing the words out of her mouth.

Without another word, Kristen quickly and carefully lifts first one foot and then the other out of the barrel and runs to join a group of children near the wall. Jill moves her head around quickly and watches Kristen's actions, then jumps out of the barrel and runs clumsily after Kristen. When she gets to her, she stands very close in front of her, juts her head out closely to Kristen, and in a very loud, shrill voice asks, "Are you my friend?" Kristen looks at her, lowers her head a bit down to her shoulders, and looks away. Jill begins to jump up and down and wave her hands at her sides. She shouts, "Are you my friend?" and continues to jump up and down. She raises her arms and makes a fist.

Kristen quickly moves her head and looks directly at Jill; Kristen's eyes narrow and she puckers her lips. Her head moves forward as she shouts loudly with all the energy in her body, "No!" Jill begins to jump up and down again and cry in a whining voice without tears.

The next episode is a typical social situation amoung four-year-olds who are using language instead of hands and feet to try to resolve a difference in views.

Jon walks determinedly up to Anthony and Alex after cleanup time, angrily pokes his finger repeatedly at the two boys, and cries bossily, "What's the big idea! I was sitting here."

Anthony and Alex ignore him by looking the other way and talking to the other children around them. Jon, however, insists. "I was sitting here! I was sitting here! I was sitting here!"

Anthony impishly raises his eyebrows, looks Jon right in the eye, points his finger at Alex, and says in self-defense, "He took your seat."

Alex starts to defend himself, "Well, I . . ." Jon haughtily breaks him off declaring, "I'm not going to give you this," taking a shiny torquoise-blue butterfly pin from his pocket and handling it admiringly.

● How much of a child's spoken language is intended as communication with others? How much only for self?

• Does a child use language to express thinking? to exchange information? to conceptualize? to reason? to describe? to ask questions? to wonder?

• Does a child's language reveal words denoting *degree?* For example, good—better; pretty—prettier; little, a lot, most; green—greener.

• Does a child's language reveal words denoting *cause?* For example, "I'm getting a bicycle for Christmas because I'm big."

• Does a child's language reveal words denoting time? For example, "Do you remember when we visited you before school started?"

• Does a child's language include words indicating place? For example, "What's that on the top shelf? "Put all the animals in the corner." "The refrigerator got to be where the kitchen is."

• Is the child's sense of humor realized and expressed in language?

Humor

Humor comes from the recognition of incongruities. Young children laugh heartily at unexpected physical incongruities, such as a sudden bump at the end of a slide, or fooling the teacher by asking for help, then laughingly helping themselves. Their newly achieved physical control makes noncontrol incongruous and therefore very funny. But it takes a certain level of maturity in comprehending both words and concepts to see incongruity in verbal terms. You have to *know* what is incongruous before you can find it funny. In the following episodes, the references were concrete and comprehensible to the four-year-old children.

ELLIOT (his eyes sparkling): "You don't eat lunch boxes!"
KEITH: "You eat Wheaties."
And both giggle at their joke.

Nils spies Candy, who has just come in out of the rain. He asks, quite seriously, "Candy, do you have a haircut today?" Candy laughs delightedly and tells him she washed her hair in the rain.

To these five-year-olds, the incongruity is in areas a bit more abstract.

Ari tells the children in an authoritative voice, "My coat is not to go in the rain." Someone asks why. Ari's face lights up and he says, delightedly, "It melts!"

BILLY (to Sara the cook, who has entered the classroom): "You cook
   good, Sara."
SARA (gushingly): "Oh, thank you, sweetie."
BILLY (giggling, and Pablo, joining in): "Sweetie?"
(Later Sara re-enters.)
BILLY: "Hello, sweetie, hello, sweetie," with a mischievous giggle.
PABLO: (imitating him): "Hello, darling," (to Sara).
BILLY (to Sara): "He called you darling."
SARA: "That's O.K. He's my boyfriend."
   Billy and Pablo look at each other with a jerk of the head,
pursed lips, and feigned surprise and shock, and then erupt into
gales of laughter.

Does a child make up chants?
Brent is in the bathroom enjoying a soapy sponge and chanting:

Aren't you glad I cleaned the mirror?
Aren't you glad I cleaned the wall?
Aren't you glad I cleaned the floor?

Jody is playing checkers and chanting:

Ha, Ha! Two against one.
I let you jump me
Only because I show you-u-u
That one . . . goes . . . there.

Comprehension

- What is the evidence that children understand what adults are
  saying? what is required of them? what choices are available to
  them? what they are to do? For example, is the evidence in

  —*facial expressions:* of agreement, irritation, anger, fear, de-
    light?
  —*actions:* positive or negative in response to adult speech?
  —*nonverbal expressions of feeling:* laughter, tears, hand clap-
    ping, foot stamping, hooting, lowering of eyes, etc.?
  —*verbal responses?*

- What is the evidence that a child listens, remembers, and does?
  For example, when the teacher says, "After you have put away
  your puzzle, you may wash your hands and come to lunch,"
  what does a child do?
- What are the children's responses to stories read by the teacher?

Do they understand the concepts and meaning? Do they understand all the words? Which words are unfamiliar? Of these, which are everyday words? literary words? culturally different words? regional words?

• Does a child require visual aids to comprehend a story?
• Does a child grasp nonverbal clues to meaning, such as the reader's facial expression, actions, pitch, and volume of voice as a story is read? (Some children, particularly bilingual children, can understand what is being said even though they may have difficulty expressing themselves adequately.)
• Does a child shut his/her eyes in order to listen better? or cover the ears to watch better? (These may indicate problems of perceptual processing.)
• Does a child pick up and use phrases, chants, and words from stories or conversations?
• Does a child repeat words spoken to her/him mechanically and without the voice change that indicates communicative response? For example:

TEACHER: Hello, dear.
CHILD: Hello, dear.
TEACHER: How are you?
CHILD: How are you?
TEACHER: What is your name?
CHILD: What is your name?

may indicate problems when it is not done in fun.

• Is the child able to relate a comprehensible story? Is the sequence logical? Does the standpoint from which the child tells the story remain consistent or does it change? Does the child wander into bypaths of unrelated items?

Vocabulary
• Is it adequate for the child's purpose?
• Is it large or small compared with others the same age?
• Does it contain unusual words for a child of that age? (As when a two-year-old knows the names of unusual animals like anteater, or colors like beige and purple; or the four-year-old, comparing his block building to others', says, "Look, it's bigger. Do your realize that? We made it so big, it's big as the world."

- Does the child like to play with words? In what way? Is the play with words within the context of dramatic play or more concerned with the relationships of sounds?

   Ron, four, climbed up onto the structure he had made and began calling, "Avocados, avocados, get your fresh avocados." The other children did not respond, but Ron continued his game, calling persistently, "A-vo-ca-dos, a-vo-ca-dos, fresh avocados."

   Micky, standing within her own climbing structure, calls out defiantly, "Those are not fresh avocados. They're poison."

   Albert, mischievous and laughing, but not mean, mimics, "Get your *nasty* avocados."

   Micky, disparagingly: "Get your *fool* avocados." Micky and Albert are both inside the climbing apparatus and laughing together.

   Ron (continuing unabashed) calls out, "Get . . your . . fresh . . a-vo-ca-dos."

- Is the child able to rhyme?

   A two-year-old sings: Butterfly, butterfly, flyeeee, flyee. Butterfly flies, bird flies, bird, bird, butterfly flies, flies, flies.

   A two-year-old chants as she plays: "Let's go sleepy in a deepy."

- Can the child make a rhyme with encouragement?
- Is the child aware of more than one meaning for words that sound alike, like pair, pear; dear, deer; see, sea?

TECHNICAL ASPECTS OF LANGUAGE DEVELOPMENT

All children by age four use the basic form and structure of their language correctly. However, the English language has many irregularities, which are usually learned between four and eight, and there are also words and forms for which a child's mental structures must develop before they can be used, for example, mixed tenses ("I used to live in the country, but after our dog died, we went to live in the city, and that's where we live now").

Speech Patterns

SENTENCE STRUCTURE

- Does the child talk in words, phrases, sentences (simple or complex, correct or incorrect for the language being used)? Does the child's speech fall into a pattern consistent with the spoken language; for instance, in English, the word order of subject, verb, complement, as in "I want milk."?

- Does the child show understanding of the regularities of the language, such as walk, walked; girl, girls? (At one stage this is an advance.)
- Does the child show knowledge of the *irregularities*, as in sing, sang; buy, bought; mouse, mice? (This is evidence of more advanced awareness of language and can be as much a result of hearing appropriate models as of stage of development.)
- How does the child use tense? For example, present tense only ("I go home." "I buy candy." "I'm playing with blocks."). Or does he/she use present, past, and future? Correctly or incorrectly? ("Where were you when I looked for you?" "I will come to your house on Saturday.")
- Does the child use pronouns appropriately, or confuse them?

Dialects of English have their own forms of regularity. If you have questions about a child's usage, be sure he or she is not following a different cultural pattern before you decide the child is confused.

PRONUNCIATION AND ENUNCIATION

- Does a child have difficulty pronouncing certain words? certain letters? Is there change over time in the clarity and precision of pronunciation and enunciation? Are some letters not sounded out in words? Can you tell which ones?

Records of children at play, of the stories a child makes up, the retelling of a known story, records of conversations, of participation in discussion, of anything a child says at any time will all provide evidence of a child's level of language use. Here are two records that show a child's pleasure in language. One situation is informal; the other is a formal reading lesson.

Adam has brought two thick packs of baseball cards to school. He has spread them out side by side, in two long lines on two railings in the center of the yard. He begins wandering around the yard, hands behind his back, head high, and chants in a clear voice, "Step right up. Look at these 74 wonderful cards. Step right up."

Occasionally he gesticulates in the direction of the cards as he continues to chant. Two girls pause to look at the cards. Adam rushes over to them. They drift off. He continues to wander around the yard, walking with a bit of a swagger, hands still behind his back, and still trying to sell his cards.

"Big ones, little ones, silly ones, all kinds of ones. Doesn't anyone want to play with any?"

He stops chanting long enough to observe two boys, Tim and James, in the block corner. He tries to get their attention with more chanting.

"Do you want to buy three? Two big, one middle? Two middle, one little? Step right up."

The first-grade teacher is distributing corrected dittos. She is seated on a low chair in front of the children, who are squatting or sitting on the floor. She calls the children one by one and comments on their work.

Carlos is seated directly in front of her, practically at her feet. He is eagerly looking up at her, awaiting his turn.

The teacher comes to his paper. "Carlos . . . Beautiful work!" She beams with approval. "Everybody wrote just one example. But Carlos wrote bat, cat, rat, hat for sat; and they, hay, may for play; and bump, hump, sump for lump . . . Only I'm not sure what that word is—sump?

Carlos appears bewildered at first. Then, looking up at the teacher directly, he lifts his shoulders and says in a clear, confident tone, "That is *sump* (emphasizing the word), like in a tree!"

Language is learned from models and through use. When opportunities for both are available to children, language develops, broadens, and deepens. Records over time will show the developmental changes that occur.

11

OBSERVING AND RECORDING THE BEHAVIOR OF INFANTS AND TODDLERS

Nancy Balaban

MAKING SENSE OF WHAT YOU SEE

OBSERVING INFANTS and toddlers in group care above all requires a keen eye and patient perseverance. The observer's pen appears to fly across the page, for the movements of children under three seem to be calibrated in milliseconds. One action follows another, often with such disjointed quality that we are roused to wonder how so small a person can think of so many things to do, so many ways to move, in so short a span of time. At the table, under the table, beside the table, on top of the table, all activities take place within a few moments, leaving the recorder, but hardly the toddler, nearly breathless.

The recorder, thus poised for action, may suddenly face another condition—that of no identifiable activity at all. The child is momentarily still, or staring into space, or repeatedly fingering or mouthing a tuft of fringe. Recorders may find themselves "tuning out," restless or possibly bored. How very unlike observing and recording three- to six-year-olds is this endeavor with the under threes!

To make sense out of all this random movement, it is wise to consider each action from the infant's or toddler's point of view—as a completed event. When seen in this way, through the eyes of the child, these seemingly disconnected events begin to take on a new meaning. For that reason, records can be taken in three- to five-minute periods and should include as much detail as possible.

146

Perhaps some activity may seem too insignificant, too trivial, or too fleeting to record. It should be written down anyway, for it is in the accumulation of these bits of lively evidence that the wider picture of this elusive baby will emerge. Every scrap of observed behavior becomes important when it is finally collated into a pattern.

For example, in this record of nineteen-month-old Danielle, no startling action occurs. Yet it is a completed behavior. It has a beginning, a middle, and an end.

> Danielle walks steadily over to a crib where seven-month-old Claudia has just awakened. Putting her two hands on the crib bars, she regards the sleepy baby with a long look. She laughs gently and then walks away.

We do not know the meaning of this action to the toddler, but as more data are collected on Danielle, other evidence of her interest in, her pleasure in, and/or her stresses with other children will begin to surface in an emerging pattern of her relations with children.

Therefore, in order to capture the mercurial lives of these under threes, it will be necessary to record as frequently as possible, without a preselection of events. In that way, some anecdotes, as that of Danielle, will be brief, and others will be more lengthy, as the following record of fifteen-month-old Jared, who is eating lunch, making connections with the caregiver and given loving attention by another toddler.

> Jared is eating cottage cheese for lunch. He holds a spoonful and examines the cheese as he bounces the spoon up and down in front of him. He sets it back in the bowl. Then he takes a spoonful again but this time the cheese drops to the table as he becomes involved in watching Robert who sits across the table. "Eating your cheese?" comments Lois, the caregiver, who did not notice that it had dropped off the spoon. He looks at her impishly out of the corner of his eye, puts the spoon to his mouth, and licks off what is left on the spoon.
>
> He moves his body forward in the small chair, perhaps to be closer to the table, or perhaps to reorganize his body in the chair's space. In doing this, he loses his balance, falls forward, strikes his head on the edge of the table and cries. Lois takes him on her lap and he molds to her body. Robert, thirty-two months, looks at Jared with wide eyes. "He's crying," he says, and leans over to plant a kiss on Jared's wet cheek. Jared slides off Lois's lap and walks steadily over to touch a toy telephone that is lying on the couch.

THE VALUE OF RECORDING

The value of these records lies in their almost microscopic focus on the tiny details of toddler and infant life that often slide by in the hurly-burly of day-to-day caregiving. The preponderant load of physical care necessary for infants and toddlers, plus their rapid developmental changes, means that caregivers must make many shifts in their own behavior in order to accommodate to these factors, often without conscious thought. Taking this sort of recording "time out" during a busy day can be viewed as putting "time in" since it provides teachers and caregivers with a deep view into the lives of the children as well as the program.

In such a yeasty situation, it is imperative that caregivers grasp as much time as possible to record these tumultous developmental changes as they occur. Such recorded data is a unique source of enrichment and growth for the infant/toddler program itself. Records, for example, lend themselves to sharing among a staff, forming the basis for regular, ongoing, content-laden meetings. The function of such record sharing is twofold. First, one or more staff members may be recording the same child over a period of time and these shared anecdotes help the staff understand not only the child in focus, but developmental characteristics of that specific age as well. Second, the very process of recording adds to staff development by serving as a basis for adult reflection about the refinements of caregiving practice as well as connecting staff members to their own individual differences in observing.

Written anecdotes provide concrete illustrations of the continually unfolding saga of development. Against this hard recorded evidence, the teacher's knowledge will be honed, for it is the teacher who must decide whether the observed characteristics fit with the age of the child, and appreciate, at the same time, the great variations produced by individual differences.

TIME

Recording at different times of the day becomes especially significant in observing children under three. The influence of the hour on the mood and the state of the very young child is often pronounced. Babies who are bubbly at 9:30 in the morning may be limp and whimpering at noon or outraged at 4:00 P.M. A record taken before lunch may be at serious odds with one taken after the meal. It might not even appear to be the same child. Time has an influence on the tempo of the child's entire environment. For instance, caregivers themselves flag and revive at different times during the day. In a day-care setting, as a further example, time dictates which staff members will be present and which absent. Obviously, different people set different tones in a classroom. Similarly, the presence and absence of some children, often dictated by the time of day, makes an impact on the environment. This, in turn, affects other children as well as the caregivers.

WHAT TO OBSERVE

An infant or toddler's day in group care is unlikely to fall into a distinct pattern of planned activity as it might in a preschool setting. Therefore, it will frequently be necessary to record at random. However, taking records in the following situations will provide a comprehensive view of the child's life in the group.

- Arrival and departure
- Caregiving routines:
    - Diapering/toileting
    - Eating/feeding
    - Napping
    - Outings
- Playing and exploring
- Interaction with adults and children
- Language

An in-depth examination of each of these situations, one by one, will illustrate the range of information that can be mined through recording.

Arrival and Departure

During the first few years of life, children form deep attachments to the person who provides them with primary care, usually a parent or a grandparent. This attachment provides the base from which children begin to separate themselves in their efforts to become individuals with a distinct sense of self. In both the arrival at group care and the departure from it the infant or toddler is, in most instances, accompanied by the primary caregiving person.

Records taken at these times provide the professional staff with an opportunity to understand the unique quality in each parent-child pair's handling of the separation as well as the reunion. Records will also help the staff focus more deliberately on the influence the child's age and developmental characteristics have on the nature of these events. A baby of five months, for example, would be unlikely to react to these events with the verve and display of feelings of a twenty-one-month-old toddler. On the other hand, certain idiosyncratic characteristics may appear as a continual thread over time. Recorded evidence will help place these developmental differences in proper perspective.

The following questions are designed to sharpen the caregiver's awareness of arrivals and departures and act as a guide in the recording process. Thinking about these items will involve an understanding that some behaviors appropriate to one age are not appropriate at another. Thus these and other questions are intended as guides and assume the teacher's familiarity with age-connected developmental differences.*

ARRIVAL OF INFANT/TODDLER—DEPARTURE OF PARENT
- Does the infant/toddler make eye contact with the parent? Does she follow the parent to the door with a gaze, or by crawling or walking?
- Does the child make any spoken sound or protest? Of what sort?
- Does the child verbally or motorically signal "goodbye"?
- Does the infant/toddler ignore the parent or behave as though the parent weren't there?
- How does the child react to the caregiver?
- If the child is distressed, is he able to find a means of self-comfort, such as thumb-sucking, becoming involved in a plaything, or accepting the caregiver's attention?

Children under three and their parents have many ambivalent feelings about leaving each other, and later rejoining, in a group-

---

*For more information about age-connected developmental characteristics, see any of the following books, which contain lists of developmental landmarks: Anne Willis and Henry Ricciuti, *A Good Beginning for Babies* (Washington, D.C.: NAEYC, 1976); Sally Provence, *Guide for the Care of Infants in Groups* (New York: Child Welfare League of America, 1971); Dorothy Huntington, Sally Provence, and Ronald K. Parker, *Day Care 2: Serving Infants*, no. (OCD) 72-8 (Washington, D.C.: U.S. Department of Health, Education, and Welfare, Office of Child Development, 1971.)

care situation. Even though parents and children are assured that the day care, nursery school, or play group offers good, loving care, it is not always easy for them to leave one another. These feelings are expressed in a multitude of ways.

Here is eighteen-month-old Ben, whose father has just brought him to the day-care center:

> Ben's dad starts to leave and Ben bolts out the door after him, without a sound. He is caught up by Ann, the caregiver, hugged, and taken over to the table for snack. He sits quietly, somewhat subdued, face blank, next to Ann. He munches on a slice of apple.

Bart, at fourteen months, is younger, and has another style of parting with his parent.

> Bart's mother brings him into the room and sits down, holding him on her lap. As Janet, the caregiver, approaches, Bart jumps down off his mother's lap and runs to her. Janet swoops him up in her arms and sets him on a chair at the table where other children are eating breakfast. He gazes blankly at the recorder, a stranger. His mother says, cheerfully, "Bye, honey," and smiles at him. He looks at her with a blank expression, sucking on his pacifier. Mother exchanges glances with caregiver and leaves.

ARRIVAL OF PARENT—DEPARTURE OF PARENT
WITH INFANT/TODDLER

Leaving group care at the end of the day (or morning) to go home presents another stress for the baby-and-parent pair. It involves a reunion that is not always totally joyous. Perhaps feelings associated with leaving one another in the morning well up when the pair is reunited. The sad, angry, and ambivalent feelings aroused by separating are usually diluted by the day's activity, but by the end of the day there is little activity to stand between those feelings and their expression, as in this incident with twenty-six-month-old Millie, usually a sweet-tempered child, when her father picked her up to go home:

> As Millie's father enters the room to take her home she picks up a book and a lunch box that is used for play. "I want the book inside the box. I want to take it home," she insisted. "You can't take the lunch box, but you can put the book inside your bag. Here," her father says in a calm tone. He holds out a small canvas bag to her. She holds on tightly to the lunch box, pouts, stands resolutely, stares into space and screams. "No! I wanna put it inside. I want it. No!"

She clutches the lunch box. "I wanna *borrow*." (The teacher has made the rule that the children may borrow one thing.) Father, becoming edgy, says, "Look, if you make a fuss, you can't even take the book. Do you want the book?" At this moment, Lucy, the teacher, steps in. "Look, Millie, I'll put the book into your bag," and begins to do this. "No!" screams Millie, holding more tightly to the lunch box. "You can't have the box and the book," her father states flatly. "I *am* going to," she insists loudly. "Are we going to have a fight?" her exasperated father groans. "I want it!" she shrieks. "I've got an idea," her father says brightly, "How about leaving the book and taking the lunch box?" She drops the book on the chair, takes her father's hand, and bounces on her toes as they go out the door.

Another child, Sally, twenty-one months, handles her ambivalent feelings about the reunion with her mother in her characteristically low-key manner:

Sally's mother comes quietly into the room. "Mommy!" Sally says aloud in a rising tone of pleasure, as she spies her mother. She stops in her tracks and looks at her mother with a blank expression for several seconds. Mother crouches down and opens her arms expectantly saying, "Sally! Sally!" Sally continues to stare blankly for a few seconds, then finally runs to her mother's open arms. Her mother lifts her up. Sally maintains a blank expression and hangs limply in her mother's arms.

Watching and recording arrival and departure situations over time provides insights into how parent-child pairs negotiate these events, what the child's particular coping style is, and how it evolves as the child grows older. Some periods of time and some stages of development may be more trying for the child and parent than others. Collecting samples of such arrival and departure events over a period of several months will reveal trends in this delicate relationship that are often the bellwether for describing parent-child attachment. (For full details on how to evolve patterns, see Chapter 13.)

Caregiving Routines

A considerable portion of an infant/toddler's day is defined through the routines of daily living. The performance of these routines is often dismissed as solely physical care. Not so! The social, emotional, and intellectual capacities of children are deeply engaged in these caretaking exchanges. Observation of routine caregiving situations, while they occur as well as before and after, may reveal the degree of children's ability to inhibit impulse and desire, ability to distract or comfort themselves, and ability to trust adults. These records may also indicate the infant/toddler's thrust toward autonomy, as sense of self expands with increasing age and experience. The observer may spot the baby's autonomous grab for the spoon during feeding, or the toddler's assertion of self in pushing another toddler out of the way.

Such observations will contain clues to the following:

- Does the child seem to feel competent about her own effectiveness and skills?
- Does the time of day and/or the style of the caregiver's handling affect the child's behavior?
- Is the child's behavior from one routine to another predictable and consistent or is it different with each routine?
- What is the salient characteristic of the child's behavior? Compliance? Restlessness? Rebellion? Teasing?
- Has the child's behavior changed significantly over time in relation to any particular routine(s)? In what ways?

Examining more closely the routines of diapering/toileting, eating/feeding, napping, and outings will also shed light on the relationship between the caregiving person and the baby or toddler. Such records can be treasures in the hands of a staff that seeks opportunities to develop itself.

DIAPERING/TOILETING

Here is thirty-month-old Joshua, who wants to control his diaper change. His preference cannot be accommodated at the moment, so the caregiver handles the situation by acknowledging his desire, but not giving in to it. A "natural phenomenon" saves the day.

Anna, the caregiver, leads Joshua by the hand into the bathroom for a diaper change. He breaks loose from her grasp by pulling away and wresting his hand from hers. He runs pell-mell out of the bathroom toward Lena, another caregiver, who is playing with two children on the floor. "Mmm. I want Lena!" he bellows, pointing at her.

Anna, who has followed him, picks him up gently. He screams a piercing, loud cry, *"Lena!"* "You want Lena, but she's busy," Anna tells him. "I think I am going to do it. Quick. Then you and Lena can read a book together. Quick, I'll do it." She smiles at him. He continues to cry and she says several times, reassuringly, "I'll do it." Suddenly a fly buzzes by him and he points at it. They both watch the fly for a moment. He stops crying and stands quietly helping to secure the diaper.

Sometimes the diapering situation is an opportunity for a special private time with a child and it becomes a social occasion. Here is two-year-old Adam, involved in a delightful give-and-take with his caregiver.

Gloria (the teacher), who is in the bathroom, calls, "Adam, come into the bathroom so I can change your diaper." Adam pushes his head forward, says an emphatic no, and pouts, jutting out his lower lip. When the teacher repeats her request, Adam starts to cry, grabs his blanket, hugging it very closely to his chest, and says, "Put in cubby." He runs out of the room, presumably to his cubby, and then runs back in. He pauses, looks at Gloria, and then with a stern look on his face, trots into the bathroom.

Gloria greets Adam as he walks over to the low table, stretches his upper body across it, and hoists himself up. Adam stands up on the table and moves very close to Gloria. She compliments him on the way he remembered exactly what to do when he is in the bathroom. As she takes down Adam's overalls, she continues to talk to him in a conversational way. Adam leans very close to her. He is playing with the buttons on her shirt and he is laughing. He stands motionless as she moves away to get a clean diaper. When he begins to scratch a slight rash on his thigh, she tells him that is not a good idea. He points to the supply cabinet, saying, "Eh, eh, eh, powder." Gloria gets the powder and he holds out his hand for some. She pours it into his hand and he pats a little on his penis. He begins to manipulate his penis, bending his legs and looking down with curiosity. When Gloria puts him down on the table to put on the diaper, she leans close to his face and talks to him. Adam smiles, reaches up, grabs her hair and pushes it in front of her eyes. The two of them laugh. Adam then starts to play with Gloria's face, saying nonsense words in a singsong way. After Adam is fully dressed he looks up at Gloria and says, "Kiss," puckering his lips. The teacher bends her head and he gives her a quick kiss on the cheek. She lifts him off the table and he shuffles into the other room, saying, "Choo, choo," pretending he is a train.

Records of diapering and toileting help to focus on children's feelings about their bodily processes as well as about those who care for them. As you record, ask yourself:

- How aware is the baby/toddler of what the diapering activity means?
- Does the child cooperate with or struggle against the person who is diapering?
- Does the child behave in the same way with all caregivers who diaper him?
- Is there any opportunity for the child to take an active role in the process, or is the diapering mostly peremptory?
- What is the quality of the adult-child interaction? Is there eye contact? Is there conversation?

In the following record, the caregiver deliberately involves the baby in her own care:

> Hannah, seventeen months, stands in front of the caregiver. They smile at each other. "Are you wet, Hannah?" the caregiver asks, stretching out her arms. When Hannah stretches out her arms, the caregiver picks her up. "Yes, indeed, you've got to be changed," she says to Hannah as she carries her to the changing table. She sets Hannah, standing, on the table. Hannah begins to pull on her slacks. "You are really good at taking off your slacks, Hannah," the caregiver grins as she gently pulls Hannah's slacks down, carefully avoiding interference with the baby's own action. "There you've done it, they're down. Now let's get your feet out." And as Hannah pulls on her feet, the caregiver removes them from the slacks. Now Hannah tugs at her diaper. The caregiver loosens the tabs; Hannah tugs again, and then hands the wet diaper to the caregiver. "Wet," says Hannah. "It *is* wet," says the caregiver, "and here's a dry one." She hands the dry one to Hannah and waits while Hannah tries to put it between her legs, then carefully arranges it so that Hannah can be involved in pressing the tabs together. After putting on her slacks half way, she waits, as Hannah begins to tug at them, then pulls them up. "What a great diaper changer you are, Hannah!" says the caregiver as she hugs Hannah before setting her down on the floor.

Since diapering and toileting occur with such frequency in an infant/toddler program, it is a situation that carries a powerful message to children. It is one way through which children learn just how adults take care of them, and how adults feel about the products of their bodies. In this record of a twenty-three-month-old, the teacher is in the bathroom with three children. One has just used the potty and another, the toilet. The third, Laurie, has other ideas.

> "It's your turn to use the potty, Laurie," the teacher tells her matter-of-factly. "Let me help you take off your diaper." Laurie pouts, turns up her head, swerves her body swiftly out of the teacher's reach, and stands resolutely, looking her in the eye. "Are you sure you don't want to use the potty?" the teacher asks again. Looking at the frozen figure of Laurie, she adds, "O.K., but let me know if you want help," and she moves toward the entry to the bathroom, discreetly looking in the other direction from which Laurie is standing. Laurie checks out the caregiver's gaze and when she is sure that it is not on her, she moves toward the potty. She turns her body in line with the potty, takes a step backward and sits on it, fully clothed, for a few moments, then gets up and walks with a confident stride out of the bathroom. She is smiling the smallest of smiles.

The tone of these episodes is revealed through the words chosen to describe the baby's facial expressions, body movements, and verbalizations. Gentleness is communicated through the description of the teacher's movements, the expression on her face. Tension, disgust, or annoyance would be revealed in the same way, through words that describe a baby's irritable crying and a caregiver's flatness or impatience of tone, choice of words, or efficient coldness.

An obvious pattern of tension or unhappiness seen over a period of time in records of diapering/toileting demands the attention of the staff. What do these repeated records say regarding the baby's feelings about diaper changes or trips to the potty? What do they tell the staff about the handling of the child at these times? Teachers can be mutually helpful if records are considered tools for their own development and learning.

EATING/FEEDING

Since eating and feeding take place with repeated regularity in an infant/toddler program, it is not difficult to take such records. Someone, it seems, is almost always eating or being fed. The range of eating situations is wide: from a baby of a few months being held for a bottle, to a two-and-one-half-year-old independently enjoying a snack or munching lunch.

Feeding and eating are situations through which the observer is able to become acquainted with the baby's style of satisfaction, level of enjoyment, and thrusts toward autonomy. Some babies are lusty lovers of the bottle and enjoy it to the last drop, often falling into a contented sleep when it is done. Others are more cautious, taking in small amounts and pausing for burps or rest between sucking. Some children experience discomfort in feeding, which may produce irritable crying or restlessness. The point is that not all babies take a bottle or solid food in the same way.

Close observation of several feeding situations with a baby will throw light on the baby's approach to the bottle. Is it eager or hesitant, lustful or langorous? Whether the baby is in or out of step with the caregiver will be detected through such details as these: does the baby mold to the caregiver's body? flail around uncomfortably? struggle to get up? Does the caregiver respond to the baby's signals and make appropriate adjustments?

Through feeding and eating, infants and toddlers form an opinion of the world. Is the world a friendly place where needs are met? Is food proffered by loving people and consumed in an atmosphere of patience and pleasure? In the following record the caregiver and the seven-month-old baby are very much in tune with one another and the level of the baby's pleasure is obviously high:

> Deirdre, held in Josephine's lap, says, "Mmmmmmm," looks around at the children who are playing nearby, moves her legs up and down, chomps slowly on the fruit and cereal, which Josephine is carefully feeding to her. Deirdre's legs circle in the air as her body reclines against Josephine's breast. "You like that? My goodness— mmmm," purrs Josephine. Deirdre begins to struggle, reaching with her arms, arching her back. Josephine shifts her own body and adjusts her position so that the baby is now sitting higher, her back straighter. She is able now to look around. She relaxes and resumes the meal, opening her mouth for the next spoonful.

Toddlers and two-year-olds, in large part, like to be very much in charge of feeding and eating. Sometimes it means waiting for the caregiver to bring the food or, as in the following case, the juice. We see Hester, seventeen months, who uses several skills to help herself wait.

> Hester is sitting on a small chair at a round table with other toddlers who have been eating pancakes for breakfast. "Ah. Du," she says to the caregiver, Ruth. "You want juice," Ruth confirms. "I'll get your juice for you." Ruth washes Hester's sticky hands with a

cloth. She willingly allows Ruth to do this and makes a squeaking sound. "O.K. I'll have to get your juice." Hester looks around at the other children. Her body is composed, her gaze relaxed. "Ruth, Ruth," she calls as the caregiver walks away from the table to take a child to the bathroom. Hester sits still and begins to suck her thumb. She screams gently, making guttural sounds and waving her hand to the caregiver, who has come back to the table without the juice. "You sound like a little tiger," Ruth says and laughs. Hester laughs, too. Then she pounds her hands on the table saying, "Ah. Ah." Two other toddlers at the table begin to pound their hands on the table. Meanwhile, Ruth, who had gone during the pounding, arrives with a small cup of juice and hands it to Hester who, with great seriousness, holds it firmly in her two hands and drinks it with gusto.

Other toddlers are not so patient or so able to distract themselves as Hester and sometimes they cannot tolerate the ministrations of adults who might attempt to feed them when they do not want to be fed.

Sarah, nineteen months, is seated next to the caregiver at a small table. The caregiver, seated between Sarah and Allan, alternately offers a spoonful of food to each child. In this position she makes eye contact with neither child, nor can she see their facial expressions. Allan willingly opens his mouth with each proferred spoonful of peas. Sarah, however, clamps her mouth shut, turns her whole body sideways in the chair, and clenches her fists on the table top. Suddenly, she emits a piercing scream, reaches over to the plate of peas, and rummaging her hands about in them, scatters the peas across the table and onto the floor.

"Well, Sarah," says the amazed caregiver, "what's gotten into you?" Another caregiver, Marian, enters the room at this moment and says, "Do you think she wants to eat the peas from the plate herself?" Marian sets the plate of peas in front of Sarah, who deftly begins to pick up one at a time with her thumb and forefinger, daintily placing them in her mouth.

While not all toddlers are such neat eaters, most of them are intent on doing it themselves. At eleven months, Nadia had a second breakfast, quite unknown to the caregivers. She was quiet and out of sight until she popped into their view.

Nadia is crawling on the floor. When she nears the high chair in which Denise sits, she pulls herself to stand, says, "Da!" and laughs. She drops deftly to the floor, crawls to a small chair, pulls herself to stand, cruises to the table next to the chair, drops to the floor, and proceeds to visually examine the floor around her. Looking ahead of her, she crawls under the table and continues slowly until she reaches the center. Seeing a paper napkin on the floor near her, she grasps it, sits up, and waves the napkin in the air. She reaches out and grabs the legs of Bill, eighteen months, who is sitting at the table for breakfast. She notices on the floor within her reach a piece of waffle that had been dropped by one of the breakfast eaters. She stuffs it into her mouth with the palm of her hand and sits, for a few seconds, chewing contentedly. Turning herself around, she crawls out from under the table. Pulling herself to stand on a nearby chair, she shifts to the table edge and cruises over to Bill, who is busy eating his waffle. She reaches over to Bill's plate and takes a big chunk of his waffle, stuffing it all into her mouth. "Don't take his food," the caregiver says gently. Nadia gives the caregiver a big grin.

What can be said of Nadia? Toddlers' persistent curiosity about the surrounding environment is very powerful and their reality testing takes place primarily through the senses. Perhaps Nadia had asked herself, "What is this stuff? It looks familiar. It really tastes good." Perhaps the heady feeling of discovering it herself and of controlling it herself fueled her continuing investigation. Had she been seen while she was under the table, would her behavior have been understood in the same way she experienced it?

Sometimes eating episodes reveal glimpses of how the toddler thinks and how the toddler's visual-motor coordination functions. Kira, twelve months, is not only involved in the joy of eating, but she is practicing the coordinated use of her hands and eyes, as well as the skill of following the path of a falling object. Both are necessary for the development of object permanence.

Kira, at her mother's side, walks through the classroom door with a bumpy gait and goes right to the caregiver, who picks her up and puts her in a high chair near the table where other children are sitting on small chairs. "Ee—ee," she says. "Say bye-bye," the caregiver instructs her. She waves to her mother as she goes out the door. The caregiver ties on Kira's bib. She plumps her hands on the high chair tray and smiles at the second caregiver, who has just come into her sight. She waves her hands in the air, smiles, pulls on her hair. When the caregiver puts some pieces of pancake on the tray, she holds one piece in her left hand while using her right hand to put pieces in her mouth. One piece drops to the floor. She looks over the side of the high chair, following the path of the fall until she locates the pancake on the floor. She shifts her gaze to the tray, takes another piece in one hand, and eats with the other. She watches the caregiver while she eats. Then she drops another piece where the first had fallen.

For infants and toddlers, feeding and eating certainly entail experiences of pleasure and satisfaction. Conversely, if problems exist, the eating itself may be uncomfortable, or a tense, unsatisfying time. Records will reveal the emotional impact of the situation over time and those characteristics that are singular to the child being observed.

However, for children under three, eating and feeding are activities unto themselves. Being fed involves trusting an adult. It means that a certain synchronism exists between child and adult—making eye contact, molding of the infant body to that of the adult, conversational give-and-take. It also involves the coordination of eye and hand as the baby begins, for example, to grasp for the spoon, and the tactile investigation through mouth and hand of the varying textures of food. We also see the dawning, budding, and flowering of autonomy, and the beginnings of language. In sum, while eating and feeding may be categorized by adults as activities of certain characteristics, important to the child, they are probably perceived by children in a multitude of other ways.

It is for these reasons that we observe eating and feeding episodes. Through them we learn about many developments occurring in these young beings. When Charlie, at fifteen months, puts his remaining two drops of juice back into the pitcher, and then puts the cup itself into the pitcher, he is continuing his experimentation with reality as an extension of the eating situation. Pouring the juice back was an exercise of eye-hand coordination and a possible imitation of adults who do the pouring. Will the cup fit into the pitcher? Reality testing of space and size are taking place.

Looking thus beyond each observed action leads to the discovery that the world looks different through the eyes of the child than through the eyes of the adult.

NAPPING

While diapering/toileting and eating/feeding are routines that occur with some regularity and frequency, napping is a routine that is frequent but not always regular, depending on the nature and age of the baby. Some very young babies sleep long stretches between feedings, some take a series of "catnaps" with alert, or fussy, periods in between. Older babies may have consolidated their daytime sleeping to one or two naps. While some babies go off willingly to nap, looking forward to the restorative interlude, others are nay-sayers, if not in word, then in deed—like the baby who refuses to lie down, but sits, instead, on the cot or in the crib, keeping eyes open at all cost; or the toddler who, shrieking and flailing about, keeps a distance from the rest space and sometimes, despite himself, falls asleep on a chair, or on the floor, late in the afternoon. Each baby has an individual style and a set of private feelings about sleep. Some are fearful and tense about sleeping in a place that is not home; others are content to sleep provided they have their favorite "cozy" from home; still others seem willing to lie down and sleep without any fanfare whatever.

Napping patterns sometimes change over time, however, from several naps to two, from two naps to one, from calm to tension-filled situations, from restless to relaxed. Recording over a period of time the baby's approach to the nap, the baby's response to the caregiver at this time, and the way in which the baby manages to fall asleep— and later to wake up—will reveal something about the baby's sense of trust in the caregiver, in the group, and in the environment in general. It will also show how willing the baby is to exchange the exciting, active, awake world for the passive world of sleep.

The following record of two children at nap time reveals their relaxed, natural, and trusting feelings about sleeping at their center.

> Kay, the caregiver, is holding Carmen's (thirty-two months old) hand as they enter the nap room. Kay says to Willie, thirty months, who is standing nearby, "Say good night to Carmen. She's going for her nap." Willie walks into the nap room with Kay and Carmen, watching as Carmen lies down and Kay covers her, patting her briefly on the back. "Have a good nap," says Kay as she and Willie leave the room, closing the door. Willie sits on the couch as Kay fixes him a bottle of juice. Bringing the bottle to him, she sits on the couch and begins to take off his shoes. He leans against her, sucking on the

bottle. "Shall we read a book?" she asks. "Yes." She begins to read *Goodnight Moon*. When it is finished, they walk into the nap room, and she covers him when he lies down. No words have been spoken, but an understanding of the routine and a pervading tenderness are apparent.

Records of the child asleep, if possible, as well as of the child waking up, may show another side of her personality. Attention to the following details will provide a rich record.

- Is the sleep restless and fidgety, or calm and quiet?
- On awakening, does the child cry, or call out, or pop out of bed and appear in the midst of activity? Is the child tense, or disoriented, or difficult to comfort? How does this behavior fit with the behavior you have seen in other situations?
- Do these reactions, to sleep and to awakening, have meanings for the baby? Can you surmise those meanings?

OUTINGS

Getting ready for an outing, the outing itself, and the return to the center are all routine situations that afford an opportunity to understand the infant/toddler in more depth. Going out involves a transition from the known to the less known and means a separation from the classroom. If not all children are taken out at the same time, it also involves a separation from some adults and children. (In such a situation, it is worthwhile observing those children who do not go out, but who stay behind.)

There are several observations that should be made.

- How does the child react to preparation for going out? Frightened? Worried? Matter of fact? With anticipation?
- Is the child able to contain excitement and attend to the necessities of dressing, or is the anticipation overwhelming, making dressing and organizing a difficult procedure?
- How does the style of the caregiver mesh with that of the child? A frantic caregiver, for example, might do little to help organ ize a toddler who is running about the room resisting wearing a coat or hat.
- How are negotiations between infant/toddler and various caregivers carried out?

- What effect do the child's manner, requests, compliances, resistances, have on different adults? Some adults, for example, are charmed and bent to the will of a child who uses facial expressions and words with finesse, where others are offended by the use of such "wiles" and refuse to comply with the child.

In the following record, Rashi, thirty-four months, wants to do things his way and the caregiver walks a careful line after making an initial error.

> Rashi starts to go out the door to get his coat. The caregiver, John, says, "Wait, I have your coat here." Rashi begins to cry and wail. "Oh," says John, "I see that you want to get it yourself. I'll put it back on the hook." "No!" screams Rashi, grabbing the coat from John. He goes out to the hall and hangs it up himself. He returns to the room, stops, whirls himself in the opposite direction, and returns to the hall, grabs his coat off the hook, carries it into the room. He lays the coat on the floor in order to flip it over his head. He flips it, but it is upside down.
>
> Casually, John says, "Rashi, your coat is upside down." Rashi ignores him. When John turns away to talk to another child, Rashi slips the coat off and tries again with an equal lack of success. He hands the coat to John without speaking and John ties it around Rashi's waist by the sleeves. "No!" he shrieks as he pulls away. John quietly removes the coat and helps Rashi on with it. Rashi allows John to hold the coat while he puts his arms into the sleeves. He stares at John and commands him, "Zip it up!" John zips it and they go out together, hand in hand.

Returning to the center after an outing involves for the very young child another transition that may ignite a range of feelings. If it is close to lunch time, for instance, toddlers may experience hunger, or worry about an impending nap, or be just plain fatigued. How does this affect their behavior? What does it mean when the caregiver says, "Juan always cries when we get within a half block of the center," or "I have to watch Harry closely because as soon as he sees our doorway he begins to run." What meaning does coming back to the center have for babies and toddlers and what is each child's special way of communicating that meaning?

Look at Carl, thirty-five months, and Mara, twenty-six months, whose feelings on returning to the center from a short walk are much larger than their vocabularies.

> Coming into the classroom through the door, Mara and Carl both take hold of the doorknob at the same time. Both scream and jump up and down, trying to be the only one to hold the knob. Amid screams, Mara pokes Carl's eye. He continues to pull on the knob while she screams, "No! No! Next time *I* close the door!" Betsy, the caregiver, reaches them at this point and says, evenly, "What's going on?" Mara shouts, "I close the door!" Betsy quietly asks, "Can I help you close the door?" Carl drops his hand from the knob and stands still, looking at Betsy. Mara continues to scream. Betsy asks her, "You want to do it yourself?" Mara looks at her openly and says, "Yes." Carl watches quietly as Betsy stands still and Mara opens the door slightly and then closes it. The three of them, without speaking, turn and head toward the snack table.

Autonomy, a central developmental issue in two-year-olds, is vigorously depicted in this anecdote. What contributed to the escalation of feeling will have to be surmised, or substantiated by further recording. Records like these shed light on normal developmental situations and point the way to further study of the special individual characteristics of the children involved. Winnowing one from the other—developmental characteristics from individual behavior—is a task that requires continual recording.

Playing and Exploring

It is surely through play that infants and toddlers learn their way about the world and exercise their burgeoning physical skills. Their ceaseless tasting, smelling, poking, prodding, looking, and touching define them as scientists, forever wanting to find out "what" and "how." Who can say where play ends and learning begins, or where, at what point, random activity becomes abstract thought? Somewhere, and everywhere, in the activity of the under threes lie the roots of all thought, all language, all conceptualization.

To record at random the play and explorations of infants and toddlers is to obtain and fully appreciate an intimate view of the young mind and body at work. Which behaviors, exactly, can truly be called play? Which can be called exploration? Which intentional? Which happenstance? Clearly no specific behaviors in the very young can be labeled as such. It is beyond question that the total of the baby's activity is a composite of play, exploration, learning, and language development. It cannot be teased apart or preselected for observation. In fact, social interaction, language activities, perceptual-cognitive activities, and both large- and small-motor activities have been included in the definition of babies' play.*

Thus, recording any behavior will most likely serve to reveal the young child playing, learning, and expressing feelings.

Here are situations that will focus on babies and toddlers playing and exploring:

- When the children are moving freely about their physical environment, either indoors or out
- When children are using any playthings, play equipment, or household items like pots and pans, boxes, spoons, etc.
- When children are engaged with specific materials such as water, dough, blocks, paint, crayons, food preparation, etc.

When collected, such observations will offer a view into the level of the child's curiosity and interest in objects, the development and control of eye-hand coordination and gross-motor ability, and the growing understanding of causes.

Within these records will be seen not only what the baby is learning but how the baby is learning it. Here is nineteen-month-old Ezra, who through imitation and random exploration is trying to understand the unknown properties of keys and keyholes, using his own familiar body as referent.

> Alex, twenty-five months, tries to open a cabinet door with a key he is holding. It doesn't work. Ezra watches Alex and then tries the same motion on the door, but without the key. Ezra turns to Alex and takes the key out of his hand. Alex does not protest. Ezra shows the key to his father, who is sitting on the floor near the cabinet, prior to taking Ezra home. Ezra plops down on the floor next to his father. He lifts up his shirt and tries to put the key into his navel. Quietly, his father says, "Don't do that."

A world of difference exists between the nineteen-month-old toddler investigating the similarities of a keyhole and a navel, and

---

*Anne Willis and Henry Ricciuti, *A Good Beginning for Babies* (Washington, D.C.: NAEYC, 1975), p. 36.

an infant of seven months who is beginning to teach herself that
objects have a permanent existence.

> Cheryl, seven months, is sitting in a walker. She holds a rubber
> squeeze animal in both hands, joyously mouthing one of its ears.
> Suddenly it drops to the floor. She leans over, her eyes riveted on the
> fallen toy. Though the caregiver picks it up, Cheryl continues to look
> at the spot where the toy had been. The caregiver hands the animal
> to Cheryl, saying, "Here's your kitty, Cheryl." Cheryl pats the
> animal with one open palm, momentarily chews the ear, then exam-
> ines it with her eyes as she turns it back and forth in her hand. Her
> expression is intent. She makes a series of "ah" sounds and returns to
> chewing seriously on the protruding ear.

With many more such experiences, plus maturation, Cheryl will
develop a more certain sense of the existence and the qualities of
things and people. In each anecdote above the behavior observed
was developmentally correct for each child at that age. But what if
the behavior of the child were not as obviously appropriate? What
if, for example, Cheryl were unable to hold and inspect the plaything, or were uninterested in, though capable of, doing so? All
behavior must be evaluated and understood within an established
framework of developmental progress and the observer must check
any hints of possible developmental delay. Before any conclusion is
made, however, records should be taken over a period of time to
determine whether the behavior is merely a lapse, possibly due to
illness or fatigue, or is, indeed, a matter for concerned attention.

One of the difficulties in recording play is that it frequently does
not look like play. Often toddler activity looks like no activity. It
looks like "fooling around" or "doing nothing." Here is Denise,
fifteen months old, engaged with a handful of plastic shapes that
were designed for preschoolers. She, however, uses (plays with)
them for her own purposes—grasping, clutching, collecting, feeling
their texture, experiencing their weight, and above all exercising
her autonomy by doing with them what she will. No one intervenes
in her explorations, so she has an opportunity to try out a range of
actions.

> Denise walks randomly about the room holding a few plastic
> shapes in her fists, plopping her feet as she goes, laughing and
> dropping some of the shapes on the floor. She momentarily puts her
> hand on the couch as she goes by, then climbs up on it, merrily

announcing, "Eeh—ahh—ehh—da—dii—di." She puts a few of the shapes on the couch while still holding others in her hand. She turns her body so that she is on her tummy, and using her fists for support, clutches the shapes as she slides off the couch. She walks over to Pat, a caregiver, swinging her arms and shoulders. She passes Pat, smiling as she goes by, and climbs over a large hollow block, sits on it, all the while still clutching the plastic shapes. Sitting there, she puts one shape at a time in her mouth, giving them rapid little licks, then drops them next to her, on the block, saying, "Da" several times in a rising inflection. She retrieves the shapes from the block, walks to the slide, and places them on the steps. She raises her hand, saying, "Ga da" as she puts the shapes on the next higher step. She leaves the shapes there and walks away.

Around the age of two, toddlers' random exploration and play begin to look more organized to the adult eye. The two- to two-and-a-half-year-old at a water basin engages in more recognizable actions with a sponge and bowl than a thirteen-month-old, who might plop a crayon in the tub or venture a splash or two with an open hand.

Using materials like crayons or felt-nib markers takes on more complex dimensions as pure investigation is overlaid with symbolic meaning. Using crayons may stimulate in the two-year-old a sense of pleasure in the colors themselves, as well as delight in mastery. A drawing by a child of thirty-four months, who carefully made, across the page, one vertical line after another, each of a separate color, evidences such delight in color.

On the other hand, observations of a thirty-month-old, drawing picture after picture containing small, knot-like circles of different colors confined to the center of the paper, may point to another dimension. As he worked, his face was set, and his body held stiffly erect in his chair. His teacher realized, both through observation and by collecting his drawings, that he did many such pictures during the first few weeks of school. Possibly he used these materials in an attempt to express his feelings about starting group life away from home.

For the eighteen- to thirty-six-month-old, playing and exploring with materials allow the sheer pleasure of making a mark where there was none before, and of expressing deep feelings and ideas nonverbally. The use of such materials as paints, water, dough, and blocks also supports the budding human need to represent the child's experience with the world. Can we say whether Lisa's drawing, at thirty-five months, of a large circle, surrounded by many attached, perpendicular lines—which she calls a "sun"—is truly a spontaneous representation or a learned convention?

Surely, the beginnings of symbolic play, which flowers openly in the preschool years into complex role-taking, can be detected in the playing two-year-olds. In the following record of vastly more elaborate action than is recorded in the previously described play of nineteen-month-old Ezra, a symbolic reorganization of two salient features of the lives of these under threes is seen. A few gestures and words represent their experience.

> Angel, thirty months, carries a block. As he strides along, he says, "I going to work. I going to work." Kristie, twenty-six months, walking with him, takes her lunch box from the shelf (these children bring their lunch to the center) and loudly announces "We're going to school." They walk along for a moment when Angel spies a doll stroller, complete with doll. He pushes it as they continue to march around the room together, Kristie holding the lunch box, he still clutching the block. As they near the phonograph, Kristie sits down to listen to a record and Angel moves to the table where the teacher is sitting.

To round out this prelude to a more developed use of expressive materials and imaginative play, look to Chapters 3 and 5, which explore the playing two- to six-year-olds in depth.

Interaction with Adults and Children

The phenomenon of infant and toddler social life has only recently been described because the opportunity to observe such young children in groups has never before been so available.

The social world of infants and toddlers is highlighted through anecdotes of interactions with both adults and other children. Records of the young child's interactions with adults may include exchanges with a wide range of people, from the familiar to the strange; from the baby's parents to the caregivers; from a student teacher to the cook; from a casual visitor to a regular delivery or service person. Including such a wide range of adults as material for observations widens the opportunity to appreciate the baby's repertoire for dealing with adults. Guidelines for these observations include the following:

- Exactly how does the child react to familiar people? Is it always the same or does it vary? Is it predictable?
- How does the child react to unfamiliar people? Is there any difference in the child's reaction if the stranger is a man or a woman? Have changes been seen in these reactions over time?
- Does the child initiate contacts with adults? How?
- What sorts of response does the child elicit from adults? What are the range and variation of these responses?
- Is the child able to communicate his needs to the adult?
- Is the child able to attract attention to herself? How?

The quality of the interactions between an infant/toddler and adults is the single most significant aspect of that baby's life in group care. It is through these relationships that babies forge an opinion of the world and a concept of their own potentiality. Therefore, records of such transactions are crucial for understanding youngsters' view of their human environment. The implications for staff development are full of promise, for the records will address both the child's experience with adults and the adults' behavior.

Some children are skilled at eliciting responses from adults. Here is a record of Earl, fifteen months, who has figured out a way to keep the universal game of peekaboo going, even after the caregiver thought it had ended.

> Ruth, the caregiver, is at one end of the fish tank and Earl is at the other. She initiates peekaboo by looking around the side of the tank and then popping her head back. Earl does the same, grinning from ear to ear. Then she catches his eye through the tank. She drops down out of sight. He giggles. She switches to the side again and he looks for her there as she repeats the game. She leaves the fish tank for a moment, but sees him looking around the tank for her, so she returns to play the game again. He laughs and peeks around. This induces her to play yet again. She begins to put the blocks away, leaving the tank. He starts to put his bottle in the tank, but she bounds over just in time to stop him. He grins.

However, experiences with adults are not always such fun. Sometimes very young children become overwhelmed with

thoughts of their absent parents and rely on adults to help them
through difficult times. The availability of an empathic adult during a surge of strong feelings is a crucial factor in the child's positive
perception of the social world. Here is twenty-three-month-old
Heather, at one moment listening placidly to a story, at the next
sobbing for her mother:

> Debbie is reading a story to Heather. Suddenly Heather begins to
> cry, and throws a small car. Soothingly, Debbie says, "Your mommy
> will be back. She'll be back." Heather cries, "Mommy!" and runs to
> the door. She begins pounding on it. Debbie puts her arms around
> Heather and says, "I'm going to pick you up and tell your bunny that
> I guess you're missing your mommy." Heather allows Debbie to pick
> her up and they settle on the floor near the photo of her mother and
> Debbie says, "Mommy will come back. We'll tell her what you did
> today." She adds, "Dirt. Right?" Debbie echoes, "Right. We went to
> see the tractor with the dirt." Debbie puts her face close to Heather's
> and they rub noses. Heather examines, with her fingers and her eyes,
> Debbie's necklace and earrings. As she does so, Debbie comments,
> "You are really interested in my earrings," and, pointing to the photo
> of Heather's mother, "Your mom has earrings, too." Suddenly,
> Heather pops out of Debbie's lap and walks steadily to the other side
> of the room to watch some children who are sticking soft plastic
> shapes to the mirror.

Such a record helps to magnify how rapidly Heather became
flooded with frightening, lonely feelings and how she was able to
use the ministrations of the adult to reorganize her briefly shattered
self. The record also spotlights the caregiver's skill.

The meaningful, everyday, social milieu of the infant and toddler
is also comprised of other children. The joy of two toddlers greeting
each other as they enter a day-care center often rivals that of the
pleasure of nine-year-old "chums," seeing one another at the start
of a school day.

Not only do such very young children enjoy one another's com-
pany but they also express preferences. It is not unusual to see a
subdued toddler "come to life" with the arrival of a friend. Reactions occur not only to friends, but to "enemies" as well. Some
toddlers seem to have a truly active distaste for one another.
Record keeping in such instances gives a staff an opportunity to
look deeply into both children's interpersonal relationships and
their own role. Staff development can be continually replenished

with new recorded observations. Such material feeds the well-springs of teacher renewal.

What are some of the instances that include what we have termed infant/toddler interaction? They appear at almost any time during the day and require only an aware adult ear as well as eye—plus the ever-ready pad of paper and a pencil. Harry, at eighteen months, is engaged in a true social exchange in the following record—first with sixteen-month-old Tina and then with his teacher.

> As dessert was served, Harry and Tina, who were sitting next to one another, began to playfully feed each other. They both laughed and looked at one another as they took turns putting their spoons of applesauce, each into the mouth of the other. Harry smiled. He really enjoyed this game. He seemed to have had his fill of food and was obviously intent on the pleasure of this interaction.
>
> It was now time to leave the dining room, so Harry ripped off his bib, wiped himself with a napkin, and then proceeded to spill and wipe milk on the table. With an expression of contentment and absorption, he wiped a little milk, spilled a little, and wiped a little more. The teacher stood quietly by for about two minutes, allowing Harry's play. Then she also wiped up the spill, took Harry's hand, and walked with him back to his room for rest. Harry willingly and happily left the dining room. He seemed to have enjoyed his lunch.

Tina and Harry were experimenting with a very early form of mutual play. They were learning that age-mates are interesting people. Further, because Harry's teacher understood the toddler's need for experimentation, she was able to help him make the transition from lunch to rest pleasant and satisfying.

How much we can glean from even the tiniest views into toddler relations! Imitation, for example, is a main avenue that connects one toddler to another. Above we saw Harry and Tina engaged in mutual imitative feeding. Here are Bradley and Maryrose caught for a slight moment at the very edge of mutual play.

> Bradley, eighteen months, climbs into an adult-sized rocking chair. He turns his body to sit down, legs splayed on the large seat, hands on the chair's arms. "Row, row," he sings in a loud voice. Maryrose, seventeen months, walks up to him, holds the arm of the chair, and rocks it, saying, "Row, row." Bradley gets off the chair and walks away.

It is often in gross-motor play that the small beginnings of peer social life lie. Exchanges of looks; pokes or pushes; empathic pats for a crying comrade; offering, giving, or grabbing an object or food, are all actions that constitute early social interaction. Imitation is a form that is als' seen in situations of more than two and has a contagious aspect.

> The caregiver turns the rocking boat over so that it has three steps on either side of a platform. She sits next to it, in a chair. Brian, seventeen months, and Dan, fifteen months, begin to climb the steps. Abby, fourteen months, climbs behind them. When Brian sits on the platform, Dan sits, then Abby sits. Brian gets up and walks down the other side, holding the caregiver's hand. Then Abby does the same. They stand at the bottom, smiling.

As children grow closer to two-and-a-half and three their imitative play displays more complexity, more use of language, perhaps more of what adults label "friendship." Such records can provide us with a short history of the ripening of a relationship. Wayne, thirty months, and Maria, thirty-two months, have discovered that jumping and falling on a mattress together is better than doing it alone.

> Wayne jumps up on the mattress, then lands on his bottom. He giggles. Maria, who has been standing by watching him, lies down on the mattress, watching him out of the corner of her eye. Wayne lies down next to her. They regard each other, smiling. Wayne, looking Maria in the eye, says, "Let's jump" with which they both jump up, and fall down on their bottoms. They look at each other and laugh heartily. Then without words they both get up and repeat the action, laughing just as hard. Maria says to Wayne, "Watch!" as she jumps and falls. Then Wayne jumps and falls as Maria watches. Maria gets up and counts "One! Two! Three! Go down!" and falls. Then Wayne does the same. They do this several more times.

Interactions are not made only of pleasant stuff. Some involve fury, provocation, hostility, spite. A seventeen-month-old who often bit was captured in the following record, about to strike. Perhaps the other child's previous experience with her saved him:

> Twenty-month-old Steven is walking out of a small doorway in a large packing crate, at the same moment that Bonnie, seventeen months, is walking in. They are squeezed body to body in this small

space. She quietly places her teeth on his arm. He silently moves his arm away before she sinks her teeth in and they continue moving in opposite directions.

Feelings of possessiveness are a frequent source of conflict to which a thoughtful caregiver can bring peace.

Eric, twenty-one months, is standing quietly, holding a small toy boat, face impassive. His body is relaxed as he stands. Charlie walks over to Eric and lightly touches the boat with one finger. "My boat! My boat!" Eric screams, looking at Charlie. The caregiver comes over and says softly, "That boat is important to you, isn't it, Eric?" Eric relaxes again. Charlie wanders off.

Angry feelings are sometimes expressed in young babies, as seen in this "fight" between two eleven-month-olds.

Kathy is sitting on the playroom floor, happily gurgling, and shaking a multicolored teething ring up and down in her right hand. She is smiling up at the caregiver, who is sitting in the rocking chair holding a younger infant on her lap. There is one other baby, eleven-month-old Randy, sitting by the doorway.

A caregiver comes into the room carrying a diaper for Randy. She bends down to Randy, intending to pick him up and change him, but he resists so much that she lets the diaper drop next to him. As Kathy spots the diaper she makes an "aarr" sound and scoots over to the diaper. At this time, Randy is picking up the diaper and happily swinging it up and down. Kathy plops down next to him and snatches the diaper away with an impish grin on her face. Randy, with an indignant shriek, reaches for it and tries to pull it away. Kathy begins to cry angrily but does not relinquish the diaper, and a tug-of-war ensues.

Kathy wins and takes off across the room in a speedy crawl with the diaper clutched tightly in her hand. Randy furiously crawls after her and overtakes her in the corner. Kathy, with an angry yet panicky expression on her face, looks to the caregiver for help as she cries and Randy determinedly reaches out for the diaper. Another tug-of-war—and this time Randy is the victor. He grunts and stuffs part of the diaper in his mouth, then waves it in front of Kathy. She is sobbing in a hurt and angry tone and waves her arms frantically up and down, then rubs her right hand behind her ear. Randy is staring at her as she reaches out and grasps the diaper. She pulls it away with a triumphant look on her face and turns away from Randy to crawl up on a nearby platform. Once on the platform, she sits and smiles at the two caregivers and flings the diaper happily up and down; her mouth forms a wide grin and her tongue is peeking out at the corner.

Kathy then spots her bottle lying across the room and, abandoning the diaper, crawls over to the bottle, cooing softly. Randy has also apparently lost interest in the diaper and is playing with a large rubber ball. The diaper is now in shreds.

Continued recording of such incidents will turn up items that can be evaluated realistically within the total range of recorded interactions. Often teachers and caregivers think there is more conflict than there really is. This misconception occurs because conflict is more dramatic and, therefore, gains more adult attention. Loving relations are taken for granted. Records help put both sorts of transactions into proper perspective.

Since the relationships of babies and toddlers contain only the rudiments of later fully formed relationships, they are often evanescent, rapidly developing and of short duration. Yet the sum total of contacts, imitation, angers, and joys will reveal to the recorder a rich and varied social life.

Language

The recording and study of infant and toddler language is an art of significant magnitude, which goes beyond the scope of this book. It is a field in which vast numbers of studies have been done. Scholars have devoted many years to unlocking the secrets of human speech by their painstaking gathering of verbatim language samples from the very young.

However, we who work with children under three cannot leave the total investigation of language development or child behavior to others. Teachers and caregivers need practice in the skill of collecting information in order to know firsthand how children learn to talk and to use language.

To this end, the collection of verbatim samples of language—sounds, as well as words and sentences—will be a most rewarding undertaking. The coos and babbles of infancy can be recorded as well as the beginning words and phrases of toddlerhood. Such notations, which will be included as a matter of course in any observations, will reveal patterns of change and increasing complexity when scrutinized over as short a period as two or three months.

There are certain characteristics to notice as records are taken. The following suggestions are highlights for observational attention:

- Which situations seem to elicit the production of sounds in the infant? (e.g., a speaking adult, a moving toy, a music box, a small child, etc.)
- Does the presence, or absence, of the parent influence the sound production of the infant? What effect does the presence, or absence, of the caregiver have? What about the presence of a stranger?
- What new sounds appear in the infant's repertoire over a period of several days? weeks?
- Does the baby, around eight to twelve months of age, attempt to repeat words spoken directly to him? Which words?
- Does the baby babble? Under what circumstances?
- Does the toddler use sounds that are not understandable, but have the rhythm and cadence of English speech or the dominant language in her home?
- Does the toddler combine sounds into two or three syllables?
- Does the toddler produce recognizable words? Does she combine any of these words to make two- or three-word sentences?
- What is the range of the baby or toddler's understanding of what is said to him?
- At what point does the child sing? chant nonsense words, or repeat words for fun, rather than understanding?

Records like the following illustrate how much of a child's language is learned from and exercised with other children and how pleasurable imitation is for the very young. Ann and Darren, both fourteen months, are sitting at a table with Ina, twenty-four months, eating apples and cheese.

ANN: Ba bee, ba bee.
DARREN: Ba bee. (He then looks across the table at Ann.)
ANN: Bo.
DARREN: Bo.
INA: I want more cheese.
DARREN (pointing to the bowl on the counter where the cheese is kept): Cheese.

The caregiver hands the cheese to Darren and Ina. Darren chews the cheese, opens his mouth, and says, "Ah. Haa Ha," looking directly at Ann, who laughs. Darren throws back his head and makes a fake laugh. "Ah. Ha! Ha!" He repeats the motion and the sound three times. Then he laughs a genuine laugh and pushes the cheese into his mouth with his fingers.

Ina, Ann, and Darren then together say, "Ba, ba, ba, ah, ha, ha."

Ann turns her face up to the ceiling and says, "Ah. ha. ha." She cackles.

Children seem to use imitation and repetition for both learning and fun. There seems to be something inherently satisfying for them in this activity.

Kelly, at thirty months, peeks into the nap room, which is empty of children. "Nobody sleeping," he says to no one in particular. "Not Matthew, not Sally, not Jamie, not Frannie, not Kelly. Nobody sleeping." He repeats his chant of nonsleeper's names, but this time he jumps in the air with each name.

As children near three, language increasingly becomes a clarifying tool. As some of the children's ideas are recorded, we can understand in the smallest detail how truly full of mystery this confusing world is to children.

At lunch time, thirty-month-old Nora was having trouble peeling her banana and asked the teacher for help. As the teacher peeled it, Nora told her, "My mommy put that peel on this morning."

Words are often interesting in and of themselves and young children seem to enjoy their feeling on the tongue.

When Joan, twenty-four months, asked her mother, "What's a budget cut?" we wonder what that phrase conjured up in her young mind.

Richard, twenty-eight months, is sitting in the caregiver's lap, observing a group of children going out with another teacher to get their snack from the kitchen. Spontaneously, unrelated to ongoing events and to no one in particular, he says, "Spring water." "Do you drink spring water?" the teacher asks. He gives the teacher a blank look.

Records also show us just how much children love to play with language. It is a special kind of plaything.

When the teacher asks Marian what she is building, she says, "I'm building a traffic clack. A traffic clack. A traffic clack. A clacking sound makes a traffic clack."

There is no true end to the recording of infant/toddler language, social interaction, play, or behavior during caregiving routines. It is an ongoing, never-ending endeavor. Each day brings new change, new development, added skills, new feelings. In records lie a deep mine of treasures. The pen is the teacher's probe. The observer's tools—those eyes, ears, and hands—are an unparalleled source of fresh and lively material that, when collected and sorted, assures constant refreshment in the practice of teaching.

12

RECORDING THE
BEHAVIOR OF CHILDREN
WITH SPECIAL PROBLEMS

IN PREVIOUS CHAPTERS we have dealt with the details to look for in observing the behavior of normal children and the methods of recording that behavior. Occasionally, references have been made to what might be considered "problem" behavior. As experienced teachers know, most young children at times exhibit behavior that is different from their usual behavior, suggesting that the child is under stress or having difficulties of some kind. This behavior may be temporary, as when there is a new baby in the family. On the other hand, it may be related to a developmental stage, as, for example, difficulty in separating from the parent (or other caregiver) at age two or three, or distress when, at the age of two, the daily routine is changed.

Here we shall focus on those behaviors that may be clues to present or future emotional disturbances or learning disabilities.* The purpose of the lists of questions presented throughout this chapter is to alert teachers to these details and to encourage them to record the behavior of the problem child in many different activities and situations over a period of time (but not to help them diagnose the problem).† All aspects of functioning—physical, social, emotional—must be taken into consideration since difficulties generally occur in more than one area. For example, although

---

*Some of these behaviors may also be associated with other types of problems, such as impairment of vision, hearing, speech, etc., or atypical or uneven development.

†These lists are, of necessity, not exhaustive.

the primary problem may involve disturbances in cognitive and perceptual functioning, there are usually attendant secondary problems, such as hyperactivity, impulsiveness, phobias, lack of self-confidence.

Records such as these should reveal whether certain behaviors occur *frequently, persistently, and/or in consistent patterns.* Such information will lead to increased understanding of the child on the part of the teacher. It is important to remember, however, that *no single behavior has any significance.* Only a combination of several that persist may signify the presence of a problem. In addition, these records may be helpful to a consultant who, if necessary, can use them along with relevant tests and assessments to provide a diagnostic evaluation of a child's problem.

As a rule, teachers cannot help but be aware that a problem exists when a child exhibits bizarre or extreme forms of behavior— inappropriate responses to stimuli, aggressiveness, excessive timidity, overdependence on adults. They are not as likely to be aware that the presence of two or more persistent but less striking kinds of behavior, such as poor large- or small-muscle coordination, inability to follow directions, and developmental lags, may also be precursors of future problems.

The relevant behavioral details to be observed are listed in six sections: Physical Functioning and Development, Relationships with People, Affective Modes, Cognitive Functioning, Language and Speech, and Ego Functioning.* At the end of each section, activities, situations, or relationships in which these behaviors are likely to be observed are identified in order to facilitate reference to the appropriate chapters in which the observing and recording methods are presented in detail.

PHYSICAL FUNCTIONING AND DEVELOPMENT
Details to Observe—Large-Muscle Skills and Spatial Orientation
- Does the child's capacity to perform large-muscle skills lag behind that of other children his age?

    For example, is a three-year-old not yet able to ride a tricycle

---

*Some of the behaviors listed may be acceptable in certain ethnic or socioeconomic groups and, therefore, may not be evidence of "disturbance." It should be noted in this connection that many of the records cited here are of Hispanic and black children who come from low-income families.

(i.e., steer and pedal)? a four-year-old, to walk up and downstairs by himself with alternating feet? a five-year-old, to skip, jump rope, "pump" himself on a swing?
- Are the child's large-body movements generally clumsy, awkward, uncoordinated?

Five-year-old Juan was engaged in block building in conjunction with dramatic play. Several times he knocked down the building of another child who was playing near him, as he passed by. Juan was surprised each time it happened. It was clearly not an intentional act.

- Is the child hyperactive (i.e., constantly in motion that is purposeless and unrelated to a specific activity or situation)? When sitting, does she tend to twist, turn, squirm?
- Is the child hypoactive? Are his movements sluggish? Does he appear sleepy or uninterested in what is happening around him?
- Are the child's movements jerky and restricted?
- Does she tend to confine her activities to an unnecessarily small area?
- Does he tend to go beyond set or natural boundaries?

When joining pieces of track for his train to go on, five-year-old Ronnie went way beyond the confines of the block corner.

- Is the child able to judge the spatial relationship of objects to each other or to himself? For example, does he know whether there is enough space between two objects to move his wagon through?
- Is the child unusually cautious and timid physically? Or is he careless about his safety?
- Is the child's energy level consistently very high or very low? Or is there extreme fluctuation in energy level?

More striking and unusual behavior may be observed:

- The child walks around in circles, or moves around the room repeatedly in the same order, e.g., from block area to easel to housekeeping corner.
- The child flaps his arms up and down when walking and there

is no overt evidence that he is pretending to fly or be an airplane or a bird.
- The child may engage in a series of seemingly meaningless bodily motions.

Bernie (age four) turned the handle on the vise for a moment; took two small jumps, twice; stuck his hand in the empty aquarium; pointed at a variety of objects in succession; rocked back and forth from one leg to another, talking to himself all the time.

Both the level and quality of the child's large-muscle coordination and spatial orientation can be observed during indoor and outdoor play, as he moves around the room or from the room to the playground and back, and, especially, during play on the jungle gym, on the slide, on a swing, jumping rope, etc.

Details to Observe—Small-Muscle Coordination
- Does the child's capacity to perform skills requiring small-muscle coordination lag behind that of other children his age? For example:
    Is a two- to three-year-old not yet able to string large beads, hold a large crayon between thumb and fingers?
    Is a three-year-old as yet unable to make balls and snakes out of clay, to button and unbutton large buttons?
    Is a four-year-old not yet able to cut on a line continuously, lace her shoes?
    Is a five-year-old not yet able to hold a pencil like an adult, to tie a bow, not yet completely left- or right-handed or clearly ambidextrous?
- Does the child have difficulty picking up or holding objects between thumb and index finger?
- Is she unable to balance one small block on another?
- Does the child have trouble fitting the proper pieces into a jigsaw puzzle (one that is age appropriate)?

The level of the child's small-muscle coordination can best be observed during routines such as eating, dressing and undressing, going to the toilet, and also when the child paints, colors with crayons, plays with clay, builds with blocks, and even when "cooking" and "serving meals" in the housekeeping corner.

RELATIONSHIPS WITH PEOPLE

Details to Observe

● Does the child have difficulty relating to other children or to adults?

Does he appear to be uncomfortable with people?

Four-and-one-half-year-old George looked up but made no other response when the teacher said hello to him. He continued with what he was doing. Shortly after, another teacher suggested that he do something. George moved away, trembling a little. When this teacher patted him a moment later, he ignored her, made no response. George ignored the teachers' overtures throughout the play period, continuing to play by himself.

● Does the child tend to play by herself? (Preference for solitary activities must be distinguished from age-level tendencies, i.e., two- and three-year-olds tend to play alone while older children tend to play with others.)
● Does the child make eye-to-eye contact with people?
● Does the child seldom talk to other children?
● Does the child tend not to join in group activities?
● When involved in a group activity, does the child tend to be shy?
● Is the child overattached to one person while appearing to be frightened of others?
● Is the child excessively resistant to the teacher's suggestions and directions?

When the teacher called four-and-a-half-year-old Michael to go wash his hands, he followed her to the bathroom. The teacher asked if he wanted to wash his hands, and he said, "No." When she told him to go back to the classroom, he went back and asked another teacher, "Will you play with me?" That teacher replied, "After you wash your hands." Michael then crawled to the bathroom, but refused to wash and came back to the room, where he went over to the housekeeping corner. Again, he asked the teacher to play with him, and the teacher said, "Not until you wash your hands." Michael screeched, as if he were in extreme pain, and then stopped suddenly. He continued to resist washing for the duration of the play period.

● Does the child cling to adults, touch them frequently?
● Is the child very dependent on and demanding of adults for help, approval, etc.?
● Is the child extremely unassertive?

Does she tend to give up materials, etc., to other children without objection? give up her turn easily?

When Isabella (age five-and-a-half) left her seat, announcing she was going to the bathroom, and another child sat in it while she was gone, she unprotestingly sat in the other child's seat.

- Does the child tend to give up quickly if he does not get an immediate response from others?
- Is the child aggressive?
  Does he fight frequently with other children?
- Does the child's aggressiveness tend to be expressed physically?
  Does he hit, scratch, bite, or kick?

Johnny, age five, tends to be physically aggressive. When Carmen said her turn came before his, Johnny hit her repeatedly. Later, when sitting in a group, Johnny waved his arms around, hitting Carmen in the nose.

- Does the child express aggression verbally?
  Does he scream, curse, or call names?

The nature of the child's relationship with others can be observed during the entire school day in a variety of activities and situations. The child's dependence on or independence of adults for help and approval can be seen particularly during routine activities (eating, dressing, resting, etc.), during play (painting, block-building, etc.), and during adult-directed group activities, such as games, rhythms, and stories. The character of a child's relationships with other children can be deduced from observations of the way she reacts to overtures by other children, the presence or absence of interest in other children or specific children, the extent to which she seeks out or avoids contacts with children, and the ways in which she initiates and responds to contacts with other children (aggressive, fearful, negative, manipulative, etc.).

AFFECTIVE MODES

Details to Observe
- Does the child tend to control his anger?
  Does he fail to express anger either verbally or physically even when the stimulus would ordinarily provoke anger?

- Is the child overly fearful?

  José (age five-and-a-half) told the teacher that, when he went to Puerto Rico on a plane, he was very scared. The teacher asked why. José said, "Bees bite plane."

- Does the child have persistent phobias (e.g., fear of dogs, of strangers)?
- Does the child tend to be passive, timid, or apprehensive?
- Does she cry a lot?
- Does the child frequently act out her anxieties in her dramatic play?

  Four-and-a-half-year-old Andy sets up a line of chairs in the middle of the room, and sits in the driver's (i.e., the first) seat. He turns an imaginary wheel and says, "I'm the bus driver." As he continues to turn the "wheel," he becomes excited, stands up, and whirls around and around. Then he pulls his chair behind him across the floor, saying, "I drive myself. I drive myself." He then yells excitedly, "The bus is out of control, the bus is out of control."

It is clear from Andy's behavior that he is expressing his anxiety that he may not be able to control his possibly aggressive impulses.

- Does the child have extreme and/or frequent changes of mood? (For example, during a twenty-minute period, Jorge's moods varied from happy to angry to depressed to almost ecstatic.)
- Does the child have sudden, seemingly unprovoked outbursts of crying or anger or laughter that he is unable to control?

  Five-year-old Alfredo was playing with a camera and humming happily to himself. Suddenly, he threw a plastic knife that was in his lap at the cabinet near him, making a stifled but angry sound. He then turned to Paula, who was sitting nearby, and said, threateningly, "Don't you hit me!"

- Does the child tend to scream frequently?
- Does the child tend to respond inappropriately to situations or stimuli?

  Five-year-old Juana smiles continually whether the situation warrants it or not. When the teacher told her she could go to snack, she smiled, threw a kiss to the teacher, and went to the table. When she sat down, she said, smiling, "I don't like chocolate milk." After she had drunk her chocolate milk very fast, she said, continuing to smile, "It's freezing in here." She then turned her cup upside down. A few drops fell on her mat. She smiled, banged her feet on the floor, still smiling, and said, "Hee hee."

● Does the child have frequent tantrums?

Chris (age 6) got very excited when the teacher said she was going to fix a book that was torn. He said he was going to "shoot" her. He then lay prone on the floor, crying and kicking his legs. Then he sat up, continuing to cry and talking unintelligibly. After the teacher taped the book, he continued to cry, refused to listen to the story, and repeatedly yelled, "Take it off" (i.e., the tape on the book).

● Does the child express expectations of disaster?

A child may display any of the above extreme behaviors in a variety of situations, e.g., when going to the toilet, at rest time, when engaged in play with materials, or in dramatic play alone or with others; or in response to many different stimuli or, even, to no observable stimulus. It is important, as always, to record the situation and the stimulus (or lack of overt stimulus) and especially the qualitative characteristics of the behavior—*how* the child did what he did.

COGNITIVE FUNCTIONING

Details to Observe
● Does the child have a short attention span?
   Does he stay with an activity for a much shorter time than do the majority of children in the group?
● Does she tend to be highly distractible—by sounds, activities of other children, etc.?
● Does the child have poor visual skills even though his eyesight is normal?
   Is he unable to judge size, shape, location, color?
   Is he unable to see similarities and differences? Is he unable to match colors, shapes?
   Is he unable to follow an object, e.g., a ball or a person, with his eyes?
● Does the child have poor auditory skills even though her hearing is normal?
   Is she unable to remember verbal directions or stories the teacher *tells* (when there are no pictures to help her remember the story)?

Does she have difficulty distinguishing between sounds, e.g., "t" and "p" (as in "ten" and "pen") and "l" and "r" (as in "lead" and "read")?

Does she have difficulty figuring out where a sound is coming from?

During outdoor play, if the teacher called four-year-old Annie to her from a distance within the range of normal hearing, she would stop and look around, indicating that she had heard her name, but she could not distinguish from what direction the sound had come.

- Does the child tend to be unaware of or, possibly, disinterested in what goes on around him?

During group discussions or story reading, Sandy (age three) would sit and play with some small object, or lie on the floor, often masturbating, apparently oblivious of what was going on around her. When she was spoken to, she showed no sign of having heard, nor did she react to subjects that were being discussed by other children.

- Does the child have few interests? (As a result, instead of engaging in activities as other children do, he may suck his thumb, masturbate, rock, etc.)
- Does the child tend to confuse "you" with "I"? "she" or "he" with "I"?

Three-year-old Angie confuses both "you" and "she" with "I," as in the following examples:

ANGIE (to teacher): Now it is morning. She gets up and has her breakfast.

TEACHER: What do you have for breakfast?

ANGIE: She has cereal. Then she has to get dressed. Then she goes to school.

ANGIE (to the teacher): You want to ride a bike. (Meaning: "I want to ride a bike.")

- Do changes tend to confuse the child?

Do changes in the location of classroom furniture, materials, etc., confuse him?

Do changes in the usual class routine, such as going on a trip and having rhythms on a different day or at a different time, confuse him?

- Is the child unable to learn, as do other children of her age, through seeing and hearing?

Does she learn only through touching or smelling, which is normal for much younger children?

When Carol (age four) arrived in the morning, the teacher was preparing the materials for a sewing project that required large yarn needles, yarn, and burlap. There were several needles on the table. Carol ran over to her as soon as she entered the room.

CAROL (to teacher): What's that? What are you doing?

TEACHER: I'm fixing these needles and yarn so we can do some sewing.

CAROL: You need to be very careful. You need to be careful so that you don't hurt your finger.

TEACHER: Yes, you do need to be careful, but these are special needles. They don't have sharp points.

CAROL: Will you hurt your finger if you touch it here (indicating the point)?

TEACHER: No, you can touch it there gently. It really isn't very sharp.

(Carol picked up one of the needles, rolled it in her fingers, and poked it gingerly.)

CAROL: Is it very shiny?

TEACHER: Yes, it is shiny.

CAROL: Is it long and shiny?

TEACHER: Yes.

CAROL: It is long and shiny, but not sharp.

TEACHER: Yes, that's exactly right. It is long and shiny, but not sharp.

(Carol fingered the needle for a few more seconds, seemingly using her sense of touch to confirm not only the tactile qualities of the needle, but the visual ones as well. Then she returned it to the table, and darted off.)

- Compared with his peers, does the child have less general knowledge about the world and self, e.g., about work roles, animals, natural processes such as birth, growth, death? (If the child comes from an impoverished environment, this category may not apply.)

When Timmy, who was not quite four years old, was asked in reference to something in the story the teacher was reading, "Can you take off your hair?" he said, "I could."

When the children were planting radish seeds in paper cups, six-year-old Tom was very much interested and wanted to plant more than the three that he had already planted. He asked when they would grow. The teacher showed him another child's cup in which the seed had begun to sprout. She said that maybe after Saturday and Sunday his would sprout. Tom, making a very large gesture with his hands, said, "It will be this big."

Lillian, almost five years old, raised her hand when the teacher asked the *boys* to raise their hands.

- Does the child have a very poor memory?
- Do the child's mental processes tend to be incoherent?

Martin, who was almost six, had been making "stoneware" dishes out of clay. He told a story about them for the teacher to write down, as follows: "The title is 'Instructional Book.' Reflections of stoneware is very good. I want to go to outer space but I can't go." (The teacher asked, "Why?") "Because I have all this 'nail' (i.e., mail) business. You have to take the cracks and always make a serving dish and two cups and two bowls. And what you have to send away to the _____ School (name of the school he was attending). And people get what they want for free."

It is impossible to pinpoint specific activities or times of day when all the above behaviors can be observed. It is possible, however, with some. For example, the extent and content of a child's knowledge might best be observed during group discussions—about a story the teacher has just read, or during or after a trip. If the teacher records the exact time at which each observation of a child's activity begins and ends, she will find out not only about his attention span in different activities, but also how distractible he tends to be. Recording a child's responses when he is spoken to may indicate whether the child can discriminate between sounds. As has been pointed out before, recording a child's behavior in many different situations and activities (or nonactivity) and at different times of the school day will undoubtedly yield the necessary information.

LANGUAGE AND SPEECH

Details to Observe
- Does the child talk infrequently?
  Does he communicate nonverbally (through body movements, facial expressions, etc.) more than verbally?

For about an hour, when David (age four-and-a-half) was engaged in a variety of activities, in all of these with one or more children (stringing beads, a color-matching game, "cooking"), he seldom spoke and tended to communicate nonverbally when necessary (shaking or nodding his head for no and yes; hitting his head with his hands when the colored die did not turn up his color in the color-matching game, smiling when it did).

- Is the child echolalic? Does he echo whatever is said to him instead of responding appropriately?

  When the teacher asked, "Do you want some apple juice?" Daryl repeated several times, "Do you want some apple juice?"

- Does the child confuse words that are associated with each other, e.g., say "table" when he means "chair"?
- Does the child have poor "receptive" language? Is she unable to understand what is said to her even though there is nothing wrong with her hearing?
- Does she have difficulty following simple directions?

  When the teacher told the children to sit "in a circle," Linda, age four, sat in the *center* of the circle. The teacher explained to her in several different ways what she meant. She told her "to sit on the tape" (which had been put on the floor to help children sit in a circle), "on the edge of the circle, on the outside of the circle, next to a (particular) child." Linda, however, continued to sit in the center of the circle. Linda was the only child in the group who could not follow the teacher's directions

- Does the child not understand the meaning of prepositions, such as "in" or "out," "up" or "down," "in front of" or "behind"?

  When the teacher was playing a game in which the children were supposed to sit or stand behind, on, in front of, etc., a chair, either when she told them to or in imitation of a doll, it was obvious that Jeff (almost six) understood the meaning of very few of the prepositions. In most cases, he either imitated the other children or did it incorrectly.

- Does the child have poor "expressive" language, i.e., does she have difficulty expressing herself verbally?
- Does the child use concrete terms instead of the usual general terms?

  Nancy (age four), when sitting on the toilet, said, "I made yellow water."

- Does the child have difficulty learning correct grammar and sentence structure? (Age is a factor here.)

  At age five, Frankie said, "I be a daddy" and "Me doctor."

- Is the child unable to remember words she knows, substituting onomatopoetic sounds, such as "baaa baaa" for sheep, "choo choo" for train (like a much younger child)?

The presence and quality of children's language (or its absence) can be observed at almost any time of the day or in any situation. Although discussions and story-time may be the best times, conversations at snack-time, when the child is playing with clay or is engaged in dramatic play, as well as social conversations with an individual teacher or child will yield good examples of children's language and speech.

EGO FUNCTIONING

Details to Observe
- Does the child have a low self-concept?
  Does he tend to be self-devaluing, self-deprecating, unsure of himself and his capabilities?

  Tony (age four) frequently called himself "stupid" and "dope."

- Does the child tend to be overly sensitive to criticism, afraid of disapproval?
- Does the child tend to be self-punishing?
  Does she bite her nails or other parts of her body, bang her head against the wall repeatedly?
- Is the child reluctant to try new materials or activities?
- Is the child highly impulsive?
  Does he tend to act without thinking of the possible consequences of his acts?

  Within a short period of time, Mike (age five) engaged in a series of impulsive actions. While playing with sand, he suddenly got up and charged toward the light switch, shouting, "Put the light switch on." As he pushed a chair across the floor, bumping into whatever was in his way, he screamed at the top of his lungs in unison with the screeching noises made by the chair. Then, after slapping himself hard on the head, he suddenly dashed off to the teacher, grabbed her hand, and rubbed his head with it in the place where he had slapped himself.

- Does the child tend to control her feelings excessively?
    When hurt, is she unable to cry?
    Is she unable to express anger despite great provocation?
    Is she unable to display joy when pleased or when she achieves her goal?

Donna was riding a large tricycle on the roof playground. She fell over onto the brick floor, and the tricycle toppled over on top of her. A teacher and another child rushed over to disentangle her from the tricycle. When Donna and the tricycle were righted, she got back on and rode off. The other child observed in amazement, "Look at Donna, teacher; she didn't even cry."

- Does the child have low tolerance for frustration?
    For example, does he have more difficulty than other children waiting for his turn on the swing when standing on line?

Most of the children were seated at tables waiting for clay. Mary was sitting between Meg and Joshua. When she received her clay, she pounded it onto the board, and then tried to lift it. To her delight, she discovered that the board was stuck to the clay. She picked it up by the clay and banged it back down on the table several times. Joshua asked her to stop, but she ignored him and continued the banging. Then the teacher called to her from the next table and asked her to stop. She yelled, "No!" repeatedly, then burst into tears.

- Is the child a perfectionist?
    For example, when drawing a picture, does she keep erasing parts of her drawing and then redraw?
- Does the child tend to engage in repetitive activity for unusually long periods of time?

On many occasions, five-year-old Jerry drew numbers repeatedly for long periods of time.

Benjy (age four-and-a-half) hung on to the post in the room with one arm. He tried to walk around the little ledge at the bottom of the post. There was a broad smile on his face, but it seemed mechanical. He slapped the post rhythmically with one hand, producing a metallic sound, as he continued to walk around the post on the ledge He persisted in this way for about fifteen minutes.

- Does the child tend to talk to himself, audibly or inaudibly?

Four-year-old Arnie was sitting at a little table, talking inaudibly to himself. He then got up, moved around, while continuing to talk to himself. He continued to talk to himself during a variety of activities such as playing with a dump truck, and walking around the room touching various objects.

- Does the child have difficulty distinguishing fantasy from reality?

FERNANDO (age five): You know, it's my aunt's birthday. (He continues after a pause.) I got married to Laura.
TEACHER: Who's Laura?
FERNANDO: Laura lives in Forest Hills.
TEACHER: When did you marry her?
FERNANDO: December 22.
TEACHER: Where is she now?
FERNANDO: She's sick. I married her nine times. Eight times when I was three years old. I married her ten or eleven times.

Alisa (age four) talked to the teacher about having a sister named Flavie, and a baby. She said her sister screamed. (Both the sister and the baby are imaginary; Alisa is an only child.)

Some of these behaviors can be observed when the child works with different materials; others, when the child does not engage in any activity at all although the other children are busy. Some characteristics can be inferred from what the child says; from the way he responds to peers and teachers; from the way he reacts when hit or called names, when he wins or loses a competitive game; and from his behavior during transition times.

GENERAL IMPRESSION

In addition to the kinds of specific behavior described above that may presage future emotional disturbances and/or learning disabilities, an outstanding characteristic of these young children with special problems is that they give the impression of being much younger than their chronological age. Jonah, for example, although four years old, seemed like a two-year-old or a very young three-year-old. The babylike quality of his skin and hair contributed to this impression, as did his high-pitched voice, his babyish pronunciation of words (such as "appoo" for apple), his unawareness that his pants were constantly falling down, and the fact that he always played alone, never with other children. In other children, this impression may stem from other sources as well, such as a developmental lag in one or more aspects of functioning—physical, social, emotional, language and speech and cognitive.

Remember. No single behavior listed above has any significance by itself. Only a combination of several, if they occur frequently and persistently, may be indicative of a problem.

13

PATTERNS— SUMMARY—
AND INTERPRETATION

PATTERNS

WE HAVE TAKEN individual children through their school day now for many months. We caught their expressions as they arrived in the morning; we observed how they removed their outer clothes; we watched them at play, noting both their use of materials and their relationships with other children. We noticed how they conducted themselves at the table, how they took care of their bodily needs, just how each responded to us, and how each behaved as a member of the group. Hopefully, we learned something of what the children think about and how they feel they are getting along. Perhaps, too, we got clues to what we could do to satisfy their particular needs for facing life now and in the future. All this material of the daily records must now be organized in such a way as to get at the nature of the children's responses more easily—their relations with adults, relations with children, uses of materials, behavior during routines, their cognitive style and how they learn, their language development, and so on. Each child has a unique pattern of response in each of these areas. To find that pattern, we must turn to our records and pull out the episodes that together reveal the pattern. Such a pulling out of episodes in one area might look like a series of small summaries. Here is how one child's responses to adults would add up. The dates refer to the original records the teacher took. Each small summary refers to a whole record, of course.

Relations with adults
10/21: Robert looks to me for support when not wanting to get into

194

game. I explain rules; he is reassured and agrees to play.

10/25: R. seeks me out to show me pipes through bricks, explaining what he sees. He brings car over and demonstrates its features. Talks a lot and shows evidence of different kinds of knowledge.

10/26: R. asks me if Darren is in charge of chairs at cleanup.

10/27: R. asks me what Liam and Paula have to do with each other.

11/1: I direct R. to let other children have turn on ropes. He follows directions, calls and asks me to watch him several times performing on ropes or tires.

11/1: Gym teacher gives R. directions which he follows. R. asks him a question later.

11/3: R. tells of discovery with Rig-a-Jig. Shares success with me.

11/10: R. enthusiastically shows me clay objects he made.

and so on. On the basis of the above digests of several episodes, the teacher was able to write up the pattern of R.'s interactions with an adult as follows:

R. feels comfortable with adults and sees them as resources for information and as people with whom to share discoveries and happy experiences. R. is at ease relying on adults when he needs them for support, e.g., 10/21, on entering attribute game or to clarify questions; 10/27 in group meeting he asks what L. and P. have to do with each other when not sure. R. likes to have adults enjoy his activities and share his appreciation of objects and knowledge, but he doesn't have an overdependence on adults. He rarely seeks the teacher out for help, nor the student teacher if she is not actually near him. He is relatively self-sufficient.

R. has positive relationships with adults and trusts them easily. He follows adult directions when in group or individual situations.

NEED FOR A SUMMARY

There comes a time when we are interested in a final summary of the child's behavior over time. It may be for the school files and next year's teacher, for consultation with the school psychologist, or for a conference with the parent. In any case, we need to put our material together in such a way that we can get a fairly complete picture of a child's behavior at school.

All the small summaries dealing with certain areas of functioning (routines, materials, etc.) will indicate a child's interaction with the environment. One can see what the patterns have been and what they have become. One will see growth, or perhaps lack of growth or even regression. The importance of any given area to the child will show up—the degree of interest and intensity, and whether these led to satisfaction or frustration. The child's behavior can be looked at in relation to that of others of the same age (they all seem able to take their clothes *off,* but not put them on again!), and to coming growth (he's finally gotten to the first rung of the jungle gym; he'll surely get to the top in the coming months). But conclusions must remain tentative (I think she'll come through . . . It looks as though . . . It seems to me . . .). All the conclusions about children's behavior need to be tested through further observation, action, and still further observation. At no time can we say about a dynamic, growing human being, "Aha, I've got him!" and be sure we are right.

Summaries of the physical functioning of a child and the overview of his/her adjustment to school give us additional clues to use at some time in interpretation. Physical functioning can be deduced from records of the daily activity, which will show such persistent aspects of functioning as the following:

- Health and the secondary effects of illnesses, operations, and physical handicaps
- Grace and coordination and their relation to emotional functioning
- Usual tempo
- Freedom or restraint of movement—expansive, abandoned, precise, vigorous, mild, lusty, strong, dainty, graceful, bouncy, earth-bound, loose, disjointed, tense, relaxed, tight, restrained, uninhibited
- Amount of energy expended in relation to activity (how quickly does child become fatigued?)
- Physical "quality" of the child—poised, restless, serene, earthbound, airy, stolid
- Attitude toward use of the body in relation to large muscular movements, such as running, climbing, etc. (eagerness, caution, fear, pleasure, etc.)
- Attitude toward use of the body in relation to fine body movements, such as writing, sewing, etc. (relaxed, tense, enjoys, tries too hard, etc.)
- Usual facial expression (frowns, smiles, looks serene, etc.)

ADJUSTMENT TO SCHOOL

Adjustment to school is something else that cannot be set to absolute standards and in its specifics will be different for different children. Yet we can get a general overall picture of a child's functioning if we do not feel too rigid about standards ourselves.

We might think of children as adjusted to school when they come readily without their mothers and know school routines, group rules, and normal daily procedures, know where materials are, who people are, what is expected of them, and what they may expect of others. Incidentally, early records that show the child's first responses to a new situation are helpful in assessing the changes that take place with familiarity. The "feeling" that a teacher has about a child's being well adjusted to school should be bolstered by tangible, concrete evidence that this is really so. One might see two levels of adjustments: (1) separation from mother—reactions to routines, knowledge of where things are, etc.; and (2) when a child is really him/herself, natural and spontaneous.

FEATURES OF THE FINAL SUMMARY

In the final summary, we include digests of the patterns of behavior at routines, with materials, with children, with adults, etc., and a survey of intellectual functioning and language. We could also include observations that show what frustrates a child and what gives satisfaction. We might include information gleaned otherwise than through observation, such as items from the admittance file, the nurse's files, or conferences with parents.

All this evidence is then looked at with fresh and objective eyes, to see which parts in one area of functioning seem to have a bearing on other parts elsewhere. For example, a summary of use of outdoor equipment (which we have not included by itself) might show a consistent picture of nonuse. The child looks sturdy enough, but he does not hang by his legs on the parallel bars, climb to heights, slide down the high slide, etc. He plays outside with apparent contentment, but only with the wagons, the sand, chalk, balls, water, etc. Anything more than two feet high is seemingly not for him. Is there anything in his play elsewhere that seems related to his behavior on the equipment? Is there anything in the information on his health and physical background that throws light on behavior in the yard? Is the child's behavior on equipment connected with his age? Is there anything in his choice of stories or activities in rhythms that offers a clue? Is there anything he said in discussion (or did not say when everyone else was clamoring to say the same thing)? Does the child behave with caution everywhere? Does he show tensions in other situations of height (for example, at the head of the stairs)? Does the child seem generally contented? In other words, how does any one piece of behavior fit in relation to whatever else we know about the child? By itself, nonuse of high equipment can be open to a variety of inept interpretations, depending on the fancy of the observer. But in relation to other aspects of a child's behavior, it takes on the specific meaning it has *for this child*, and that can be anything from simple inexperience and normal caution to undeveloped muscles, malnutrition, or fear of heights.

Let us take other possible relationships. A child has certain attitudes toward other children. Is there anything in her attitude toward adults that seems to be of a piece? Is her attitude toward herself and her accomplishments with materials involved here? Does her capacity to take frustration, as evidenced in numerous situations, relate to her getting along with children?

What behavior at routines is related to behavior with adults? What behavior at play is related to behavior with adults? What behavior at the table is related to behavior with children? Is there a common thread running throughout? the same happy-go-lucky attitudes at routines, at play, and with adults? the same inability to find satisfaction? the same even keel? the same passionate outbursts, etc.?

Trends

The final record includes the *trends* of behavior.

Apparently Simon is outgrowing his need to suck his thumb. Over the months he has left off perpetual sucking for brief returns at rest hour.

Bill stops now for a good look when someone comes toward him fast. Instead of screaming, he sizes up the situation. He turns and runs without looking back.

Tammy sits with books and really seems to be enjoying them. She sits through a short story too, apparently able to follow it. Last week she asked a question about the character in the story. Tammy is learning to concentrate on happenings outside herself!

Problems

Perhaps if we recognize that the growing-up process is not accomplished with smoothness and evenness by anyone, we can use the word *problems* in its proper context. Every child at some time or other has a problem or hurdle to overcome and conquer if he or she is to grow. These problems, or hurdles, might also be indicated in the final summary.

Lucy has yet to learn not to cry when she is denied something she asks for. Her disappointment is so keen, whether it is over a cracker before lunch, a doll in someone else's possession, or no place at the easel when she wants to paint, that it seems quite out of proportion to the many real satisfactions she has in her life. She has come to expect gratification for all her wants, and of course life is not like that. She is generally a happy child and really enjoys herself immensely at school. But it is important that she learn to accept frustration with somewhat better grace. This is true more for her own sake than for her relationships with children. The children like her and play with her. But she makes herself unhappy unnecessarily.

Evaluating Growth

The trends and problems merge into an evaluation of growth. "He has grown so much" has real meaning when it is qualified: She has learned to . . ., he used to . . ., but now . . .; . . . she uses so many colors, so many materials, so many ideas and words; he makes, he says, he does." It is all in the record. And how easily we forget what children did three months ago if we do not write it down!

Prognosis

We can guess at what the future holds for a child's growth and can recommend what that child should have for the best chances for growth. We can make recommendations to the next teacher and perhaps to the parents.

The record shows that Luke has just begun to take an interest in classroom responsibilities. He should have a chance to continue this experience and gain satisfaction from it. He is not yet ready to take on responsibility without adult help, and he should not be expected to do so for a while. But if it can be doled out to him at his pace, he will surely grow into independent responsibility too.

Kathy will probably sail through next year like a charm. Although her adjustment to school was somewhat stormy for a while (she cried

when her mother left, she clung to the teacher, she attacked anyone
who touched her clay, her puzzle, her doll, etc.), she has come to feel
so at home that one would not know it was the same child. She plays
with two other children (Margery and Theresa) who will go on with
her next year. She uses materials with creative pleasure. She is
relaxed with the teacher and has visited in next year's classroom several times. The worst seems to be over, and she should be able to get
real satisfaction from her new group from the very beginning. My
guess is that if there is an initial readjustment again (which is possible) she will get over it comparatively easily.

Extremes

In the final record we would note *extremes* of behavior, such as
overdependence, overall immaturity with materials, complete rejection of routines, or overall extraordinary competence. Every child
can be expected to show some inconsistency, but extremes of behavior may mean real trouble or special talent and should be noted.
Along the same lines are such special problems as stuttering, excessive thumb-sucking, accident-proneness, persistent reluctance to
become involved, frequent expression of fear, passivity, etc. These
behaviors are normal to young children but cause us concern when
they take up so much of a child's energy that there is little left for
wholesome play.

The Whole Child

We must also note the special quality of the personality as we see
it—dramatic, charming, gentle, sturdy, slithery, bright, etc.—the
first thing we think of as we think about a child, the overallness of
that unique person. After recording minutiae, we have the right to
give our own sensory impression! Not every child calls forth the one
apt word. But many do, and we need not hesitate to include it in
the final summary. We may well begin or end a summary of a
child's behavior with "He is an imp," "She is all daintiness," "He
is perpetual motion itself," "She is an utterly competent person,"
etc. On their own, these words and phrases are open to question.
But with evidence piled up in the summary of many aspects of behavior, the teacher is justified in adding this wholly understandable
personal reaction.

INTERPRETATION

By this time we seem to know our child well. There does not seem to be much that we have missed. The next question the teachers usually ask is why? Why does the child do as he or she does? Is it because the child was "spoiled"? Is it because of a loving or a rejecting mother, grandmother, brother, or sister? Is it because he or she feels inadequate, overconfident? Is it. . .? Is it. . .? Of course we want to know. We work closely with children and do many things for and with them. It is impossible not to hypothesize as to the causes of their behavior.

Whether we are right or wrong can make an important difference to a child's growth and happiness. It is dangerous to interpret incorrectly. Any interpretation at all must not only be tentative and subject to change if new facts emerge, but must definitely relate to a background of information.

What Teachers Need to Know to Understand the Causes of a Child's Behavior

- The physical side of behavior:
    Do we know what is a well or ill child?
    Do we know the effects of illness on a child? the effects of malnutrition?
    Are we sure that a timely piece of bread and butter won't be as effective as a hug? or vice versa?
    Do we understand the relationship between physical state and emotional? between physical and intellectual?
- Facts about child development:
    Do we know how children grow in our culture?
    Do we understand what stages are?
    Is there an orderly progression? Is it the same for everyone?
    Can we have reasonable expectations about a child's behavior at any given age? What determines these?
    Is temperament real? Is there a pace and a pattern of growth for each child?
    Is personality inherited?
- Cultural influences on personality and growth:
    Does every neighborhood place a premium on the same kind of behavior?
    Does every family conform to neighborhood expectations?
    Do ethnic standards and values play a part in parent and child behavior?
- Individual experience:

Do we know the specific events that have affected this particular child?

Have this child's life stresses been identical with anyone else's?

What kinds of people have shaped the child and passed on their views of the world to him or her?

Interpretation is difficult because it involves knowing so much. It involves feelings too, *our* feelings. Can we put outselves in a child's place? Can we do it and remain objectively adult? Or do we respond to what we like or don't like, agree with or disagree with, as we interpret? Are we competing with the parents when we find fault with the child? Are we boosting our own morale when we say the child has made superior progress at school?

Interpreting causes of behavior is dangerous unless we tread carefully. Can we verify every statement we make? Do we have evidence for our hunches and our guesses? Is the child more important to us than being right? Are we willing to give up a pet theory because it really does not fit the child?

The same behavior can mean different things in different children. Children hit out of anger, fear, resentment, jealousy, panic, and defiance. They can withdraw into silence out of anger, fear, resentment, jealousy, panic, and defiance. A child will not necessarily do what we do, although some will. We must learn to study children in general in order to find the answers for the individual child about whom we are concerned. We must also study individuals and extend our understanding to all. Each human being is unique, as we ourselves are. Each human being wants to be understood for his/her unique self, as we ourselves do. Let us be just to the children we teach, and guard their precious individualities. If we would understand them, let us learn to gather accurately the evidence that will give us the clues we need. To our clues we must bring the illumination offered by knowledge of human behavior.

The following is a final summary prepared at the end of the school year by one little boy's teacher.

FINAL SUMMARY

Lee M.; age four years, five months:

Lee has accomplished much in his adjustment to school. His first days at school were quite unhappy. He was reluctant to leave home and mother and registered his disapproval in no uncertain terms. His favorite quote seemed to be "My mother says I don't have to do that." Now he rarely mentions his family and is only occasionally anxious to take some of his work home. He still brings possessions from home to show, or share with us. Other than these material bridges between home and school, we hear very little about Lee's life away from school.

Upon entering school Lee resisted vigorously any and all routines; only gradually did he accept them, one by one. He has never had a toilet accident at school, but called for the utmost privacy in toileting, and usually postponed the process until he reached home. It was not until December that he went willingly without signs of stress. I was delighted last week to have him come to me and say, "You know, I went to the bathroom twice already." He knows when we wash our hands, and washes his in methodical fashion. He eats his snack matter-of-factly, placing cup and napkin in wastebasket when finished. He rests quietly after settling down on his rug. He dresses and undresses himself, asking for help only when necessary. He knows where to hang his clothes, and is careful to hang them up correctly.

Lee's work with creative materials has been largely teacher-initiated. Before he begins any activity he usually spends some time watching the other children. Then when he apparently feels more sure of himself he begins. His attention span is adequate to complete the activity. He works deliberately and quietly, absorbed and interested in the task at hand. It is quite evident that this is real work. His work is neat and carefully done. When he abandons this approach to materials, he seems worried, and seeks reassurance from the teacher that his untidiness is accepted comfortably by her. He verbalizes as he works, a running commentary to teacher, children, or no one. He shows pride in accomplishment and again often seeks approval from the teacher. His work with clay is delightful and imaginative and he seems to feel more freedom here than in the use of other media. Considering Lee's relationships with the teachers, he is an extremely articulate child who makes his wants known easily and often—in case of emergency, with loud calls for help. He finds it easy to verbalize his feelings in many cases, and he also reveals the intensity of these feelings. In everything he does we can see a real need for love and approval from the teacher, and an undercurrent of worry that she may possibly disapprove of his behavior.

With his peers Lee shows a pattern of caution, observing them closely before he joins them. It has just been during the past few weeks that he has taken part in singing and rhythmic group activities. He seems to derive great satisfaction from this type of activity, asking, "Are we going to play the Jingle Bell game today?" etc. If sufficiently absorbed in a certain task, he ignores others in his immediate vicinity completely. He is friendly with most children, but tends to seek out one particular child to play with. This child changes on a day-to-day or week-to-week basis. When a third child enters (in my notes, it seems always Michael) he feels very insecure, covering his feelings of hostility with a sulky withdrawal, seldom with an overt act of aggression. (This week I did see him pounce unexpectedly upon Michael's back and wrestle him to the floor with triumphant laughter on his part and complete bewilderment on Michael's.) Although Lee talks a great deal, he seems to be talking *at* the children most times, not *with* them. They all delight in listening to his tall stories. He has a good sense of humor and his hearty laugh can be heard throughout the room. He often uses laughter as a release from tension.

Lee seems well able to think things through. He has good ideas and definite concepts of the world about him (size, time, etc.) although sometimes these emerge in his conversation in a slightly garbled form (e.g., while attempting to crawl from the top of one packing case to another about two-and-one-half feet away, he looked around for a plank to bridge the gap. Seeing none, he surveyed his prone figure solemnly, and then said in resigned tones, "I need more long . . .").

When he is happy, Lee is happy from head to toe. His eyes dance; he roars with laughter and quivers with delight. He sparkles long after the experience has ended, and seems to be reliving the pleasure he found. He is evidently able to absorb quite a few hard knocks physically—I have only one notation of his being hurt and crying. His cautious approach to life may partly account for this. When fearful or anxious he quickly seeks security in contact with the teacher. Certain defensive techniques have been noted during the year. As I have mentioned, he quoted his mother constantly in his first days at school. Also, he used such alibis as "I'm tired," or "It's too noisy," especially when making up his mind to conquer a certain task confronting him. Then too, he creates choices for himself as a face-saving gesture (e.g., "I'll rest, but I won't eat my cooky"). Just lately he has shown signs of an approaching readiness to take aggressive action (e.g., wrestling with Michael and Paul). His mother says that he reported proudly at home, "I had a big fight and I made that kid almost cry." Actually it was a very little fight, but its importance to Lee in his self-picture is very evident, for here is a child who *never* will tell anything at all about school to his mother. However, Lee will still need a great deal of encouragement to face up to his difficulties.

Lee finds great satisfaction in measuring up to what is expected of him. This is very noticeable in routines in which he now accepts his weaknesses as a matter of course. The other day he, in turn, reassured Bobby, who needed help with a zipper, "Everybody needs help. Everybody but mommies, daddies, and teachers."

Children are complicated creatures, as all human beings are. But because they are still openly revealing their feelings and are uninhibited in reaching out to life, sensitive adults can get to know them well enough to gauge their needs with a fair degree of accuracy.

Each child is a unique combination of the inherited unknowns interacting with particular family and cultural influences. As such, each child is unlike anyone else. Each child is also representative of a stage of development in the life of a human being, and as such shares many characteristics with other children at the same stage. And finally, each child at school is a member of a society of peers in which the struggle both to be oneself and yet belong to the group calls forth particular responses to the demands of all the others who are equally engaged in balancing out their separate, individual needs with the satisfactions of belonging to the whole group.

Although there is much we can learn about children, no teacher can ever know any child so well that there will be no surprises. The very nature of children's ongoing growth implies change, and that requires a constant state of open-mindedness from a teacher. We can only make educated guesses today as to how a child responds to life. Tomorrow we start all over again, because every growing child's tomorrow is a little different from that child's today.

SUGGESTED READING

Almy, Millie, and Genishi, Celia. *Ways of Studying Young Children: An Observation Manual for Early Childhood Teachers*. Rev. ed. New York: Teachers College Press, 1979.

American Council on Education, Commission on Teacher Education. *Helping Teachers Understand Children*. Washington, D.C.: American Council on Education, 1945.

Biber, Barbara; Murphy, Lois; and others. *Child Life in School: A Study of a Seven-Year-Old Group*. New York: E. P. Dutton, 1942.

Carew, Jean W.; Chan, Itty; and Halfar, Christine. *Observing Intelligence in Young Children: Eight Case Studies*. Englewood Cliffs, N.J.: Prentice-Hall, 1976.

Cass, Joan E. *Helping Children Grow Through Play*. New York: Schocken Books, 1973.

Chan, Itty. "Observing Young Children, a Science, Working with Them, an Art." *Young Children* 33, no. 2 (January 1978): 55–63.

Child Welfare League of America. *A Guide for Teacher Recording in Day Care Agencies*. New York, 1965.*

Flapan, Dorothy, and Neubauer, Peter B. *The Assessment of Early Childhood Development*. Rev. ed. New York: Jason Aronson, 1976.

Freud, Anna. *Normality and Pathology in Childhood* (Chapters 1 and 3). New York: International Universities Press, 1965.

Gardner, Howard. *Developmental Psychology: An Introduction*. 2nd ed. Boston: Little Brown, 1982.

Gellert, Elizabeth. "Systematic Observation: A Method in Child Study." *Harvard Educational Review* 25, no. 3 (Summer 1955): 179–195.

Gordon, Ira. *Studying the Child in School*. New York: John Wiley, 1966.

Hartley, Ruth; Frank, Lawrence; and Goldenson, Robert. *Understanding Children's Play*. New York: Columbia University Press, 1952.

*Child Welfare League of America, 67 Irving Place, New York, NY 10003.

Hayden, A. H.; Smith, R. K.; von Hippel, C. S.; and Baer, S. A. *Mainstreaming Preschoolers: Children with Learning Disabilities*. DHEW Publication no. (OHDS) 79-31117. U.S. Department of Health, Education and Welfare. Office of Human Development Services, Administration for Children, Youth and Families, Head Start Bureau. 1979.

Huntington, Dorothy; Provence, Sally; and Parker, Ronald K. *Day Care 2: Serving Infants*. No. (OCD) 72-8. Washington, D.C.: U.S. Department of Health, Education, and Welfare, Office of Child Development, 1971.

Irwin, D. Michelle, and Bushnell, M. M. *Observational Strategies for Child Study*. New York: Holt, Rinehart and Winston, 1980.

Isaacs, Susan. *Intellectual Growth in Young Children*. New York: Schocken Books, 1966.

————. *Social Development in Young Children*. New York: Schocken Books, 1972.

Koste, Virginia G. *Dramatic Play in Childhood: Rehearsal for Life*. New Orleans: Anchorage Press, 1978.

Lasher, Miriam G.; Mattick, Ilse; Perkins, Frances J.; von Hippel, C. S.; and Hailey, L. G. *Mainstreaming Preschoolers: Children with Emotional Disturbances*. DHEW Publication no. (OHDS) 79-31115. U.S. Department of Health, Education and Welfare. Office of Human Development Services, Administration for Children, Youth and Families, Head Start Bureau. 1979.

Marot, Mary S. "School Records: An Experiment." In Charlotte B. Winsor, ed., *Experimental Schools Revisited*. New York: Agathon Press, 1973.

Murphy, Lois B. *Personality in Young Children*. 2 vols. New York: Basic Books, 1956.

Peller, Lilli. "Significant Symptoms in the Behavior of Young Children." *Mental Hygiene* 30 (1946): 285–295.

Prescott, Daniel. *The Child in the Educative Process*. New York: McGraw-Hill, 1957.

Provence, Sally. *Guide for the Care of Infants in Groups*. New York: Child Welfare League of America, 1971.*

Raskin, Larry W.; Taylor, William J.; and Kerchoff, Florence G. "The Teacher as Observer: A Guideline." *Young Children* 30, no. 5 (July 1975): 330–334.

Rowen, Betty. *The Children We See: An Observational Approach to Child Study*. New York: Holt, Rinehart and Winston, 1973.

Safford, Philip L. *Teaching Young Children with Special Needs*. St. Louis: C. V. Mosby Co., 1978.

Stone, L. Joseph, and Church, Joseph. *Childhood and Adolescence: A Psychology of the Growing Person*. 4th ed. New York: Random House, 1979.

Taylor, Edith Clark. "Teacher's Role in a Therapeutic Preschool." *Exceptional Children* 36 (1969): 273–276

Walker, Evangeline. *Effective Observations for Educators*. Urbana, Ill.: ERIC Publications, University of Illinois, 1972.†

Willis, Anne, and Ricciuti, Henry. *A Good Beginning for Babies*. Washington, D.C.: NAEYC, 1976.

†ERIC Publications, University of Illinois, 805 West Pennsylvania Ave., Urbana, IL 61801.

INDEX